BEYOND RELIGION

ADVANCE PRAISE FOR BEYOND RELIGION

"This book is unique. There is nothing like it! In an era where most of the old religions have not been able to sacrifice their rigidity in light of new world problems, *Beyond Religion* offers readers a way to nourish and enhance their souls."

— Stanley Krippner, Ph.D., coauthor of
Personal Mythology and *Spiritual Dimensions of Healing*

"A fine book. Appealing and powerful views and practices that people both in formal religions and informal paths will find attractive."

— Thomas Greening, Ph.D., Editor of
The Journal of Humanistic Psychology

"An annotated guide to an array of nonreligious paths to spiritual fulfillment. Elkins affirms the spiritual potential of human activities not often thought of as spiritual. As a humanistic psychotherapist, this is the kind of book I can comfortably recommend to my clients."

— Maureen O'Hara, Ph.D., Vice President for
Academic Affairs, Saybrook Graduate School

"This book is an idea whose time has come. I know of no other book that so intriguingly covers the spiritual revolution of our day."

— William S. Banowsky, Ph.D., former President of
Pepperdine University and the University of Oklahoma

BEYOND RELIGION

A Personal Program For Building A Spiritual Life Outside The Walls Of Traditional Religion

David N. Elkins, Ph.D.

A publication supported by
THE KERN FOUNDATION

Quest Books
Theosophical Publishing House

Wheaton, Illinois ♦ Chennai (Madras), India

The Theosophical Publishing House
P.O. Box 270
Wheaton, IL 60189-0270

A publication of the Theosophical Publishing House,
a department of the Theosophical Society in America

Library of Congress Cataloging-in-Publication Data

Elkins, David N.
    Beyond religion: a personal program for building a spiritual life outside the
walls of traditional religion / David N. Elkins. — 1st Quest ed.
        p.   cm.
    "Quest books."
    Includes bibliographical references and index.
    ISBN 0-8356-0764-X
    1. Spiritual life.   2. Psychology, Religious.   I. Title.
BL624.E445   1998   98-14775
291.4 — dc21   CIP

4   3   2   1   *   98   99   00   01   02   03   04

Printed in the United States of America

Dedication

For Sara

In the silence of this page
I hope you will hear the ineffable richness
you have brought into my life for more than thirty years.

You nurture and sustain my soul.

CONTENTS

ACKNOWLEDGMENTS   ix

PREFACE   xi

INTRODUCTION   1

PART I — THE SPIRITUAL REVOLUTION

CHAPTER 1   The Spiritual Revolution: 9
   The Movement Away from Religion to Spirituality

CHAPTER 2   Toward a New Spirituality: 23
   A Nonreligious Approach

CHAPTER 3   The Soul: 37
   Doorway to the Imaginal World

CHAPTER 4   The Sacred: 61
   The Mysterious Dimension of Human Experience

PART II — EIGHT ALTERNATIVE PATHS TO THE SACRED

PATH 1   The Feminine: 103
   The Path of the Anima

PATH 2   The Arts: 121
   The Path of the Muses

PATH 3   The Body: 141
   The Path of Eros, Sex, and Sensuality

PATH 4   Psychology: 167
   The Path of Counseling and Psychotherapy

PATH 5   Mythology: 191
   The Path of Story, Ritual, and Symbol

PATH 6   Nature: 209
  The Path of the Earth and Heavens

PATH 7   Relationships: 225
  The Path of Friendship, Family, and Community

PATH 8   Dark Nights of the Soul: 247
  The Path of Existential Crises

WALKING THE PATHS: 261
  A Personal Program for Spiritual Growth

EPILOGUE   277

NOTES   279

INDEX   297

ACKNOWLEDGMENTS

This book is an expression of my personal and professional journey over the last twenty years. Many people have contributed to my growth and to the ideas contained in this book. I am grateful to all of them but would especially like to acknowledge the following:

I wish to thank all the clients, students, and workshop participants who have helped me clarify these principles through the years. I am especially grateful to those who have given me permission to include their stories here. Some of the examples in the book are actual persons; others are composites based on my personal and clinical experience. In all cases, except where explicit permission was obtained, names and identifying information have been changed to protect privacy and confidentiality.

Through the years various colleagues have worked with me on projects related to spirituality. I would especially like to acknowledge Stephen Brown, James Hedstrom, Edward Shafranske, Olivia de la Rocha, and Robert Weathers. Many psychology graduate students have also helped. In particular, I wish to thank Lori Hughes, Andrew Leaf, Stephanie McElheney, Terry McClanahan, and Cheryl Saunders. I also wish to thank those colleagues who read portions of this manuscript, giving me constructive feedback and encouraging endorsements. These include William Banowsky, Emily Coleman, Thomas Greening, Robert Johnson, James Kavanaugh, Stanley Krippner, Maureen O'Hara, Kirk Schneider, Elizabeth Strahan, and Robert Weathers.

I wish to thank my university and the administrators who have provided support through the years for my research and writing. I especially wish to acknowledge Dean Nancy Fagan, Associate Dean Cary Mitchell, and former Associate Dean James Hedstrom.

I am deeply grateful to my family and relatives who have encouraged my work. In particular, I would like to thank my wife Sara and my two sons, David Alan and Jody Lynn, for their love and support through the years and for their assistance with this project. I also thank Monica, my daughter-in-law, for her information and assistance related to computers and word processing.

I wish to thank Melanie Coughlin, a true friend who listened with enthusiasm to each chapter as it was completed and who provided me with relevant books and materials along the way.

I am also grateful to Brenda Rosen, executive editor at Quest Books, for her professionalism and assistance with each phase of this project. She provided editorial guidance when needed and also gave me the freedom I needed to pursue my own creative vision. I also thank Carolyn Bond and Vija Bremanis for their expert assistance with this project.

Finally, I would like to make it clear that those named in these acknowledgments are not responsible for the perspective taken in this book nor for any of the weaknesses it may contain.

PREFACE

Speaking of spirituality, a Sufi master once said, "A river passes through many countries, and each claims it for its own. But there is only one river."

We don't know exactly when the first human being knelt beside that river and drank of its spiritual waters. All we know is that the river stretches back into the primordial ancestry of the human race and its headwaters have never been found. For thousands of years and in every culture, human beings have sat on the banks of that river and felt the stir of sacred impulses as the river spoke to them of mystical worlds and unseen things.

My own spiritual life began along one small stretch of that river which ran through the backwoods of the rural South. As a young boy I loved the mystery of its spiritual waters and the calming silence it brought to my soul. My small church claimed the river for its own, and it was many years before I understood the wisdom of the Sufi master's statement, before I realized that the river which nourishes my own soul also flows to every tribe and nation.

This book is about that river. It describes spirituality as a universal phenomenon available to every person, whether religious or not. The first half of the book defines spirituality, the soul, and the sacred in nonreligious terms. The second half of the book describes eight alternative paths to the sacred and shows readers how to develop a life of spiritual passion and depth.

If your soul is thirsty and life is hard, I hope you will find an oasis in these pages, a place to drink and be refreshed. But more than this, I hope you will come to see that the river is always there, and that all you have to do is cup your hand, reach down, and drink its life-giving waters—any time, any place, even now.

It is not true that we have to give up the concern for the soul if we do not accept the tenets of religion.
— Erich Fromm

INTRODUCTION

If you are one of the millions of Americans who find that traditional religion no longer meets your spiritual needs, this book is for you.

As a clinical psychologist and university professor, I have been studying spirituality for the last twenty years. This book is the result of that study. It is not a pop psychology book, and it will not give you easy answers. Authentic spirituality involves the development of depth, wisdom, passion, and love and is not something you can get by simply reading a book.

But don't misunderstand. This is a powerful book that contains field-tested principles. If you take this book to heart, it will show you a path and set you on a journey that could change your life forever. I know this not only because I have seen hundreds of clients, students, and others changed by these principles, but because I have experienced these changes in my own life.

I grew up in the foothills of the Ozark Mountains of northeastern Arkansas. This remote section of the country is deep in the Bible Belt, and practically everyone I knew was religious. My father was a leader in the local church, and my family attended worship at least three times a week, sometimes more.

While still a boy, I decided that I wanted to be a minister. After graduating from high school, I enrolled in a church-related college to study religion. I did well in my ministerial training, and in 1966 I was ordained as a minister. This was the realization of a long-held dream, and I was deeply happy. At the time I fully intended to spend the rest of my life serving God in that profession.

Today, thirty years later, I am no longer a minister. In fact, I am not involved with organized religion at all. Yet I am deeply interested in spirituality and believe I am taking better care of my soul today than ever before.

My disillusionment with religion began while I was still a minister. Ironically, it was as a result of my theological training that I began to outgrow my church and to realize that it was no longer meeting my spiritual needs. I found that I could no longer believe many of the things my church taught, and in the worship services I began to experience an emptiness that had not been there before. No matter how much I wanted to believe and how hard I tried to believe, I found that I could not believe what I didn't believe. It was that simple.

And that painful. Because I could no longer support the conservative views of my church, I eventually came into conflict with the leaders of my congregation and was fired. Needless to say, my family and friends were shocked. Later, when I decided to actually leave the church, almost no one could understand that decision. Nor could I fully understand it myself. All I knew was that life seemed to be pointing me in a new direction, and I felt compelled to go.

For several years I visited other churches, hoping to find one that would be in accord with my journey and be able to nurture my soul. While I met some caring people, I eventually realized that traditional religion was simply no longer relevant to my life. This was an overwhelming realization. The church had always been the center of my life. Since now it no longer spoke to my soul, I felt very lost and alone. I was afraid my spiritual life might have reached its end.

But in 1976 all of this changed. That was the year my personal lessons in the nonreligious care of the soul began. By that time I had enrolled in graduate school to pursue a doctorate in psychology. Because of the changes in my life and the fact that I was no longer taking care of my soul, I began to feel depressed. Unable to pull myself out of this unhappy state, I decided to enter therapy.

My therapist was seventy-three years of age, a former professor of philosophy and a Jungian analyst who had studied at the C. G. Jung Institute in Zurich. After listening carefully to the half-articulate longings I expressed during my first therapy session, he said gently, "You are spiritually hungry." His diagnosis proved to be profoundly correct. My soul *was* spiritually hungry, and for the next two years this wise, kind man was my spiritual mentor. Under the guise of psychotherapy he taught me about the care and feeding of the human soul.

When I told him about my disillusionment with organized religion, he assured me that there are many ways to nurture the soul that do not depend on traditional religion. He said that while religion is one path to spiritual development, there are many nonreligious paths as well.

As I learned to care for my soul in new ways, significant changes began to occur in my life. I began to feel for the first time that I knew who I was, that I was touching something of my fundamental identity, that I was coming home to myself. I felt more confidence, more personal power. Life took on depth and passion; I experienced things more intensely. I was more in touch with my body, my sensuality, my creativity. The world, which had seemed like a television program playing in black and white, now switched to living color. In time, my depression completely lifted and I felt healthy and whole.

That therapy experience was the major turning point of my life. By showing me how to care for my soul in alternative ways, my analyst provided me with the skills I needed to create a spiritual life outside the walls of established religion. In the twenty years since, I have applied this wisdom to my own life and shared it with clients and students. I have learned from my own experience the truth of psychoanalyst Erich Fromm's statement: "It is not true that we have to give up the concern for the soul if we do not accept the tenets of religion."[1]

This is vitally important. The care of the soul is essential for psychological health, and spiritual development is not an option that we can take or leave. Like the body, the soul needs care. But we live in a society that pays little attention to the soul. As a result, we find ourselves spiritually thirsty and drying up for lack of soulfulness.

In *Man and His Symbols* Carl Jung wrote, "We have stripped all things of their mystery and numinosity; nothing is holy any longer."[2] In my practice as a psychologist I see the casualties of a desacralized society. Underneath the depression, anxiety, and despair of many clients is a soul hungering for attention and care. Such spiritual hunger is rampant in America, and spiritual deprivation is at the root of many clinical pathologies. When I nurture the souls of my clients, they begin to improve. When they learn to nurture their own souls, the end of therapy is in sight.

But spiritual development is not only essential for psychological health; it is also the key to a life of passion and depth. Authentic spirituality awakens the soul, reconnects us with the sacred, and fills us with the passion of life. Spiritual development is not about religious rituals and practices; it is about waking up to the wonder of life.

What I am talking about here is reclaiming something we all seem to have naturally in childhood but then lose somewhere along the way. What happens to us as we grow up? What happens to the wonder and joy of existence? Is the death of the soul the price of adulthood? Unfortunately, when we become adults, many of us lose our vitality and our passion for life. Some fall into depression, others seek escape in compulsions or addictions, far more slip quietly into resignation and disillusionment. We stop living from our soul; we stop nurturing our soul. Some of us even forget we ever had a soul.

I live near Los Angeles. On many days the smog hangs low over the city and spreads its haze through the valleys and along the lower slopes of the mountains. But at certain times, when the Santa Ana winds blow or after a steady, cleansing rain has fallen, the smog disappears and the original beauty of this land once again sparkles in the California sun, reminding one of the beauty the early settlers must have seen when they came over the mountains or sailed up the California coast.

So it is also with our souls. In childhood the soul has a natural beauty and sparkles with life. But in adulthood the smog moves in to obscure the soul. We don't intentionally lose our soul; it simply disappears under the haze of mortgages, work schedules, and other stresses of adult life. Yet underneath the haze the soul is still alive. If we can clear away the smog, we can lay claim once again to our soul's original beauty and know again the wonder of our own existence.

Buried deep in the heart of every adult is a longing for a life that matters. We want to drink deeply from the stream of existence and know the passion of being truly alive. The purpose of this book is to say that such a life is possible, and that it all begins by learning how to nurture and care for the soul.

Ironically, one of the major obstacles to this kind of spiritual development is organized religion. In Western culture we have associated spirituality almost exclusively with traditional religion and, as a result, many people think nurturing the soul means going to church and actively embracing the rituals, beliefs, and practices of organized religion. This is unfortunate, for those who have no interest in institutional religion tend to assume that matters of the soul have nothing to do with them. To make matters worse, some churches continue to teach that one cannot be spiritual without being religious, and they discount the spirituality of those not affiliated with their particular religion or set of theological beliefs. Such religious groups have done great damage to the spiritual development of those who have no interest in formal religion.

Nevertheless, today there are many highly spiritual people who are not religious, as well as many highly religious people who are not particularly spiritual. I believe it is time for our society to acknowledge that spirituality and religiosity are not the same and that genuine spirituality deserves respect, whether we find it inside or outside the walls of organized religion. Therefore, to every spiritually thirsty man or woman, I would say this: The sacred is all around you and no one can stop you from touching the transcendent or drinking from the sacred stream. This is your birthright as a human being. No religious organization has yet captured God or imprisoned the sacred within the walls of a church building. So if organized religion no longer speaks to your soul, perhaps you are being called to go beyond religion to build a spiritual life outside the walls.

This book is written especially for those who find themselves outside those walls. The first half of the book provides a foundation for a new, nonreligious spirituality. It focuses on such words as *soul, sacred,* and *spirituality,* redefining these terms in nonreligious ways and showing that they point to something that is accessible to every person. The second half of the book provides an in-depth description of eight alternative paths to the sacred and shows you step-by-step how to develop your spiritual life.

While this book is about nonreligious spirituality, I want to make it clear that my intention is not to denigrate religion. For thousands of years religion has served as a path to transcendence for millions of people, and it will continue to serve this function for years to come. But traditional religion must realize that it does not hold a monopoly on spirituality. Spirituality is a universal human phenomenon found in all cultures and in every age; it is not the exclusive possession of any religious group. So while this book is not anti-religious, it is opposed to narrow forms of religion that build walls around the sacred and lay exclusive claim to spirituality.

My hope for this book is that it will speak to all those, religious and nonreligious alike, who once yearned for more in life, who longed to live at the growing edge of their being, who dreamed of dancing on the burning tip of life. I know that many who once dreamed such dreams have lost touch with their souls somewhere along the way.

From my own experience, I can assure you that souls can be found and spiritual life can flourish once again. If, as a result of this book, even one person arises from despair to fall in love once again with the spiritual quest, my efforts will be made worthwhile.

This book has one basic message: Life is a gift, and it is so short. Live it with all the depth and passion of your soul.

Part I

Part I lays the foundations for a new, nonreligious spirituality. It describes the spiritual revolution of our time and then redefines spirituality, the soul, and the sacred in nonreligious terms.

These chapters affirm that spirituality is a universal human phenomenon and that all people, whether religious or not, can learn to access the sacred and thereby nurture their souls and deepen their spiritual lives.

*I am deeply interested in spirituality, in being a spiritual
person. But I have no interest in religion at all. I guess
you could say that I'm spiritual but not religious.*
—a graduate student

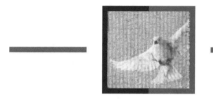

CHAPTER ONE

THE SPIRITUAL REVOLUTION
The Movement Away from
Religion to Spirituality

A spiritual revolution is quietly taking place in our society.

Millions of Americans have left traditional religion to pursue alternative paths to spiritual development. They are realizing that they can be spiritual without being religious and that they can nurture their souls without going to church or temple. This separation of spirituality from religion is one of the major sociological changes of our time and is at the heart of the greatest spiritual revolution in the West since the Protestant Reformation.

Joan, a successful artist, is a typical example. She grew up in a religious family in the Midwest but dropped out of church during her college years. Yet she remained interested in spirituality and through the years learned to nurture her soul with art, music, poetry, and literature. Now, at thirty-seven, Joan is a deeply spiritual person and, perhaps without knowing it, is on the cutting edge of the revolution I am talking about. Joan is spiritual but not religious; she has gone beyond religion to build a spiritual life outside the walls of traditional religion.

In *Megatrends 2000*, John Naisbitt named increased interest in spirituality as one of the ten megatrends in contemporary American

9

society. He pointed out that while attendance in mainline churches has declined, interest in personal spirituality is on the rise. This is especially true among educated baby boomers now reaching midlife, half of whom said they had become more spiritual in the last few years. According to Naisbitt, churches are not meeting the spiritual needs of many Americans, and "college educated people are particularly critical of this lack of spiritual nurturing."[1]

Wade Clark Roof, professor of religion and society at the University of California, Santa Barbara, recently completed a survey of 1600 baby boomers.[2] He found that this generation, which he defined as those born between 1946 and 1962, dropped out from organized religion in large numbers in the 1960s and 1970s. Of those with a religious background, 84 percent of Jews, 69 percent of mainline Protestants, 61 percent of conservative Protestants, and 67 percent of Catholics dropped out. In his survey, Roof distinguished three categories. He termed *loyalists* those who are committed to traditional religion, tend to be politically conservative on issues such as abortion, and may never have left the church. The group he labeled *returnees* tend to be more liberal and often go from one church to another "church shopping." They often find themselves in conflict with the more conservative loyalists. *Dropouts,* those in the third and largest group, show no signs of returning to church or temple. While not rejecting the notion of God, they have no interest in institutional religion. College-educated baby boomers and those without children are most likely to belong to this group.

While 25 percent of the baby boomers who left organized religion in the 1960s and 1970s have now returned to mainstream churches, 42 percent—an estimated 32 million—remain unaffiliated with any church. Yet many of these people are deeply interested in spirituality and have turned to Eastern religions, Native American traditions, Greek mythology, Twelve Step programs, Jungian psychology, New Age philosophies, shamanic practices, meditation, massage, yoga, and a host of other traditions and practices in an attempt to feed their souls.

But unfulfilled longings remain and many Americans seem lost. Having rejected organized religion, some find themselves running from one spiritual practice to the next in an effort to find spiritual meaning. Others seem to have traded their old dependency on religion for a new dependency on the latest spiritual guru or program.

The truth is, most of us have always looked to religion to guide us in spiritual matters, and we are not very good at caring for our own spirituality.

THE HISTORICAL RELATIONSHIP OF RELIGION AND SPIRITUALITY

For nearly two thousand years the Christian Church held a monopoly on spirituality in the West, and during this time nurturing the soul was the task of religion. In the Catholic Church of the Middle Ages, the parish priest was officially charged with *cura animarum,* the cure and care of the soul. Throughout medieval Europe, the Church was the center of spiritual activity and the priest was the director of all spiritual matters. Religion and spirituality were inextricably bound together.

When the Protestant Reformation broke out in the 1500s, the reformers challenged the spiritual monopoly of the Catholic Church by emphasizing the priesthood of all believers. They argued that all Christians have the right to interpret the Bible for themselves and to approach God directly, without having to go through the priest or the church. The reformers recognized that one's spirituality should not be under the control of the institutional church. This was the first crack in the solidarity of religion and spirituality.

The essence of the Protestant Reformation was that it honored the individual conscience over the power of the institution. This marked the emerging of the spirit of Western individualism in religious garb and was a major turning point in the history of the West. After centuries of religious control, individuals were free to work out their own salvation without the Church telling them what to do, think, and believe. By elevating the individual over the institution, the Reformation weakened the power of the Catholic Church and contributed to the Renaissance that was spreading across Europe at the time.

The Renaissance, the name of which means literally "being born again," began in the fourteenth century and continued until the seventeenth century. It was the transitional period between medieval and modern times and was marked by a return to the classics, a revival of humanism, an emphasis on the arts, and the beginnings of modern science. But the real fire of the Renaissance, like that of the Reformation, was the rising sense of the freedom of the individual—the intoxicating realization that one's own heart, not the dictates of any institution, is the ultimate court of appeals.

Ironically, as time went by, many Protestant churches became just as controlling as the Catholic Church that Protestantism had rebelled against. Some church leaders became obsessed with doctrinal purity and, backed by the power of Protestant governments, dealt harshly with those who disagreed with their theology. Thus many Protestants, like the Catholics before them, found that they were not in charge of their own spirituality after all. They were severely limited and circumscribed by the theology and dogma of their particular denomination.

Thus, in Europe and later in the New World, the institutional church in both its Catholic and Protestant forms continued to hold a monopoly on spirituality, and the priest or pastor remained in charge of the soul.

Religion and Spirituality Today

However, in our day this situation has changed. Millions of people no longer consider the church or temple the center of their lives, nor do they look to a priest, pastor, or rabbi for the care of their souls.

This radically different perspective is the result of the changes that came during the modern era. In medieval times the Church was the ultimate authority not only in religious matters but also in the arts and sciences. During the Renaissance the arts and sciences broke away from the Church and began to establish themselves as separate disciplines. Over the next 350 years, science slowly established itself as the ultimate authority in Western culture, and we came to look to science in much the way medieval people looked to the church. During the modern era, science expanded our knowledge and gave us new, non-theological explanations of the origin and nature of the universe and of the human species itself. These scientific explanations often contradicted what was taught in churches and Sunday schools, and slowly the scientific stories made their way into our minds, often eroding the old religious stories.

As students of theology know, science also turned its penetrating eye on religion itself. For example, modern scholars, using the tools of science, raised major questions about the origin and history of the Bible. Comparing the earliest manuscripts, they discovered differences, contradictions, additions, and deletions. Their work revealed the arbitrary and sometimes politically motivated way choices were made to include some books in the Bible and exclude others. Moreover, scholars have demonstrated that major parts of the Bible could not have been written at the time and by the authors that the Bible itself claims they were. Those who once believed the Bible was a divine book, given as a direct gift from God to humanity, have had to face the fact that it appears to be a far more human work than we had thought. Even if we maintain that the Bible is still in some sense an inspired book and a source of spiritual wisdom, this is very different from believing it to be the literal word of God and the source of all spiritual truth.

The basic problem here is that all of our traditional religious belief systems originated in a premodern era, yet we keep trying to make them fit our times. Despite our best intentions and efforts, this is becoming increasingly difficult to do.

To complicate matters even more, today we are moving out of the modern era into a postmodern age. Many of the religious belief systems that managed to hold together during the modern era in spite of the undermining influence of science are now crumbling as postmodernism adds another blow. In the modern era we believed truth was out there waiting to be discovered and that science was the way to that truth. Postmodernism, which questions our basic assumptions about knowledge itself, challenges this view. It focuses on how knowledge and belief systems are constructed and suggests that what is regarded as truth depends on the assumptions operating in a particular culture. For example, in medieval times, because theological assumptions underpinned that culture, the Church was regarded as the ultimate source of knowledge. Today, given the scientific assumptions of our culture, we look to science as the ultimate authority. We like to think that the medieval worldview was inferior, based on superstition, and that science is the true path to knowledge. But postmodernism reminds us that all knowledge systems, including our own, are social constructions. Thus our cultural assumptions, along with the politics of power, have much to do with what we decide to accept as truth. In other words, we *construct* or *invent* truth rather than simply *discover* it.[3]

The social construction of reality, as this piece of postmodernism is called, is a radically new perspective. Yet, it has strong appeal because of its usefulness in helping us to understand our diverse and confusing world. Anyone who has contact with other cultures learns firsthand that there are other realities. A businessperson who travels to Japan finds very quickly that Japanese "reality" is quite different from

American "reality." Working with Native Americans as a psychologist gave me the opportunity to appreciate the very different assumptions Native Americans hold about life, nature, God, and human relationships. As our planet becomes a global village through jet travel and electronic communications, more and more of us are exposed to diverse cultures and realities every day. Every major U.S. city is a mix of different races, ethnicities, and cultures. Dozens of realities are intermingling, often creating confusion, and sometimes violence. Many of us experience a postmodern culture shock as we try to adapt to the multiple realities in which we live our lives. Never before in the history of the world have so many people had so much contact with so many cultures different from their own.

As we are exposed to these multiple realities, it becomes increasingly difficult to maintain our own reality as the only truth. Only the most defended among us are able to do so. Most of us are forced to acknowledge that there are other realities just as viable as our own and that what we hold to be true may be far more relative than we would like to acknowledge.

This has profound implications for understanding the breakdown of Western religion and the spiritual revolution that is the focus of this book. Through contact with other cultures we have come to see that our own constructions of reality are relative and that this applies to our religious traditions as much as to any other aspect of culture. As a result, many Americans no longer consider their own religious tradition to be the only true religion, but have come to believe that all religions have something to offer, that all are legitimate ways to nurture the spiritual longings of human beings. This is a postmodern perspective.

This breakdown of our religious centrism and the opening of ourselves to other traditions is the first step in our spiritual evolution. An insular mentality that closes itself to other perspectives is simply not viable in a postmodern, pluralistic world. When we can value our own religious tradition while realizing it holds no monopoly on spiritual truth, we can then respect other traditions and open our hearts to what they may have to offer.

But it is not easy to open ourselves to other perspectives. Many of us have been taught that it is wrong to question our own religion or to investigate the religions of others, or even that to do so is an act of blasphemy against God and a betrayal of our tradition. Such religious taboos are often deeply rooted in the human psyche, and it takes great courage to transcend them. But difficult as this may be, I see the relativizing of our own tradition and the opening of ourselves to other perspectives as the first step toward spiritual maturity.

The second and perhaps even bigger step, which is the focus of this book, is the realization that spirituality and religion are not synonymous and that there are many ways to nurture the soul that have nothing to do with religion at all. The first step breaks the container of our own tradition and opens us to other religions; the second step breaks the container of religion itself and opens us to life. When we take the second step, we see that all of life is sacred and that the entire universe is a garden from which we can nourish our souls.

At this stage in our spiritual development we stop looking to priests, pastors, rabbis, or gurus to tell us what is best for our souls, and we begin to take *cura animarum* as our personal responsibility. While we may value religion as one path to spiritual development, we no longer see it as the *only* path, and we are cautious about turning over our souls to any religious leader or spiritual discipline.

Personal spirituality in its most radical form means taking responsibility for our own spiritual development and learning how to nurture our own soul. For many of us it means going beyond religion to build our own spiritual life outside the walls.

The journey toward spiritual maturity is not simply an intellectual journey but one that involves the heart as well. The death of old beliefs is intensely painful, and the lack of understanding from family and friends can be almost devastating. Yet our birth into a wider spiritual consciousness makes it ultimately worthwhile. We break into a new reality that transcends the narrow confines of our own culture and creed. Our identification moves beyond our own clan to the human species at large as we realize that the spiritual longings of our own hearts are the universal song of humankind. The universe becomes our temple, the earth our altar, and daily life our sacred bread. The oral traditions, wisdom literature, and spiritual libraries of the world become our scriptures, and all humanity, regardless of nation, race, color, or creed, becomes our congregation.

Millions of people have already taken these steps, and millions more will do so in the future. The movement away from traditional religion to new forms of spirituality is a major revolution, part of the general *zeitgeist* as Western culture moves into a postmodern age. Before this revolution is finished, it will have changed the nature of spirituality in the West for all time to come.

THE SEPARATION OF SPIRITUALITY FROM RELIGION

The core of the spiritual revolution is that for the first time in 2000 years of Western history, spirituality is breaking away from traditional religion. In America we can see recent manifestations of this in the form of three waves of change that have occurred over the past thirty years.

The First Wave: The Human Potential Movement

The first wave was the human potential movement of the 1960s. Abraham Maslow, one of the founders of this movement, considered personal spirituality a major component of one's psychological growth, or self-actualization. Maslow was not impressed by most organized religions, but he was deeply committed to spirituality. In *Religions, Values, and Peak Experiences* he wrote:

> I want to demonstrate that spiritual values have naturalistic mean-
> ing, that they are not the exclusive possession of organized churches,
> that they do not need supernatural concepts to validate them, that
> they are well within the jurisdiction of a suitably enlarged science,
> and that, therefore, they are the general responsibility of all man-
> kind.[4]

Maslow was not opposed to organized religion per se, but he was critical of any church or religion that claimed a monopoly on spirituality and that refused to acknowledge its universal human character.

Inspired by people like Maslow and caught up in the *zeitgeist* of that decade, in the 1960s many young people left the religion of their parents in quest of more personal and relevant forms of spirituality. While the human potential movement itself began to fade in the 1970s, the search for spirituality it had spawned continued. A Gallup poll taken in 1978 showed that ten million Americans had turned to Eastern religions and nine million were involved in some form of spiritual healing.[5]

The Second Wave: The New Age Movement

In the 1980s the second wave broke across America in the form of the New Age movement. *New Age Journal* was launched in 1983 with a circulation of 50,000, which grew to nearly 200,000 by the end of the decade. Ninety-five percent of its readers were college-educated and had household incomes averaging $47,500.[6]

Millions of Americans were intrigued by the New Age movement —by channeling, reincarnation, past-lives therapy, spiritual healing, New Age music, even the beads, pyramids, and crystals that were the movement's physical trappings. The movement generated countless articles, books, tapes, videos, groups, and workshops. In many ways the New Age movement was a spiritual collage, a smorgasbord of spirituality imported from many lands and traditions and eagerly sampled by spiritually hungry Americans.

Early in its history, parts of the New Age movement seemed to overlap and join forces with Alcoholics Anonymous and other Twelve Step programs that for years had emphasized the importance of spirituality in the recovery process. Although New Age spirituality and the spirituality of the recovery movement were not the same, they supported and enhanced each other. Thus the movement toward spirituality in America grew even larger. Books on love, healing, and spirituality hit the bestseller lists. It became almost fashionable to be a recovering addict on a spiritual journey; prominent persons, from Hollywood stars to political figures, came forward to confess their addictions and to testify about the spiritual reorientation that was part of their healing.

The Third Wave: The Movement toward the Soul

In the early 1990s, a third wave began to form, distinctly different from the previous two. This was the movement toward the soul.

In 1991, Thomas Moore's *Care of the Soul* was published and within a few months was on the bestseller lists.[7] Soon the market was flooded with books, tapes, workshops, and conferences on the soul. The word *soul*, which until then had been associated primarily with religion or the blues, moved out from these confines and was used to describe everything from inspirational stories to intimate relationships.

These three waves have had a powerful impact on spirituality in America. They helped break the historical tie between religion and spirituality, and they produced a generation of Americans who knew that it was possible to be spiritual but not religious.

How the Baby Boomers Are Shaping America's Spirituality

The baby boom generation has been the force behind the human potential, New Age, and soul movements. Members of this generation bought the books, attended the workshops, and provided the impetus for the spiritual revolution. Because they will continue to shape America's spirituality for years to come, we need to take a closer look at this unusual group.

The baby boomers are the largest generation of Americans in history. Defined by the U.S. Bureau of the Census as those born between 1946 and 1964, the sheer numbers of this generation, estimated at 75,862,000, are staggering.[8] This population bulge changes our culture as it passes through each stage of life.

The baby boomers are now reaching midlife. Midlife forces us to face our mortality. As we watch our parents grow old and die, we cannot help but reflect on ourselves, for we are next in the generational line. Midlife calls on us to examine our values, to sort out what is truly important from what is not. For many it is a time of turmoil and confusion. Some leave their mates or have affairs. Others change occupations or move to new places. Even those who do not make major life changes often make radical shifts in their values and priorities. And some fail to make it through the midlife passage altogether; they become lost in the turbulence of those years. "Midlife crisis" is more than a cliché.

If we define the midlife years as between the ages of thirty-five and fifty-five, this generation will not complete the midlife passage until the year 2020. This means that for another two decades, millions of Americans will be struggling with the existential issues of midlife and will continue to look for ways to address these spiritual needs.

Midlife spirituality has it own character, and it is distinctly different from that of youth. One way to describe this difference is to say that the spirituality of youth has to do with spirit while that of midlife has to do with soul.

Jungian scholar James Hillman has pointed out that spirit and soul, two words we often use interchangeably, are actually quite different in meaning.[9] Spirit is about height; soul is about depth. Youth is a time of the spirit; it is about climbing, striving for success, achieving. Midlife is a time of the soul; it is about descending into our depths to forge new values for the second half of life. Over the door of youth the sign reads: "The workshop of the spirit," while the sign over the door of midlife says: "The smithy of the soul."

The human potential and New Age movements were primarily spirit movements. They were about ascending, growing, actualizing, and expanding. The human potential movement, reflecting the exuberant spirit of youth as the baby boomers came of age, told us that, like Jonathan Livingston Seagull, our potential was limitless, that we could fly ever higher, ever faster. Maslow told us we could climb the ladder of self-actualization and achieve our highest potentials. Likewise, the New Age movement, reflecting the expansive spirit of this generation as it moved into young adulthood and the optimistic spirit and economic expansion of the 1980s, told us that spiritual growth and economic success had no ceilings.

Now, in the 1990s, as the baby boomers reach midlife, they have begun to descend, creating the movement toward the soul. Because of its large numbers, the baby boom generation is like a weather vane that indicates the nature and direction of spirituality in this country. If we wish to understand future spiritual trends, we must continue to watch this generation as it passes through midlife and into its older years.

The spiritual revolution has found its army in the populous baby boom generation. However, it would be a mistake to conclude that this revolution is simply a baby boom phenomenon. The spiritual revolution is part of a much larger cultural *zeitgeist* that has been gathering force for centuries and is now sweeping Western society into a new world and toward a new kind of spirituality.

The baby boomers have not caused the breakdown of religion in the West. They are merely the first generation to express, en masse, the new reality—that traditional religion has already broken down.

They will not be the last.

JUNGIAN PSYCHOLOGY AND SPIRITUALITY

As we survey the spiritual landscape in the throes of the spiritual revolution, we see a great deal of confusion and chaos. The territory of spirituality has changed, and we need all the help we can get to find our way in this new land. Here psychology, which literally means "the study of the soul," can be of assistance. While the field of modern psychology is dominated by medical and mechanistic models that leave little room for the soul, there are some theorists, such as Carl Jung, who have a great deal to teach us about the soul. Because I will be referring to his ideas throughout the book, I would like to introduce him to those who are not familiar with his views.

Jung, a contemporary of Freud, was once his protégé. But whereas Freud had little interest in spirituality and even considered it a sign of neurosis, Jung made spirituality the center of his work and believed the major task of midlife was the recovery of the soul. In *Modern Man in Search of a Soul* Jung said that, among his patients over the age of thirty-five, not one was healed who did not recover a spiritual orientation to life.[10] Jung's work is now experiencing a momentous revival. Jungian themes, such as archetypes, mythology, spirituality, and the soul, are being discussed widely, and books and programs reflecting these themes are attracting the attention of millions.

The Collective Unconscious and the Archetypes

Through his study of religion and mythology, Jung developed his theory of the collective unconscious.[11] He considered the collective unconscious to be the deepest region of the mind, containing the *archetypes*, literally the "old patterns," from our primordial past. These universal patterns, which are found in all cultures, are the roots of our religions and mythologies and the sources of our deepest passions. When the ancient Greeks created their pantheon of gods and goddesses, they were expressing the polytheism of the collective unconscious, the archetypes that we project into our mythologies.

But archetypes are not only found in religion and myth; they are also present in art, literature, poetry, plays, movies, stories, and almost any other medium that deals with the universal themes of human life. When thousands of women were drawn to the image of the "wild woman" in Clarissa Pinkola Estes' best-selling book, *Women Who Run with the Wolves*, they were being stirred at the archetypal level.[12] Likewise, when Robert Bly and others in the men's movement talked about recovering the primitive "wild man," they were referring to a Jungian archetype that men have lost touch with in the context of modern society.[13] When mythologist Joseph Campbell was interviewed by Bill Moyers for television and fascinated television audiences with mythological stories from many cultures, he was speaking the universal language of the human soul, the language of Jungian psychology.[14] Spirituality has much to do with the collective unconscious and the archetypes. That is, spirituality has to do with the deepest levels of the human psyche and the universal patterns of the human soul. If we wish to create a new spirituality and learn how to nurture the soul in new ways, we will not find a better guide than Carl Jung as we move into these uncharted regions.

Jung's Developmental Theory

Jung's developmental theory is especially helpful for understanding some of the issues discussed in this book.[15] Jung compared our life span to the course of the sun as it ascends in the morning, reaches its zenith at noon, and descends in the afternoon. Thus youth is the morning of life—a time to ascend, achieve, try our wings, discover our potentials. But at midlife, when our journey is half complete, we must change direction as we enter the afternoon of life. Midlife is thus a time for reflection and spiritual reorientation, a time to forge the kind of spirituality that can carry us through the second half of life and even into the face of death itself. As Dante knew, midlife is like entering a dark wood. It is a time to travel into the underworld, into the shadows and depths of the soul. Here we must confront our own darkness, look old age and death in the face, and understand more fully the tragic and noble realities of human existence. This is the central task of midlife. Through it we come to appreciate life in its fullness, valuing every precious moment, and we find the kind of spirituality that can only be forged in the dark smithy of the midlife soul.

We are living in a time when one age is dying and another is trying to be born. For many, the old wineskins of traditional religion are breaking and the symbols of the past no longer speak to the soul. Thus the task of our generation is to find new symbols for the sacred, new ways to nurture and care for our souls. We need a new spirituality, one that cannot be contained by the wineskins of the past, one that is based on universal spiritual principles and is therefore relevant to the postmodern soul.

*I believe deeply that we must find, all of us together,
a new spirituality.*
—the Dalai Lama

CHAPTER TWO

TOWARD A NEW SPIRITUALITY
A Nonreligious Approach

According to Jungian analyst Robert Johnson, the following story was Carl Jung's favorite.

> The water of life, wishing to make itself known on the face of the earth, bubbled up in an artesian well and flowed without effort or limit. People came to drink of the magic water and were nourished by it, since it was so clean and pure and invigorating. But humankind was not content to leave things in this Edenic state. Gradually they began to fence the well, charge admission, claim ownership of the property around it, make elaborate laws as to who could come to the well, put locks on the gates. Soon the well was the property of the powerful and the elite. The water was angry and offended; it stopped flowing and began to bubble up in another place. The people who owned the property around the first well were so engrossed in their power systems and ownership that they did not notice that the water had vanished. They continued selling the nonexistent water, and few people noticed that the true power was gone. But some dissatisfied people searched with great courage and found the new artesian well. Soon that well was under the control of the property owners, and the same fate overtook it. The spring took itself to yet another place—and this has been going on throughout recorded history.

Johnson commented on this story:

> Water has often been used as a symbol for the deepest spiritual nour-
> ishment of humanity. It is flowing in our time in history, as always,
> for the well is faithful to its mission; but it flows in some odd places.
> It has often ceased to flow in the accustomed sites and turned up
> in some most surprising locations. But, thank God, the water is still
> there.[1]

Spirituality is sustained by the free-flowing water of life. But, as the
story implies, throughout history institutional religion has fenced off
the water, put locks on the gates, and made rules as to who can and
cannot have access. Religion has often proclaimed itself the sole cus-
todian of the water, telling the nonreligious, no matter how spiritually
inclined, that they have no water rights unless they become members
of the church and abide by its rules.

Frustrated by such exclusion, many people today have turned away
from the gates, unwilling to pay the price of admission, and have gone
in search of new wells. Others, who once paid the price and were admitted, have found their religion to be barren and dry. Realizing they
were buying empty promises and nonexistent water, they have left to
join the ranks of those searching for a new spirituality outside the
walls of traditional religion.

But what does it mean to create a spiritual life outside the walls?
What is spirituality stripped of its ecclesiastical robes? What does it
mean to drink from the sacred waters in their purity, undiluted and
unaltered by religion? How does one define and describe such a spirituality?

THE MEANING OF THE WORD *SPIRITUALITY*

The word *spirituality* comes from the Latin root *spiritus*, which means
"breath" and refers to the breath of life, or the animating principle.
This same idea is expressed in Genesis 2:7, which reads, "And the
Lord God formed man of the dust of the ground, and breathed into
his nostrils the breath of life; and man became a living soul."

Spirituality is based on the belief that there are two dimensions of
reality, the material and the nonmaterial. Material reality refers to the
world of tangible things, the things we know through the five senses.
The earth, trees, soil, rocks, this desk in front of me, even my own
body are all tangible realities, parts of the material world.

But there is another dimension that is just as real; this is the
nonmaterial realm, the world that artists, mystics, poets, prophets,

shamans, and philosophers have described for thousands of years. This dimension is not part of the material realm; it is not tangible and cannot be known through the five senses. Yet, it is vitally important to human life. In this dimension we anchor our lives and find our deepest values and meanings. This is the world of spiritual and phenomenological realities. Spirituality lives in this nonmaterial world.

In their book *The Spirituality of Imperfection*, Ernest Kurtz and Katherine Ketcham pointed out that in ancient times the word spirituality was used in contrast to materialism. The word then fell out of usage for almost sixteen hundred years until the postmodern age resurrected it, again as a contrast—but now less in contrast to materialism than to religion.[2] Today, when people say they consider themselves spiritual but not religious, they are making this distinction. And in this distinction lies the seed of the new spirituality.

THE NEW SPIRITUALITY AND RELIGION

My father was a farmer who had a homespun way of stating some profound truths. One of his favorite sayings was, "Sitting in a church house will no more make you a Christian than sitting in a chicken house will make you a chicken!" Dad knew the difference between institutional affiliation and personal spirituality.

Many scholars, using more academic language, have made this same point. The psychologist and philosopher William James said there are two basic types of religion: institutional and personal.[3] Abraham Maslow agreed, calling institutional religion "big R" religion and personal spirituality "little r" religion.[4] Gordon Allport, a psychologist who spent his life studying religion, also concluded that there are two basic forms of religion, which he called "extrinsic" and "intrinsic."[5] Extrinsic refers primarily to the public or external aspects of religion, while intrinsic refers more to one's personal or inner devotion.

Thus, a line of demarcation runs through the field of religion. On one side is public or institutional religion with its buildings, programs, clergy, theology, rituals, and ceremonies. On the other is private or personal religion with its emphasis on nurturing the soul and developing one's spiritual life.

So far nothing new has been said. Most people, including those who are religious, would agree that affiliation with a religious institution and personal spirituality are not the same. Priests, pastors, and rabbis continually remind their congregations that true spirituality involves a commitment of the heart, not simply an outward show of religiosity.

But we must go a step farther. The new spirituality is not only different from institutional affiliation; it is also different from personal spirituality based on religion. What makes the new spirituality so unprecedented is that for many people it has nothing to do with religion at all, in either its institutional or personal forms. If people were merely rejecting organized religion to practice the same religion at home, though this would certainly have an impact, it would not be nearly so revolutionary as what is actually taking place. Today people are rejecting not only organized religion but also the religious belief system that goes along with it. They are searching for radically new forms of spirituality, which is what makes this spiritual movement so significant.

I am convinced that this movement is revolutionary only because traditional religion has been so exclusive about spirituality. Is it really so radical to think that spirituality is a universal phenomenon and that everyone has a right to drink from the sacred spring without the mediation of a particular religion? If the artesian well is flowing freely outside the walls of conventional religion, doesn't everyone have a right to drink its life-giving water? From this perspective, the new spirituality is not really new at all; it is simply an effort to reclaim what has always belonged to us—the right, whether we are religious or not, to drink from the sacred spring.

In keeping with this vision, I would suggest the following as a working definition of spirituality:

> Spirituality is the process and result of nurturing one's soul and developing one's spiritual life. While many do this in the context of traditional religion, it must be recognized that religion is only one path to spiritual development and that there are many alternative paths as well. Therefore, spirituality is accessible to all those who are nurturing their souls and cultivating their spiritual lives, whether inside or outside the walls of traditional religion.

THE CONTENT OF SPIRITUALITY

While the above definition helps clarify and extend the boundaries of spirituality, it really tells us little about the content of spirituality itself. What is spirituality when it is divorced from religion? In other words, what is the essence of spirituality once all the religious trappings have been removed?

A friend of mine who is a member of a conservative church says the problem with nonreligious spirituality is that it has no content— it has no systematic beliefs, no specific moral teachings, no identifiable social community, and no set of rituals, ceremonies, and symbols. What my friend is really saying is that the new spirituality is not a religion—but we already knew that. What he fails to understand is that this is exactly why those who see themselves as spiritual but not religious prefer this new vision of spirituality over the traditional religious one. While the old religious forms bring comfort to some, others find them to be oppressive. Those who are spiritual but not religious do not like the massive yoke of religious rules, requirements, and directives which typically go along with religion. They prefer to engage life in a fresh, authentic manner, seeking new and creative solutions to the complex problems of existence.

The new spirituality *does* have content—perhaps not a content of specific religious beliefs, rules, and rituals, but a content of foundational spiritual values. My friend prefers a spiritual house where all the rooms, and even the furniture and decorations, are already in place. And traditional religion offers this. The new spirituality is more concerned with the house's foundations. The foundations of a genuine spirituality have both vertical and horizontal dimensions. They involve loving God, or the transcendent, and also treating our fellow human beings with mercy, compassion, and justice. The new spirituality believes that individuals have the right to build their own spiritual house provided they build it on solid values.

The new spirituality is more prophetic than priestly. The priests of the Old Testament tended to be concerned with rules, rituals, and ceremonies, while the prophets were the ones who cut through religious forms and went to the heart of the matter, calling for a return to foundational principles. For example, when the prophet Micah tried to call the people back to God, he said, "What does the Lord require of you but to treat others with justice, to love mercy, and to walk humbly with your God?"

We find the same in the New Testament. Jesus himself was in the prophetic tradition. He challenged the institutional religion of his day and emphasized foundational values. The Pharisees, who were immersed in religious rules and rituals, asked him, "What is the great commandment?" Going straight to the heart of the matter, Jesus answered that the greatest commandment is to love God and the second is to love one's neighbor as one's self, and that on these two commandments hang all the law and the prophets.

Of course, those who prefer elaborate rules and ready-made answers to life's problems will be uncomfortable with foundational spiritual principles. They will see such principles as too ambiguous and a spirituality based on them as having no content. But I believe that those who live from such principles, working to apply them to each life situation, are expressing a more mature spirituality than those who operate at the legalistic level. Life is complex, and ready-made answers do not always fit. In fact, sometimes ready-made answers are damaging and immoral because they ignore the complexity of a situation and trample people, and compassion, underfoot. True spirituality means entering the arena of life with a heart of compassion and then doing the best we can. It means getting our hands dirty at times and not being so concerned with our own legalistic purity. This is not a content-less spirituality, because the principles themselves are the content. Personally, I know of no content of spirituality more powerful than such principles as love, compassion, mercy, and justice. If sincerely followed, these principles would impact everything we are and everything we do.

Spirituality and Theological Correctness

One of the major objections to a universal spirituality comes from those who believe spirituality is only accessible to those who hold certain religious beliefs. Fundamentalist religions are especially insistent on this point. Adherents will tell you in no uncertain terms that unless you believe what they believe and practice what they practice, your spirituality cannot be valid. The history of religion is filled with groups that have taken this view.

Must one be a "true believer" in a particular religion in order to develop an authentic spirituality? Must we be a member of a certain religious group or hold a particular set of theological beliefs? Or is spirituality something bigger, more universal than fundamentalists would lead us to believe? Is it possible that a certain attitude of the heart, rather than one's creed or theological position, is the key that opens the doors to an authentic spiritual life?

The following scholars have struggled with this issue and provide important insights.

Paul Tillich: Ultimate Concern

Paul Tillich, one of the most influential theologians of this century, believed the word *faith* is best understood as "ultimate concern."[6] Faith is an existential attitude of the heart rather than commitment to a particular theological view. Faith means to invest something with our ultimate concern. In this act we say, "This is the most important thing in life and it deserves my commitment, passion, and soul." Tillich was well aware of the risk involved in faith; he knew we could devote ourselves to the wrong things and come to realize at the end of our lives that we had completely missed the meaning and purpose of our existence. The authenticity of our spiritual life depends on the depth and level of concern with which we address this central task. In Tillich's view, every human being, whether religious or not, is confronted with the question of faith: What will be the organizing principle, the ultimate concern, to which I give my life?

James Fowler: The Deeper Meaning of Faith

James Fowler, a contemporary theologian trained at Harvard, takes a similar view in his discussion of the deeper meanings of the word *faith*. Like Tillich, Fowler believes faith is universal and has to do with the heart rather than with commitment to a particular belief system. In his book *Stages of Faith*, Fowler pointed out that the Latin word *credo*, usually translated "I believe," comes from *cordia* or "heart" and literally means "to set one's heart upon." Thus, faith is an action of the heart rather than an intellectual assent to theological propositions.

Fowler emphasized that faith is not always religious in nature. He wrote:

> Prior to our being religious or irreligious, before we come to think of ourselves as Catholics, Protestants, Jews or Muslims, we are already engaged with issues of faith. Whether we become nonbelievers, agnostics or atheists, we are concerned with how to put our lives together and with what will make life worth living.[7]

Fowler sees faith as an effort to find a center for our lives, an ultimate concern that we can believe in and give ourselves to. As he put it, faith is a "way of moving into the force field of our lives" and of finding "an overarching, integrating and grounding trust in a center of value and power sufficiently worthy to give our lives unity and meaning."

Fowler used an incident from his eighth grade science class to illustrate the nature of faith. One day his science teacher brought two electromagnets and some iron filings to school. The students sprinkled the iron filings onto a sheet of paper, set the magnets at either end, and turned on the current. Fowler told what happened: "Impressively, the iron filings danced into a symmetrical overall pattern. As we tapped the paper lightly they formed force lines running smoothly from one magnet to the other, spreading like the seams of a cantaloupe. The lines graphically revealed the patterns of the magnetic force field." So also, faith is a way of bringing "order, unity and coherence in the force field of our lives."

To those who hold narrow, exclusivistic views, Fowler said:

> To you I want to affirm the largeness and mystery of faith. So fundamental that none of us can live well for very long without it, so universal that when we move beneath the symbols, rituals and ethical patterns that express it, faith is recognizably the same phenomenon to Christians, Marxists, Hindus and Dinka, yet it is so infinitely varied that each person's faith is unique. . . . Any of us can be illumined in our efforts to relate to the holy by the integrity we find in the faith stances of others, whether they are religious or nonreligious.[8]

William James: Primal Truth

In *The Varieties of Religious Experience* William James also affirmed the universal nature of spirituality. He defined religion as "the feelings, acts, and experiences of individual men in their solitude, so far as they apprehend themselves to stand in relation to whatever they may consider the divine." He went on to define the divine in very broad terms, saying that it could mean any primal truth or overarching principle to which one is committed. James wrote, "A man's religion might thus be identified with his attitude, whatever it might be, toward what he felt to be the primal truth." Refining this point, however, James said that he could not call all such commitments religious or spiritual. He gave examples of some primal truths that are shallow and cynical, indicating that, in his opinion, they did not deserve to be called religious. Finally, he stated his own view of the religious attitude in the following words:

> There must be something solemn, serious, and tender about any attitude which we denominate religious. If glad, it must not grin or

snicker; if sad, it must not scream or curse. It is precisely as being solemn experiences that I wish to interest you in religious experiences. . . . The divine shall mean for us only such a primal reality as the individual feels impelled to respond to solemnly and gravely, and neither by a curse nor a jest.[9]

Like Tillich and Fowler, James made it clear that spirituality is an attitude of the heart, a solemn and serious approach to the task of choosing and living in relation to a primal truth. For all three men spirituality depends on a certain existential attitude toward life, rather than on a particular set of theological beliefs. Of course, some people will not accept this enlarged view of faith. They are convinced that their religion is the only correct one and that their theological beliefs are the only key to the spiritual kingdom. In the meantime, however, the world goes on; in every culture, including our own, people are finding their way to the sacred. God is not as small as many people think.

Paul Tillich's idea of faith as ultimate concern and James's idea of primal truth hold much meaning for me. These ideas deliver faith from being an assent to narrow theological propositions and reframe it as an existential attitude of the heart. Yet, in agreement with James, I cannot equate all ultimate concerns or primal truths with spirituality. For example, if my ultimate concern or primal truth is to eat, drink, and be merry, I am a hedonist, not a spiritual person. So it seems that one must always ask about the object of the ultimate concern. With regard to spirituality, the object must always be the sacred, or what James called the divine. I do not believe that one must hold a certain theological position or have the sacred all figured out; but I do believe spirituality is always connected with our yearning for the divine, the sacred, the mystery, the numinous, the transcendent, the ultimate, or whatever one wishes to call that which lies beyond.

What I am suggesting is that the sacred is an essential ingredient in the formula for spirituality. It is the proper object of our ultimate concerns, primal truths, and searches within. The sacred is revealed through those experiences in life that touch the soul and fill us with a sense of poignancy, wonder, and awe. Where the soul is stirred, nurtured, and moved by the sacred, there is spirituality. In these moments one's latent ultimate concern may rise up, know itself, and lay claim to what is truly important in life.

Research in Nonreligious Spirituality

I first became interested in a new, nonreligious vision of spirituality in 1985 after attending a symposium at a California Psychological Association (CPA) meeting in San Francisco. A CPA task force had conducted a state-wide survey of psychologists to determine their attitudes toward religion and spirituality.[10] The survey found that over 70 percent of California psychologists considered spirituality relevant to their personal lives and clinical work, yet only 9 percent reported a high level of involvement with organized religion. Almost half (49 percent) said they were following an alternative spiritual path, and 74 percent indicated organized religion was not the primary source of their spirituality.[11]

I was intrigued by these findings, which confirmed my own informal observations that many people were developing their spirituality outside organized religion. Pursuing my interest in this area, in 1986 I formed a research group at my university to study nonreligious spirituality. Since then this has been the major focus of my scholarly activities.

My Personal Views on Spirituality

My studies, reflections, and experiences related to spirituality have led me to the following conclusions:

First: Spirituality is universal. By this I mean that spirituality is available to every human being. It is not limited to one religion, one culture, or one group of people. In every part of the world one finds those who have cultivated their souls and developed their spiritual lives.

Second: Spirituality is a human phenomenon. This does not mean that it has no divine component, but it does mean that spirituality is an inborn, natural potential of the human being. It also means that authentic spirituality is grounded in our humanity; it is not imposed from above or from without.

Third: The common core of spirituality is found at the inner, phenomenological level. Spirituality manifests in countless outer forms— from the rain dances of Native Americans to the prayer services of Southern Baptists, from the whirling dervishes of Islam to the meditating monks of Zen Buddhism, from the ecstatic worship services of charismatic churches to the solemn, silent meetings of the Quakers.

But underneath these outward forms, there is a common longing for the sacred, a universal desire to touch and celebrate the mystery of life. It is in the depths of the soul that one discovers the essential and universal dimensions of spirituality.

Fourth: Spirituality has to do with our capacity to respond to the numinous. The essential character of spirituality is mystical, a fact easily overlooked in a scientific and material age. Spirituality is rooted in the soul and cultivated by experiences of the sacred; it feeds on poignancy, wonder, and awe. Its very nature is an expression of the mystery of life and the unfathomable depths of our own being.

Fifth: There is a certain mysterious energy associated with spirituality. Every culture has recognized a life force that moves through all creation. Mystics, poets, artists, shamans, and others are familiar with this force and have described it through the centuries. The soul comes alive when it is nurtured by this sacred energy, and one's existence becomes infused with passion, power, and depth.

Sixth: The aim of spirituality is compassion. The word *compassion* literally means "to suffer with." Spiritual life springs from the tenderness of the heart, and authentic spirituality expresses itself through loving action toward others. Compassion has always been the hallmark of authentic spirituality and the highest teaching of religion. Loveless spirituality is an oxymoron and an ontological impossibility.

The Components of Spirituality

One of the goals of my original research group was to define and describe spirituality from a nonreligious perspective. We found that many people, including researchers themselves, often confused spirituality with certain religious beliefs and practices. We believed there is a difference between spirituality and religiosity, and we wanted to clarify this difference.

As we reviewed articles and books on this subject, it became increasingly clear that spirituality is a complex construct composed of several major factors. Eventually, our research group arrived at the following definition of spirituality:

> Spirituality, which comes from the Latin *spiritus*, meaning "breath of life," is a way of being and experiencing that comes about through awareness of a transcendent dimension and that is characterized by certain identifiable values in regard to self, others, nature, life, and whatever one considers to be the Ultimate.[12]

We elaborated on this definition to arrive at a description of spirituality as a multidimensional construct having the following nine major components:

1. Transcendent dimension. The spiritual person has an experientially based belief that there is a transcendent dimension to life. The content of this belief may range from the traditional view of a personal God to a psychological view that the transcendent dimension is simply a natural extension of the conscious self into the regions of the unconscious or Greater Self. But whatever the content, typology, metaphors, or models used to describe the transcendent dimension, the spiritual person believes in the "more," that what is seen is not all there is. She believes in an unseen dimension and believes that harmonious contact with and adjustment to this unseen dimension is beneficial. The spiritual person is one who has experienced the transcendent dimension, often through what Maslow referred to as peak experiences, and she draws personal power through contact with this dimension.

2. Meaning and purpose in life. The spiritual person has known the quest for meaning and purpose and has emerged from this quest with confidence that life is deeply meaningful and that his own existence has purpose. The actual ground and content of this meaning vary from person to person, but the common factor is that each person has filled the existential vacuum with an authentic sense that life has meaning and purpose.

3. Mission in life. The spiritual person has a sense of vocation. She feels a sense of responsibility to life, a calling to answer, a mission to accomplish, even a destiny to fulfill. The spiritual person is "meta-motivated" and understands that it is in losing one's life that one finds it.

4. Sacredness of life. The spiritual person believes life is infused with sacredness and often experiences a sense of awe, reverence, and wonder in nonreligious settings. He does not dichotomize life into sacred and secular, but believes all of life is holy and that the sacred is in the ordinary.

5. Spiritual vs. material values. The spiritual person may appreciate material goods such as money and possessions but does not seek ultimate satisfaction from them nor attempt to use them as substitutes for frustrated spiritual needs. The spiritual person knows that ontological thirst can only quenched by the spiritual and that ultimate satisfaction is found in spiritual, not material, things.

6. Altruism. The spiritual person believes we are our brother's keeper and is touched by the pain and suffering of others. She has a strong sense of social justice and is committed to altruistic love and action. The spiritual person knows that no man is an island—rather, that we are all part of the continent of humanity.

7. Idealism. The spiritual person is a visionary committed to the betterment of the world. He loves things for what they are, yet also for what they can become. The spiritual person is committed to high ideals and to the actualization of positive potential in all aspects of life.

8. Awareness of the tragic. The spiritual person is solemnly conscious of the tragic realities of human existence. Deep awareness of human pain, suffering, and death gives depth to the spiritual person and provides her with an existential seriousness toward life. Somewhat paradoxically, however, awareness of the tragic enhances the spiritual person's joy, appreciation, and valuing of life.

9. Fruits of spirituality. The spiritual person is one whose spirituality has borne fruit in her life. True spirituality has a discernible effect upon one's relation to self, others, nature, life, and whatever one considers to be the Ultimate.

The Spiritual Orientation Inventory

The first phase of our research, as described above, provided us with a nonreligious definition and description of spirituality. The second phase focused on the construction of the *Spiritual Orientation Inventory*, a measure of nonreligious spirituality, since we wanted to produce a test that psychologists and others could use in research and clinical work.[13]

At first we were reluctant to try to measure spirituality. But in time we came to believe this could be done if it was approached in a sensitive manner. Two things convinced us of this. First: we noted that most people have an intuitive sense of what is meant when someone is described as very spiritual. We believed that by basing our assessment on the above nine components, we could make this intuitive process more conscious, systematic, and accurate. Second: we knew that the history of psychology has proven that subtle phenomenological realities can be assessed and even quantified if this is done gently and carefully.

We found that existing tests for studying spirituality often were not based on a comprehensive theory of spirituality and that they measured only some of the dimensions in our model. Further, some of them included items reflecting a traditional religious point of view and therefore were not sensitive to the spirituality of those not involved with traditional religion.

So we became convinced that it was important to develop a theoretically based inventory that would assess spirituality from a nonreligious perspective. We eventually produced a preliminary form of what would become the *Spiritual Orientation Inventory*. After our research group dissolved, I continued to develop this inventory, which is now used rather widely by those doing research on spirituality.

The work I have described here is only a beginning. Nevertheless, I believe it lays down some important theoretical foundations and shows that spirituality can be defined in nonreligious ways. I hope these efforts will inspire others to do research and theoretical work in this area.

As we move into the postmodern age, we can no longer afford the luxury of tribal gods and narrow spiritual views. We simply must see that God is everywhere, that artesian wells of spirituality exist across the land. We must recognize that spirituality is universal and that the spiritual blood, as it were, that flows in our own veins is no different from that which flows in the veins of every other man and woman. To develop a new, universal vision of spirituality, we must be willing to open our hearts and let go of narrow religious views. We must be willing to join hands with others and work toward a common faith. As the Dalai Lama said, "We must find, all of us together, a new spirituality."[14]

Everyone should know that you can't live in any other way than by cultivating the soul.
—Apuleius

Chapter Three

The Soul
Doorway to the Imaginal World

According to an old Hindu legend, there was once a time when all human beings were gods, but they so abused their divinity that Brahma, the chief god, decided to take it away from them and hide it where it could never be found. Where to hide their divinity was the question. So Brahma called a council of the gods to help him decide. "Let's bury it deep in the earth," said the gods. But Brahma answered, "No, that will not do because humans will dig into the earth and find it." Then the gods said, "Let's sink it in the deepest ocean." But Brahma said, "No, not there, for they will learn to dive into the ocean and will find it." Then the gods said, "Let's take it to the top of the highest mountain and hide it there." But once again Brahma replied, "No, that will not do either, because they will eventually climb every mountain and once again take up their divinity." Then the gods gave up and said, "We do not know where to hide it, because it seems that there is no place on earth or in the sea that human beings will not eventually reach." Brahma thought for a long time and then said, "Here is what we will do. We will hide their divinity deep in the center of their own being, for humans will never think to look for it there." All the gods agreed that this was the perfect hiding place, and the deed was done. And, since that time humans have been going

up and down the earth, digging, diving, climbing, and exploring—
searching for something that is already within themselves.

THE REALITY OF THE SOUL

This Hindu story tells us that we have a divine nature that lies hidden at the core of our being. Many great spiritual leaders have given us
this same message. Jesus, for example, said, "The kingdom of heaven is
within," and asked, "What is a man profited if he gains the whole
world but loses his own soul?"

Throughout history the religions of the world have panned the
stream of human experience, seeking the gold it will yield. And these
religions, almost without exception, have concluded that the most
valuable nugget they have found is that we have a spiritual dimension
that transcends everything else. If we lose this part of our nature,
we have lost everything. If we betray our soul, we have betrayed our
essence. If we sell our soul, we have forfeited our existence.

Literature and art also bear witness to the existence of a spiritual
stream that flows at the core of our being. What are literature and art
but the working out of soul, the perpetual dipping into this eternal
stream? And what is artistic genius but a special gift for accessing and
articulating the subtle nuances and powerful passions of the soul?
Take soul out of the writings of Homer, Dante, Goethe, Shakespeare,
Nietzsche, Rilke, Rumi, Joyce, to name but a few, and nothing would
be left but barren lines and fleshless facts. Literature and art come from
the soul, they speak to soul, they are soul. Speaking for all creative
artists, James Joyce said, "I go to encounter for the millionth time the
reality of experience and to forge in the smithy of my soul the uncreated conscience of my race."[1] Great literature and art are forged
in the soul, and they penetrate into the depths of our soul, revealing
to us the contours of our own being. And in these moments of recognition, when art reveals us to ourselves, we cannot help but fall to our
knees and acknowledge the power and reality of soul.

THE DEATH OF THE SOUL

We live in a culture that has forgotten the soul. In so many ways
America is a barren landscape, a desert of computers and corporate

buildings, a place where lonely winds scatter the dust of the poetic spirit, and soul cannot be found. We hunger for something we cannot name and go up and down the earth searching for something we cannot find, never realizing that what we are really looking for is the soul that lies at the core of our being.

Thomas Moore said, "The greatest malady of the twentieth century, implicated in all our troubles and afflicting us individually and socially, is 'loss of soul.'"[2]

The present course of Western culture was set over three hundred years ago when Descartes said, "I think; therefore I am." This was not simply an axiom of his philosophy but an omen of the god we would come to worship. Descartes exalted rational thought and, in Hillman's words, banished the soul to the "pea-sized pineal gland in the middle of the brain."[3] Since that time Western society has worshipped at the altar of rational thought and paid little attention to the soul.

So today we know much about the mind and little about the soul, much about critical thinking and little about the imagination, much about logic and little about passion. From kindergarten through college we are trained to question, to argue, to analyze, to criticize, to debate. In short, to think, think, think!

In the meantime, our souls are dying. And when the soul dies, it does so quietly, unobtrusively. We hardly notice. There is no sound, no mourning, no funeral, no tears for the soul. One day it simply folds in upon itself and the candle goes out. The body goes on, almost as though nothing has happened, eating, drinking, sleeping, working. The mind too, like a spiritless machine, continues to click and whirr and do its work. But the soul has died and the passion is gone.

Something is desperately wrong in our culture. We are in unconscious mass mourning for the soul we have lost. Whether we know it or not, we are starving for what the Spanish call *duende*, for an opening of the heart, a return to the soul.

Fortunately, lost souls can be found, and the candle that has gone out can be lit once again. Over eight hundred years ago the poet Adi al-Riga wrote:

> I was sleeping, and being comforted
> by a cool breeze, when suddenly a gray dove
> from a thicket sang and sobbed with longing,
> and reminded me of my own passion.

> I had been away from my soul so long,
> so late-sleeping, but that dove's crying
> woke me and made me cry. Praise
> to all early-waking grievers![4]

Sometimes it takes so little to bring us back to our souls—the cry of a dove, a piece of music, a poignant poem, the touch of a friend. When we have been away from our souls too long, the smallest things can wake us up and bring us back to ourselves.

When James Joyce had graduated from college and was about to leave home, he wrote in his diary, "Mother is putting my new second-hand clothes in order. She prays now, she says, that I may learn in my own life and away from home and friends what the heart is and what it feels."[5]

Here is the map we need. In a culture obsessed with what the mind is and what it thinks, we must follow the road less traveled and learn what the heart is and what it feels. Or as Rilke put it, "Work of sight is done; now do heart work."[6]

DEFINING THE SOUL

In Greek the word for soul is *psyche,* and in Latin it is *anima.* The English word *soul* itself derives from the Old English *sawol* and the Anglo-Saxon *sawal,* words which had to do with breath or life force.

But when we try to define the soul, we immediately run into a problem. The word *soul* has been religionized in our culture, and most people associate the soul with theology and religion. By contrast, in ancient Greece the word *psyche* was a human term that referred to the center and deepest passions of the human being. In the Greek myth of Psyche and Eros, for example, Psyche was a beautiful young woman who fell passionately in love with the god Eros. Together they gave birth to a daughter named Pleasure. The word *psyche* was also associated with the word for butterflies, which again had feminine connotations of life and beauty. Thus, while *psyche* was associated with the spiritual dimension, it was in no way a religious word in the modern sense. So also, the word *soul* belongs to humanity; it points to a universal dimension of human experience. It is not the exclusive possession of traditional religion. And if we are ever to recover the soul in the West, if soulfulness is ever to become a part of everyday life, we must free the soul from organized religion and give it back in all its passion and fullness to the men and women of our time.

As Thomas Moore said in *Care of the Soul*, "'Soul' is not a thing, but a quality or a dimension of experiencing life and ourselves. It has to do with depth, value, relatedness, heart, and personal substance."[7]

But even after we free the soul from its ecclesiastical associations and recover its humanistic meanings from ancient Greece, the soul is still very difficult to define. As James Hillman said, "The soul is immeasureably deep and can only be illumined by insights, flashes in a great cavern of incomprehension."[8]

Paradoxically, our very difficulty in defining the soul gives us our first clue to its nature. The soul resists our Western need for abstract, operational definitions. We are reminded that there is another world, a world far deeper and more primordial than our logical processes. Soul is the door to this ancient imaginal world; she is mythic and poetic in the deepest sense of these terms.

So if we wish to know the soul, we must lay aside our rational ways of knowing and open ourselves to the world of imagination. We meet the soul when we are stirred by music, moved by a poem, absorbed in a painting, or touched by a ceremony or symbol. Soul is the deep, empathic resonance that vibrates within us at such moments. The catch of the breath, the awe in the heart, the lump in the throat, the tears in the eyes—these are the signs of the soul that let us know we have touched her or she has touched us.

Thus, the soul can be felt, touched, and known, but never defined. She will slip through the net of every conceptual system and elude every scientific expedition that goes in search of her. To know the soul, we must seek her not in dictionaries or denotative definitions but in art galleries, poetry readings, concerts, theater performances, symbols, ceremonies, dreams, intimate relationships, and other places more sympathetic to her imaginal nature.

Understanding the Soul

If the soul cannot be defined, how do we arrive at a common understanding of the soul? I believe that each of us must seek to know the soul personally and experientially. If we come to know the soul in our own lives, we will find common understandings and shared meanings with others who are exploring this same realm. We only fool ourselves that we understand when we come up with an abstract definition or logical construct to represent the soul. Without a personal, experiential knowing of the soul, such intellectual abstractions simply hang in space, empty and devoid of meaning.

One of the best ways to know the soul is to place ourselves in those arenas where she is most likely to be found. And while words can never define the soul, they can point to her and help illumine her nature. The following sections explore the soul through key words with which she is associated.

The Soul and Depth

The soul is associated with depth. Centuries ago the Greek philosopher Heraclitus brought soul and depth together when he said, "You could not discover the limits of soul, even if you traveled every road to do so; such is the depth of its meaning." James Hillman has pointed out, "Ever since Heraclitus brought soul and depth together in one formulation, the dimension of soul is depth (not breadth or height) and the direction of soul travel is downward."[10]

Spatial metaphors permeate our language. We speak of feeling up or down. We talk of a friend as being close or distant. We say a poem moved us deeply or a conversation raised our spirits. Spatial metaphors move in psychological and ontological space; they help structure our inner worlds of experience and being.

When psychologist Carl Rogers and theologian Paul Tillich engaged in their famous dialogue in 1958, they discussed the subject of depth. Rogers said that in his psychotherapeutic work the most significant moments had to do with going down, making deep contact with his clients.

> What I mean is this: I feel at times when I'm really being helpful to a client of mine, in those sort of rare moments when there is something approximating an I-Thou relationship between us, then I feel as though I am somehow in tune with the forces of the universe or that forces are operating through me in regard to this helping relationship.

Tillich replied:

> And you will be interested to hear from me that I am accused very often by my theological colleagues that I speak too much of down instead of up and that is true; when I want to give a name to that with

which I am ultimately concerned, then I call it the "ground of being" and ground is, of course, down and not up.[11]

Tillich went on to say that we can make contact with this creative ground in many ways, including the sort of deep person-to-person encounters with his clients that Rogers had described.

As mentioned earlier, James Hillman has pointed out that the words *soul* and *spirit* share the vertical plane in spatial metaphor—spirit having to do with going up while soul has to do with going down.[12] Spirit is the phoenix rising from the ashes; soul is the ashes from which the phoenix rises. Spirit is Icarus flying toward the sun; soul is Icarus as he plummets from the sky, falling back to the earth. Soul is always about coming back to the ground, about coming down, about descending into our depths. Soul is about learning the lessons that triumph and achievement cannot teach.

Because of its connotations of depth, the soul teaches us a new kind of spirituality, providing the balance our culture so desperately needs. Western spirituality, particularly its American form, tends to be masculine and heroic. Much of our spirituality is about questing, overcoming, ascending, transcending, and transforming. These are all movements of the spirit, having to do with going up the vertical plane.

While the heroic venture is an important part of life and should not be denigrated, we must realize that it is only half of the polarity. Life is more than climbing mountains and overcoming the next challenge. Life is also about going down, descending into the valleys and experiencing the pain and tragedies of life. We need a spirituality that can support us not only when we are planting our flag at the top of the mountain but also when we have fallen off the mountain or cannot even find the courage to begin the climb. We need to balance our masculine, heroic "*spirit*-uality" with a deeper, more feminine *soul*-fulness."

Soul provides in our lives a place for depth as well as height, for failure as well as triumph, for weakness as well as strength, for infirmity as well as health, for poverty as well as riches, for wisdom as well as knowledge, for woundedness as well as healing, for flaws as well as perfection, for depression as well as joy, for the loser as well as the winner, for the beaten as well as the triumphant, for the outcast as well as the accepted, for the downtrodden as well as the privileged, for tears as well as laughter, for roots as well as wings, even for death as well as life.

Soul enters when our spirits have been crushed and our egos have fallen apart. She moves gently amid the ruins of a destroyed life and begins to tidy up and build again. She stays with us when everyone else has left and holds us through the night until the dawn breaks again. And through the night she sings us songs we have never heard yet somehow know by heart. She tells us stories of courage—not the courage of dashing heroes and heroines, but a deeper courage that only grows in the valleys of defeat and despair. And in the cracks of our shattered life she plants the painful seeds of hope. This is the work of the soul—a work that spirit can never do.

As the soul has to do with depth, we are not likely to encounter her if we move in the horizontal dimension, skimming the surface of life; nor are we likely to find her if, in spirit fashion, we are always ascending, achieving, going up the vertical plane. Rather, we must go down into the depths of our being, down into the depths of our relationships, down into the depths of life itself. This is the first clue for understanding the soul.

The Soul and Art

The second clue has to do with art. Soul and art are closely connected. Soul is the creative and inspirational force behind all artistic creation. In ancient Greece there were nine muses who were thought to inspire poetry, music, lyrics, dance, passion, eloquence, comedy, theater, the playing of instruments, and other forms of artistic expression. Each of the nine muses was a facet of soul; or one could say that soul differentiated herself into these minor goddesses of creativity. Soul as embodied in the muses was the source of all creative art.

Art is the perfect container for the soul. Like soul, art belongs to the nonrational, imaginal world and can contain and mediate the soul without doing damage to her nature. Try to hold the soul in rational concepts and you will pierce and kill her with the spear-like linearity of logical thought. But place the soul gently in a painting, poem, or sculpture, and she will live for hundreds or even thousands of years, long after the artist has died and turned to dust. Art is the body of soul, an incarnation that allows soul to appear in the world. But art is not a passive container; it fuses with soul and becomes active and alive. Art stirs the imagination. It inflames the passions; it starts new fires. All creative art forms, including painting, poetry, dance, sculpture, and music, are boiling cauldrons of hot soul; they are forges that belch fire and sparks through time and space. Art touches every emotion, every string of the lyre of human passion. Art soothes, heals, and warms us inside. It also incites us to anger, rebellion, and revolution. Its beauty inspires and its power fills us with awe. Its truth breaks us open to new places in ourselves. Sometimes art can reach so deeply into us that, as Rilke said, "You must change your life."

The mystery of art, like that of the soul, remains impenetrable. One cannot explain a painting of Van Gogh or a symphony of Beethoven. The paint on the canvas or the electronic imprints on the CD tell us nothing. Even the structure of the painting or the movements of the music do not reveal the mystery. In art, as in every other realm, *psyche* cannot be reduced to *techne*. Ultimately, we can speak only of art's beauty, power, and truth. And with these words we enter the world of Being. This is where art begins and where art ultimately takes us. Soul gives us art; art gives us soul. Together they connect us to and saturate us with Being.

The Soul and the Feminine

The soul is associated with the feminine. In Latin and Greek the words for soul, *anima* and *psyche,* are both feminine nouns. To my knowledge, in every language that assigns gender to its nouns the word for soul is feminine. Carl Jung called the soul the anima and made her a central construct of his psychological theory. In his autobiography Jung described how he discovered the anima. He said that he was descending into his own unconscious when suddenly he heard a woman's voice speak to him. Intrigued, Jung began talking with her in an effort to discover who she was. He said, "My conclusion was that she must be the 'soul,' in the primitive sense, and I began to speculate on the reasons why the name 'anima' was given to the soul."[13] Jung came to believe that the anima was the major feminine archetype of the collective unconscious.

But what does it mean that the soul is feminine? And what does the word *feminine* itself mean? I think of the soul as that part of us, whether we are male or female, that is relational, intuitive, mystical, imaginative, artistic, creative, emotional, flowing, and right-brained. The soul is the complement of the masculine side of ourselves, which is logical, rational, analytical, linear, sequential, organized, structured, and left-brained.

I realize the terms *feminine* and *masculine* are problematic, since they tend to perpetuate gender stereotypes by implying that women cannot have masculine qualities and men cannot have feminine qualities. So it must be emphasized that everyone, whether male or female, has the potential for both feminine and masculine qualities. Once this point is made clear, these terms become useful and in fact may communicate better than others that have been suggested.

We cannot discuss the feminine without placing it in a societal context. We live in a patriarchal society. That is, the politics, economics, institutions, structures, and values of our society operate from masculine rather than feminine principles. This does not mean that the feminine is absent or that it is not valued in some contexts. But in a patriarchal society it is the masculine that ultimately holds the power, while the feminine is assigned a subordinate or inferior status.

The religion or mythology of a culture often provides insight into its values. The two major religions in Western culture, Christianity and Judaism, are both extremely patriarchal. In Judaism God is male; in Christianity there is God the Father and God the Son. Neither Judaism nor Christianity has a place for God the Mother or God the Daughter. The closest to this is probably the reverence in Catholicism for Mary, who symbolizes the feminine principle. But in both Judaism and Christianity the idea of a goddess, or even of addressing God as "she," is often regarded as blasphemous, even though an elementary understanding of theology should convince us that all such gender characterizations are purely anthropomorphic and that the Ultimate, whatever we may consider it to be, is beyond gender classification. It says something about our tremendous investment in patriarchy that we elect few females to Congress and none to our pantheon.

All this is very important to our discussion of the soul. From a Jungian perspective, the mythological system of a culture is a projection or externalization of our deepest archetypes. In turn, these external symbols stimulate individuals of that culture at the archetypal level and provide a way for them to express and develop these deeper parts of themselves. But according to Christianity and Judaism, the heavens are empty of the transcendent female. No little girl is able to go to a church or temple to find a goddess to serve as her ideal. No little boy is able to experience the benefits of a religion that prizes the feminine and gives him a transcendent female personage to stir his soul and help him develop his feminine qualities. If the soul is the major feminine archetype as Jung maintained, yet we have no transcendent female in our religion or mythology, it suggests we have repressed the soul and that individuals in our culture may not be getting much help from their religious symbols for developing their souls. Perhaps, then, it is no mystery that our patriarchal society has so little soulfulness. When we repress the feminine—whether in ourselves, in our religion, or in our society—we do damage to the soul.

This sheds light on the fact that in our culture masculine institutions such as science, technology, and defense are given the big pieces of the economic pie, while more feminine projects, such as the arts, human services, environmental issues, and efforts for peace and cooperation, are given the leftovers, the crumbs that fall from the tables of power. A patriarchal society will never give women, feminine values, or the soul an equal place at the table, and with good reason. The feminine principle is dangerous to patriarchal systems, for feminine values subvert masculine assumptions, and the soul has more power than patriarchy ever dreamed. If soulfulness ever infiltrated our institutions of power, it could destroy them and leave them in rubble. But on those ruins the soul would build a more balanced and humane world.

This leads to an important point: The soul is not simply a psychological construct to be explored through introspective activities; soul must be taken into the marketplace and made a part of our society. If we are ever to become a soulful society, we will have to do not only the individual work of cultivating our own souls, but also the political work of bringing soul into the religions, institutions, and power centers of our society. Anything less will only perpetuate the death of the soul in Western culture.

The Soul and Imagination

The soul is also associated with imagination. Imagination is the modality of soul as thinking is the modality of mind. The word *imagination* has to do with image-making. The soul produces images, fantasies, dreams, and symbols, just as the mind produces ideas, thoughts, and abstractions. The soul works in the medium of imagination; she knows herself, creates herself, and reveals herself through images. In fact, soul and imagination are so closely related that it is almost impossible to tell them apart. One of James Hillman's definitions of soul is "the imaginative possibility in our natures." He said that "fantasy images are both the raw materials and finished products of psyche," and "to be in touch with soul means to live in sensuous connection with fantasy."[14]

Our culture is ambivalent about imagination. We worry about the little girl who daydreams too much or the little boy who prefers water colors to soccer. We discourage our children from becoming artists and feel much better if they pursue careers in business, law, or medicine. In psychology we associate primary process, which involves fantasy, with pathology and secondary process, which involves thinking, with psychological health. On the other hand, we spend billions of dollars each year on movies, novels, plays, music, paintings, sculptures, crafts, and other products of the imagination. Clearly, we are ambivalent about imagination; we love its products but do little to support and develop the imaginal capacity that produces them. It is as though our soul knows it needs these things, but our mind can't quite figure out why. As Rollo May said, "Throughout Western history our dilemma has been whether imagination shall turn out to be artifice or the source of being."[15]

Carl Jung had no doubts about the importance of imagination. He wrote, "All the works of humanity have their origin in creative imagination. What right, then, have we to disparage fantasy?... Not the artist alone but every creative individual owes all that is greatest in his or her life to fantasy."[16]

We owe much to imagination, for it is the creative womb where every cultural reality was once conceived. Imagination is the *tenemos,* the sacred place, where trembling visionaries spin their dreams and fashion future worlds. Imagination is the smithy of cultural revolutions and the birthing rock of new nations. It is the source of inspiration for artists, prophets, philosophers, and all those who have re-imagined and thereby changed our world.

If we wish to deepen and nurture the soul, we must open ourselves to imagination. James Hillman said that imagination is a "royal road to soul-making."[17] Soul-making, a powerful image itself, evokes images of a farmer cultivating his field, a woman weaving at her loom, a sculptor working his clay. Soul-making implies that we do not receive the soul fully grown and mature, but rather, it is given to us *in potentia.* Its unique character is present from the beginning. But like the acorn that contains the oak, it must be nurtured, cultivated, and exposed to the rain, wind, and sun in order to grow into the rugged, sturdy full manifestation of its character.

Imagination is the loom on which we weave our souls. *Ex nihilo*, "out of nothing," we create the psyche, our inner life. The loom itself is fashioned of mystery, silence, darkness, and love. We wrestle with angels or devils for every piece of yarn and weave it in with sadness or joy. From the blacks, blues, yellows, greens, reds, silvers, and golds of life we make our soul, a mandala of the heart, where each fiber is a hope, a dream, a friend, a lover, a mate, a child, a parent, a joy, a longing, a heartache, a death, or some lonely night of our lives. As time goes by, the rich and textured tapestry of our soul emerges. Through imagination we weave images of meaning with the existential events of our lives. This is what is meant by soul-making.

The Soul and the Archetypal World

The soul is also associated with the archetypal world. Jung called the deepest part of the mind the collective unconscious and said that it contains the universal archetypes of the human race.[18] Archetypes are inherited patterns in the human psyche that predispose us to react to certain life events in a somewhat predictable manner. They arise from human experiences, repeated generation after generation, until they cut deep tracks in the human soul. Like riverbeds in the desert which direct the flow of water when the rains come, archetypes channel our experience when we are exposed to certain life events. Archetypes are affectively-charged, which means they are infused with emotional energy. One of the ways we can tell that we are in the grips of an archetypal experience is by the intensity and passion of our feelings.

Jung maintained that we project our archetypes into our religions, and thus that one of the best ways to identify archetypes is to look for the universal themes that appear in the religions and mythologies of the world. Birth and death, for example, are major archetypes that appear in every religion. Christianity, for instance, is filled with rituals, ceremonies, and symbols related to birth and death. There is the new birth that comes after dying to old sins. Christenings mark the birth of a child, and last rites and religious funerals ritualize death; baptism is the new birth and itself is a symbolic reenactment of the death, burial, and resurrection of Christ; the Eucharist, or Mass, is a ritual reflecting the death of Christ, his body and blood; and Christmas celebrates Christ's birth and Easter week his death and resurrection from the grave.

One finds major archetypal themes not only in the religions of the world but also in literature, poetry, art, and cultural stories. Archetypes permeate life and are so much a part of our existence that we hardly notice them. Those who grow up in the Christian faith, for example, usually take its rituals, ceremonies, and symbols for granted, never realizing that at the archetypal level Christianity is not that different from other world religions. Archetypes form the common spiritual core of every religion and culture. They tie us together as a species and reflect the fact that, despite outward differences, we are one at the level of the heart.

The soul lives in the archetypal world and thrives on archetypal experiences. Soul-making occurs best in the emotional heat of archetypal events. Fortunately, we do not have to personally go through an archetypal event in order to benefit from its soul-making power. Archetypes can be worked with vicariously. Religion, literature, and the arts are filled with archetypal themes and by participating in these, we can experience archetypal material vicariously. We do not have to die, for example, in order to experience the archetypal theme of death. A book such as Tolstoy's *The Death of Ivan Ilyich* or a play such as Arthur Miller's *Death of a Salesman* may provide us with ample material for soul-making related to this theme. Nor do we have to sell our own souls to the devil in order to explore our own darkness, thanks to Goethe's *Faust*. There are countless books, stories, plays, movies, paintings, poems, rituals, ceremonies, and symbols which reflect archetypal themes and which can help us explore the archetypal dimensions of our own soul.

The Soul and Darkness

The soul is associated with darkness, the moon, and things of the night. Carl Jung spoke of the soul as that "primeval cosmic night that was soul long before there was a conscious ego and will be soul far beyond what a conscious ego could ever reach."[19]

In our culture we tend to associate darkness with evil. But darkness is also associated with power, substance, mystery, and the feminine principle. For example, the Black Madonna, an image that has survived in Catholicism, is highly revered and thought to have great spiritual power. The Christian mystic St. John of the Cross said that spiritual insights and experiences come by night.[20] Carl Jung spoke of the shadow archetype, knowing it is both dangerous and the source of passion and power. Poets and other artists have found that authentic creativity often comes from the darkness of the soul.

On the other hand, there is also an evil, destructive side to the soul's darkness. This is something we do not like to face, especially when it rears its head in our own lives. But if we accept the goodness of the collective unconscious, we must also acknowledge its dark, evil side. The history of the human race is filled with violence. Human beings continue to kill, rape, abuse, and commit terrible, bloody crimes against one another. People become caught up in the fervor of war and march off to slaughter their fellow human beings. Domestic violence—doing violence to those we are supposed to love—continues to be a problem throughout the world. While few like to admit it, most of us are fascinated by violence, death, and destruction, witnessed by the fact that we read the books and go the movies which feature these themes.

"The Lottery," a fictional story about a small community that ritually kills one of its members each year, had great impact when it was first published in the 1940s.[21] Various theories were put forth as to why people found it so compelling. My own view is that the story brings a shock of recognition. At some inaccessible level in the soul, I suspect we all know that our ancestors once did such horrible things. Ritual death and human sacrifice were part of tribal life in many parts of the world. If, as Jung believed, the collective unconscious contains imprints of our evolutionary history, then perhaps we all know about such atrocities in the dark depths of the soul.

Given its dark possibilities, we must approach the soul with respect, even with fear and trembling. When I began writing this chapter, a poem arose from my depths which I titled "Tremble, Tremble."

> I tremble, tremble
> Something dark and monstrous
> Rises up, towers over me
>
> The soul is not
> Some pristine light
> That shines at the center of the heart
>
> She is a dark, foreboding mountain
> Filled with rags and bones and blood
> Debris of past lives
> Human remains, both evil and good

I cannot name Soul
I can only tremble, tremble
As She names me[22]

This poem, like most poems, seemed to come from some unknown place. I felt my soul was telling me, "Don't be presumptuous in writing about me. I am also a dark and monstrous power. I shake people at the core of their beings. I am that eternal, cosmic night from which you came and to which you will return."

Two weeks after I wrote this poem, a colleague in New York whom I had not seen for more than a year asked if I would write an article for his journal. I was astonished when he told me the title of the issue, which was to be *Tremble, Tremble—Patients in Panic, Patients in Awe*.[23] I rarely use the word tremble, and, as far as I know, I had never used the phrase "tremble, tremble" before. Nor had my friend. I cannot explain this strange occurrence. I can only say that it felt mysterious, almost as though I was being given a mandate from beyond to make sure that I paid proper respect to the dark and destructive power of the soul. The dark side of the soul is not to be trifled with nor taken for granted. Her dark power is to be approached with fear, trembling, wonder, and awe. This is the dark, fierce side of soul-making.

The Soul and Mystery

The soul is also associated with mystery. The soul is a vast cavern of secret passageways and archetypal rooms full of old bones and whispered voices from ancient times and places. She is the tattered journal of the long and arduous evolution of the human species. She is the great womb of the world that has given birth to countless civilizations that now lie in silence. And she is, even now, pregnant with new worlds to come. Soul is our connection with the Mystery of mysteries. She channels mystery into the world and into our own individual lives.

To say this less metaphorically, the soul is that dimension of our own being that reaches into the unknown. When we descend into this mysterious realm, we find that it is a place of immense depth, magnitude, and darkness. When Carl Jung descended into this region, he was overwhelmed and apparently lost his way for a time. Artists poets, writers, shamans, prophets, and seers have also gotten lost in these dark passageways and inner chambers of the soul. Yet here we also discover our greatest gifts: artists find their own true voice, shamans learn to heal, and prophets receive their fiery truths.

To know the deepest levels of the soul we must, in a sense, become mystics. I believe we become mystics by following that deep, nostalgic longing that stirs at the core of our souls. We sometimes feel it when we listen to music, read a piece of great literature, watch a sunrise, look at our children, or simply reflect on time, mortality, and the existential poignancy of life. This longing has no name, nor does it always know what it is longing for. Yet it is overwhelmingly poignant and plaintive. I suspect this is the primal spiritual impulse and that it is the longing for the Mystery—for what mystics call union with God and what Paul Tillich called reunion with the Ground of Being. Not everyone will travel into these mystical regions of the soul, but those who do will find nurturance for the soul and rich opportunities for soul-making.

Soul and "the More"

William James used the term "the more" to describe that which lies beyond the seen world, beyond what we can say or define.[24] To suggest that the soul is associated with "the more" is to say that she lives in the subtleties and ineffabilities of life. As the thirteenth-century Sufi poet Rumi said, "The world of the soul follows things rejected and almost forgotten."[25]

Our culture has given primacy to hard facts, operational definitions, and linear ways of knowing. These approaches leave out "the more," the rich, ineffable nuances that hover around the hard facts and between the lines. Denotative and linear ways of knowing are narrow, constrictive. By contrast, nonlinear knowing and connotative words—metaphors, similes, and images—allow us to move out into the regions of "the more" where the soul lives, where we find the real substance and depth of life.

James Hillman has said that our culture has a monotheistic bias.[26] That is, we do not like what he calls multiple or polytheistic perspectives. We find relativism and pluralistic thinking upsetting and prefer neat, singular ideas of truth. Yet the soul is by nature pluralistic. She contains multitudes, holds countless perspectives and points of view. Thus, monotheistic thinking and linear ways of knowing tend to be incongruent with the soul. They are narrow, constricting ways of approaching the world. They fail to honor the multiple perspectives of the soul, and they prevent us from seeing the nuances of "the more."

One of my graduate students recently spent a month living with a family in southern France. She was amazed at how much time and soul were put into preparing the evening meal. Fresh vegetables and meats were purchased daily, and great care was taken to wash and prepare them. Herbs were added to each dish, which was then cooked slowly to bring out its full flavor. The meal was served in several courses over a period of about three hours. A sense of community filled the room as the family drank wine, discussed politics, told stories, and shared their hearts and lives. For my student those evening meals were an authentic experience in soul, and she found it hard to return to the United States with its fast foods and prepackaged meals. One might say that in America, eating tends to be just another linear event, to be done as quickly and efficiently as possible. But, as my student learned, in Southern France people seem to appreciate "the more" of dining.

To use a different example, let's say you attend a concert by your favorite performing artist. The evening is magical, the music powerful, and for three hours you are lost in the performance. The next day a friend asks, "How was the concert?" Perhaps you will say, "Oh, it was great. It was really powerful." But no matter what you say, you will not be able to capture the fullness of what you experienced. In such situations "the more" is so large, so far beyond words, that we often end such conversations by saying, "I can't describe it. You just had to have been there." And in the silence of that ineffability the soul lives.

The linear approach to life, which fails to appreciate "the more," is, metaphorically, as though we cut a narrow swath through a field of wheat and then think we know wheat fields. But we know nothing compared to the old farmer who, season after season, has planted the wheat, watched it grow, rolled it between his rough palms, tasted its ripeness, cut it down, hauled it to the mill, ground it into flour, and eaten the bread at his table. This man knows "the more" of wheat and wheatfields. And if you want an experience in soul, sit some summer evening on his front porch and listen as he tells you of mules and ploughs, rains and dry spells, hard times and hope.

"The more" is also at work in the area of values and morality. As a child, I was taught that right is right and wrong is wrong. Morality was a matter of black and white, with no place for gray. But when I grew up and went out into the world, I found that things were not always so black and white. Sometimes choices were complex. Sometimes two values, both important, were in competition, and it was hard to know which one to follow and which one to set aside. Sometimes legalistic morality seemed to be in conflict with compassion, with the needs of a human being who was suffering and desperately needed mercy instead of judgment. Sometimes when a "sinner" was being stoned, I knew I was no better; so I dropped my stone and walked away, convicted by my own conscience. Life has a way of breaking down our self-righteousness and undermining simplistic moral prescriptions. Life is messy and, in spite of our moralistic pretensions, we don't have all the answers for our own lives, much less the answers for someone else's. Theologian Joseph Fletcher, in his book *Situation Ethics,* said that we have to grow beyond rules-oriented thinking and really grapple with the difficult decisions of life. Quoting Jesus, Fletcher said that the underlying principle of all morality is love and that in every moral decision we must ask, "What is the most loving thing to do?"[27] Fletcher was suggesting to us an ethic of compassion or, as Harvard psychologist Carol Gilligan called it, an ethic of care.[28] The law kills but the spirit gives life.

"The more" spreads out beyond the rule, the code, the law, the blacks and whites of moral dogmatism, and often it is in "the more" that we find the answers to the moral dilemmas we face. When we grow beyond rules and struggle with "the more" of moral questions, we cultivate and enlarge our soul. The chains of judgment begin to drop away; we can admit we do not have all the answers, and we can extend a richer compassion to others and have greater compassion for ourselves. As Rumi put it, "Out beyond ideas of wrongdoing and right-doing, there is a field. I'll meet you there."[29]

"The more" also exists in human relationships. Sara and I have been married for more than thirty years, but I cannot capture her in words. "The more" spreads out far beyond any words that I can say. I can tell you that Sara is bright, creative, caring, attractive, a strong woman, a good accountant, a wonderful wife, and my best friend. But how can I possibly capture the nuances of what she means to me—the knowing smile, the mischievous look, the intimate touch, the cozy feelings, the shared memories, the feeling of safety, the unconditional acceptance, and the thousands of other ineffable fibers that weave the tapestry of our love. We are sustained by "the more."

If we wish to nurture the soul, we must learn to cultivate "the more." We must quit taking the interstate highways of life, the shortest distance between two points, and learn to take the scenic routes, the

sideroads and backroads with their potholes and surprises. We need to
relax, wade a stream, listen to the cry of a jay. We need to stop and
smell the roses, or better yet, sit in a rose garden on a warm summer
morning and feel "the more" of the roses penetrate our pores and wash
over our souls. To cultivate "the more" means to taste life deeply, immerse ourselves in its sensuous fullness, suck the marrow out of it, as
Thoreau put it. Rich and voluptuous, "the more" waits for those who
will cultivate her fertile soil; and by cultivating her soil, we nurture
and grow our souls.

The Soul and Mood

Soul is also connected with mood. Paul Tillich pointed out that the
word mood comes from the German *mut* which refers to a movement
of the soul or a matter of the heart.[30] The philosopher Martin Heidegger said that mood is a mode of Being.[31] I believe mood is also a mode
of soul.

There are certain identifiable moods associated with the experience
of soul. If we are in one of these moods, the heart is open and the soul
is accessible. If we are not, it is almost impossible to touch the soul.
When I give poetry readings, I always begin with a piece of soulful
music. I find that if the listeners are in a soulful mood, the poetry can
reach their hearts. I have also experimented with mood in my university classes. In a doctoral class on existential themes, I often use music
or poetry to set the mood for the topic we are about to discuss. I find
that students are far more receptive to existential material when their
hearts are open and they are in a reflective, soulful mood.

Mood may be the common denominator in all experiences of soul.
It has always puzzled me how such diverse things as music, poems,
plays, oceans, mountains, and even cities can produce such similar
moods. Listening to music is certainly different from looking at paintings in a museum, yet both may evoke a similar mood. Watching a
sunset is nothing like going to a play, yet both may put us in a soulful
mood.

Sara and I have a cabin in the mountains. One snowy afternoon we
sat by the fireplace and listened to an audiotape of poetry readings.
Later, when we took a walk in the snow, we stopped at the edge of a
forest and gazed into its darkness. Strangely, those woods, silent and
dark as twilight fell, produced almost the same mood we had experienced earlier while listening to poetry.

I suspect that mood is our most direct experience of soul. Like a pregnant woman feeling her baby move in her womb, we feel the soul through the mood that rises up from the depths of our inner life. This phenomenological experience lets us know that our soul is alive and well at the center of our being.

The Soul and the True Self

Finally, the soul is associated with the true self and impels us toward radical individuality. The soul is tied up with our personal destiny, our true calling. She knows our daimon, that inner spirit that contains our true destiny and presses for individual expression. If we wish to find our own voice and live authentically, we must continually make the soul our reference point. The soul contains the code of individual destiny.

Shaun McNiff said, "The word soul suggests the essential nature of persons. . . . It is characterized by individuality, the aesthetic quality, or aura, that distinguishes one thing from another."[32]

Thomas Moore wrote, "Many of us spend time and energy trying to be something that we are not. But this is a move against soul, because individuality rises out of the soul as water rises out of the depths of the earth."[33]

I am not sure how seriously most of us take this idea of personal destiny or authentic commitment to the true self. But I have been impressed by the number and caliber of the people who have come to the conclusion that this is what life is all about.

Sören Kierkegaard, the founder of existentialism, believed that the goal of life is "to be that self one truly is."[34] He said that he wanted his epitaph simply to read, "That individual."[35]

Friedrich Nietzsche, one of the most brilliant thinkers of all time, also believed that the task of life is to become oneself. He asked, "What does your conscience say? You shall become who you are."[36] And in a very moving passage he wrote:

> The soul in its essence will say to herself: no one can build the bridge on which you in particular will have to cross the river of life—no one but yourself. Of course there are countless paths and bridges and demigods ready to carry you over the river, but only at the price of your own self. In all the world, there is one specific way that no one but you can take. Whither does it lead? Do not ask, but walk it. As soon as one says, "I want to remain myself," he discovers that

it is a frightful resolve. Now he must descend to the depths of his existence.[37]

Tillich said, "Man's being . . . is not only given to him but also demanded of him. . . . He is asked to make of himself what he is supposed to become, to fulfill his destiny."[38]

In his essay "Self-Reliance," Ralph Waldo Emerson said:

> There is a time in every man's education when he arrives at the conviction that envy is ignorance; that imitation is suicide; that he must take himself for better or worse as his portion; that though the wide universe is full of good, no kernel of nourishing corn can come to him but through his toil bestowed on that plot of ground which is given to him to till. The power which resides in him is new in nature, and none but he knows what that is which he can do, nor does he know until he has tried.[39]

In *The Soul's Code* James Hillman takes the position that each of us, like an acorn, contains our own destiny. Agreeing with Pablo Picasso who said, "I don't develop; I am," Hillman believes the soul's code is written on our hearts from the beginning and that life is an opportunity to express, with increasing authenticity, that which we essentially are. Hillman encourages us to give ourselves to our destiny, to "recognize the call as a prime fact of human existence [and to] align life with it." He reminds us: "A calling may be postponed, avoided, intermittently missed. It may also possess you completely. Whatever; eventually it will out. It makes its claim. The daimon does not go away."[40]

Psychoanalyst Karen Horney tells us that if we are prevented from expressing our real self as children, we will, instead, actualize an ideal self. As a result, we will eventually feel self-contempt as we sense the discrepancy between who we really are and the false self we have created.[41]

Alice Miller makes the same point, telling us that depression is the result of being separated from one's true self.[42]

Similarly, Abraham Maslow said:

> If this essential core of the person is denied or suppressed, he gets sick, sometimes in obvious ways, sometimes in subtle ways. . . . This inner nature . . . is weak and delicate and subtle and easily overcome by habit, and cultural pressure. . . . Even though denied, it persists underground, forever pressing for actualization.[43]

Rabbi Susya said, "When I get to heaven they will not ask me, 'Why were you not Moses?' Instead they will ask, 'Why were you not Susya?'"[44]

And Robert Frost wrote, "Something we were withholding made us weak, until we realized it was ourselves."[45]

I would like to add my own testimony to these voices. My daimon knew that I was meant to be an artist—a writer and poet. But all my life I fought this artistic calling. Raised in an isolated rural area, as a child I had no one to tell me about art, creativity, and the world of imagination. Yet I was always drawn to this world and at some level always knew that it was my destiny. When I decided to become a minister, my daimon was at work, drawing me to a profession where I could at times feel the numinous. Later, when I became a psychologist, I was responding to this same pull of destiny, since for me psychology was a way to explore the soul. I was drawn to the humanistic and existential psychologies, never to the medical or mechanistic approaches, because I saw in the former the imaginative depth and creative possibilities I craved. But both the ministry and psychology were only approximations, stations along the way. They were, in fact, substitutes for a whole-hearted response to the call of destiny.

Then, at midlife, the call became more insistent. My defenses began breaking down. I cried the first time I read Rumi's poem which says:

> Inside you there's an artist
> you don't know about. . . .
> Is what I say true? Say yes quickly,
> if you know, if you've known it
> from the beginning of the universe.[46]

When I was forty-nine, I finally saw with clarity the destiny I had avoided. I shrank back, afraid. I wrote in my journal, "It's taken me forty-nine years to know who I am, and now I fear I'm too old to be it. What do I do with the accumulations of what I'm not? Can an older body contain the passions of new dreams? Can I start at the beginning again and honor that young boy who, with the best of intentions, went down so many wrong roads?"

I have learned the answers to those questions: It is never too late to go to Nineveh, never too late to be coughed up onto the shores of one's destiny. Older bodies *can* contain the passion of new dreams. New wine does *not* burst old wineskins; it makes them moist, supple, and strong. One can always start again; one *must* always start again.

So, after many years of resisting, I finally listened to my daimon and took the plunge. I began to write and even, in time, to think of myself as a writer, a poet, an artist. When asked my profession, instead of saying "psychologist" or "professor," I sometimes found the courage to say "writer" or even "poet." I still feel embarrassed by those designations, afraid that I am not worthy to be called by those titles. Perhaps this is how it is with destiny. We know that this is serious business, the stuff of ultimate concerns. When we give ourselves to destiny, we feel tremendous awe and great humility. This is not ego or pride, nor a grandiose delusion about our gift or about saving the world. Rather, this is the quiet celebration of a heart that has finally found itself; it is the grateful humility of a prodigal soul that has finally come home.

The daimon is always playing its flute out there on the mountain. The soul is always calling, singing her gentle song of homecoming. But we continue going up and down the earth doing what we feel we must, hanging back, buying time. Destiny waits, endlessly patient yet increasingly insistent, until one day we finally give up, give in, and go home to the only place we were ever meant to be—the place of personal destiny which James Joyce described as near to the wild heart of life.[47]

Nothing is more important than being true to ourselves, to the daimon that lives at the core of our soul. And what if this means that we walk alone, that no one understands, that no one knows our name? Rilke gives us the answer:

> And if the earthly no longer knows your name,
> whisper to the earth: I'm flowing.
> To the flashing water say: I am.[48]

The old Hindu legend, which began this chapter, raises a serious warning. It reminds us of how easy it is to forget that we have a soul. But for some people, the legend does not apply. After searching "up and down the earth," they finally come home to the soul hidden at the core of their being.

Future and past cannot live off the present forms of religious experience for these are too shallow; the future can live only from the most primordial communion with the sacred.
—Thomas Berry

CHAPTER FOUR

THE SACRED

The Mysterious Dimension of Human Experience

The following is a true story, first reported in 1926 by two anthropologists working in Australia.

> A small group of nomadic Australian aborigines, the Achilpa clan of the Arunta tribe, always carried a sacred pole with them as they moved from place to place. While no one could recall how long the pole had been in the clan, they all believed it was a gift from the god Numbakula who had, according to legend, fashioned it from a gum tree, climbed it, and then disappeared into the heavens. The clan believed the pole had sacred powers, and they built their lives around it. Each morning they decided the direction of their travels by the way the pole bent. Each evening they erected the pole in the midst of their encampment, thus establishing their world wherever they went. They believed that the pole, reaching toward the sky, connected them with the heavens and their god Numbakula. Thus, the sacred pole was both literally and symbolically the very center of the Achilpa clan.
>
> Then one day the sacred pole broke. This threw the clan into chaos. Without the sacred pole to create their world, connect them with their god, and guide their journeys, they were lost. The clan wandered about aimlessly, becoming increasingly anxious, confused,

and disoriented. Finally, convinced all was lost and life was over, the entire clan—over one hundred men, women and children—lay down in the desert to await death.[1]

This dramatic story illustrates the nature and power of the sacred in human life and the disorientation that occurs when our connection to the sacred is severed.

Today, the plight of Western culture is similar to that of the Achilpa clan. Traditional religion once served as the sacred pole of the West. It answered our questions, oriented us in our world, connected us to the heavens, and provided directions for our own nomadic journey through life.

But today millions of people are no longer moved by the rituals, symbols, and theology of traditional religion. It no longer meets their intellectual, psychological, and spiritual needs. The sacred pole of traditional religion, which once stood at the very center of Western culture, now lies broken and splintered at our feet.

When the sacred pole breaks, whether among the Achilpa clan or in Western society, there are powerful repercussions. Symbols and mythological systems constitute the psychological and existential ground on which a culture stands. When symbols break down or mythological systems shift or disintegrate, we are thrown into existential chaos. The earth rumbles and quakes beneath our feet; the foundations shake and crack; and we desperately hang on to avoid falling into nothingness.

We may find it amazing that a clan of primitive people would become anxious, disoriented, and ready to die simply because their sacred pole was broken. But an existential analysis of our age would suggest that we have reacted no less dramatically to the loss of our own spiritual center. Anxiety is now the leading emotional disorder in the United States, followed closely by clinical depression. Existential angst permeates our society. It is in our art, music, literature, movies, and plays; it is behind the increasing rates of anxiety, depression, and suicide; it is the ennui and sense of hopelessness that threaten to swallow our children.

The breakdown of our spiritual center affects us all at a very personal level. Some of you have seen everything you once believed in disintegrate. You have looked into the abyss of anxiety and depression and wondered if hope could ever return. Others of you have watched your own children as they were sucked into the swirling vortex of addiction, violence, or other forms of existential despair. Some of you have known dark nights of the soul and long, weary days that had to be lived one at a time because courage was insufficient to do more. For those of you who have suffered such things, existential agony is not a textbook cliché; it is the living reality of your life, leaving indelible scars on your heart.

Make no mistake. Our sacred pole has broken and we are living in an age of unprecedented spiritual disorientation.

But it is important that we diagnose the problem correctly. Our problem is not that the sacred has ceased to exist, but rather that we have lost our connection to it. Religious symbols are the cultural code words by which societies access the sacred. When these code words break down, as is now happening in Western culture, people feel cut off from their spiritual center. This is exactly what happened to the Achilpa people. When their sacred pole broke, they could no longer access the sacred, and they felt cut off and lost. Had they been able to realize that the sacred was still there, perhaps they would not have fallen into despair.

In the same way, if we today can recognize that the sacred still exists, perhaps we can regain hope and find new paths to the sacred, new code words that will allow us to reconnect with that dimension. This is vitally important, because the sacred is the eternal source from which the soul draws its energy and power. When we are cut off from the sacred, the soul withers and dies; but when we reconnect with the sacred, the soul comes alive and we grow spiritually. Thus the well-being of the soul and of our spirituality itself depends on our connection to the sacred.

UNDERSTANDING THE SACRED: THE VIEWS OF SCHOLARS

As it has with other spiritual concepts, religion has monopolized the sacred and given it a strictly religious meaning. Like a masterpiece that has been painted over by later artists, the sacred was originally a beautiful human phenomenon that has been obscured by the forms and conventions of religion through the centuries. Our task, then, is to see if we can remove the accumulated layers of old paint and reveal the beauty of the original masterpiece.

Fortunately, many scholars have worked to understand the sacred in its original form and can help us with our task. I will begin with a brief excursion through some of the more important theories and then describe my own approach to the sacred.

Rudolph Otto: The Sacred as the Numinous

In 1923 Rudolph Otto, a German theologian, published a little book entitled *The Idea of the Holy* that was destined to have a profound effect on the phenomenology of religion.[2] Though Otto was a Christian and used the language of that tradition, he was interested in the universal human dimensions of sacred experience.

Otto maintained that throughout history human beings have had encounters with the sacred. These are strange and mysterious events, and they always have a profound emotional impact on those who experience them. Modern theology, with its emphasis on the rational and conceptual aspects of religious experience, has generally neglected these events. Otto's aim, however, was to explore the affective dimension of these experiences.

Otto began by defining the word *sacred*, or *holy*. He said that people usually think of the word as meaning "completely good," emphasizing its moral or ethical component. For example, we think of a holy person as one who embodies goodness. But Otto said that this common usage of the term is inaccurate and went on to show that the moral or ethical element was either not present or not emphasized in the original meaning of the term as found in Latin, Greek, Semitic, and other ancient languages.

According to Otto, the most fundamental element of sacred experience is the feeling response of the believer. The sacred encounters the person at a deep, nonrational level, and powerful emotions are stirred. Otto called this the numinous experience and said that it constitutes the profounder level of religion, that "there is no religion in which it does not live as the real innermost core."

Otto then did a careful phenomenological analysis of these numinous experiences. He concluded that they are characterized by various elements, including a sense of being overwhelmed, a feeling of mystical awe, a sense of fascination, and an experience of intense energy or urgency. He said that in these experiences "the soul, held speechless, trembles inwardly to the farthest fibre of its being."

I would like to call special attention to the last element, energy. When we encounter the sacred, we experience what Otto called the energy of the numen, which expresses itself as "vitality, passion, emotional temper, will, force, movement, excitement, activity, impetus." Otto described this energy as "a force that knows not stint nor stay, which is urgent, active, compelling, and alive," and as "that 'consuming fire' of love whose burning strength the mystic can hardly bear, but begs that the heat that has scorched him may be mitigated, lest he be himself destroyed by it."

Here Otto has given us an important clue about the recovery of passion in our lives. Passion is the fire of the soul, but the ultimate source of this energy, according to Otto, is the sacred, the energy of the numen. So if our passion has died, if the fires of the soul have gone out, the key is to reconnect with the sacred and rekindle our souls from its powerful energy.

This may seem a strange prescription to Western ears. While Eastern traditions often focus on meditative and spiritual approaches to energy, we do not. And when we read about the Christian mystics, their encounters with the sacred seem so overwhelming that most of us cannot relate to those experiences. In their more intense forms, encounters with the sacred can be incinerating; and even if we did have such an experience, trying to rekindle our souls from it would be like walking into a wall of flames. Of course, if we could endure the intensity, we might experience transformative effects, as did the mystics. But most of us are not mystics, and we will never have such overwhelming encounters with the sacred. Nevertheless, we can learn to warm ourselves, as it were, beside the sacred fire, taking a few hot coals now and then to keep our passion alive. This more moderate experience of the sacred is both nurturing to the soul and sufficient for energizing and reconnecting us with the passion and vitality of existence.

Mircea Eliade: The Sacred as Reality, Power, and Being

Mircea Eliade was a French religious historian who served as chair of the Department of the History of Religions at the University of Chicago for seventeen years. His classic work, *The Sacred and the Profane*, was published in 1959.[3]

Eliade considered the sacred and the profane to be two modes of being in the world. Indigenous cultures are permeated by the sacred. They have many sacred places and times, and even the daily functions of life, such as eating and sex, are considered sacred. Eliade said, "For the primitive, such an act is never simply physiological; it is, or can become, a sacrament, that is, a communion with the sacred."

By contrast, modern societies live in the profane, or secular, mode of being. They have little sense of the sacred and life has very few sacred places or times. And while eating and sex are enjoyed as pleasurable physiological activities, they are rarely regarded as sacred or holy. Thus, while indigenous people live in daily contact with the sacred, we have lost this connection. As Eliade said, "Desacralization pervades the entire experience of the nonreligious man of modern societies." He devoted himself to studying the sacred in order to bring an understanding of it to men and women living in modern society.

Eliade emphasized that the sacred manifests itself to us and that we are not in control of these encounters. For these manifestations he proposed the term *hierophany*, which literally means "something sacred shows itself to us." Eliade did not mean that there is nothing we can do to encourage the sacred to appear. Certainly we can create an arena and an atmosphere conducive to such an experience. However, we cannot manipulate the sacred. After all our preparations, ministrations, and evocations, the sacred still may not appear. If it does show itself to us, it is always a matter of grace. Therefore, the proper attitude before all hierophanies is one of gratitude and humility.

Eliade began defining the sacred by saying that "the first possible definition of the sacred is that it is the opposite of the profane." He pointed out that we first become aware of the sacred because of its dramatic contrast with everyday experience. When the sacred breaks into our secular sphere, we recognize it as "something of a wholly different order, a reality that does not belong to our world" and as "something wholly different from the profane." Eliade then gave a more specific definition of the sacred:

> The *sacred* is equivalent to a *power*, and, in the last analysis, to *reality*. The sacred is saturated with *being*. Sacred power means reality and at the same time enduringness and efficacy. The polarity sacred-profane is often expressed as an opposition between *real* and *unreal* or pseudoreal. . . . Thus, it is easy to understand that religious man deeply desires *to be*, to participate in *reality*, to be saturated with power.[4]

This is a remarkable definition. Eliade is taking the philosophical position that reality is not what it seems, that there are both real and unreal levels of existence; the sacred has to do with the real, while the secular has to do with the unreal or pseudoreal. In other words, the sacred is the "really real" world. One might say that it is a more intense, more concentrated level of reality. A person who connects with the sacred participates in this more intense level of reality, which is saturated with being and power.

It is important to recognize that Eliade does not psychologize the sacred. In other words, he does not explain these powerful experiences as simply occurring in the mind or emotions. Eliade grounds his theory of the sacred not in psychology but in metaphysics, in the nature of reality itself. He believes the sacred is a manifestation of a deeper dimension of reality and that the powerful psychological effects we experience in an encounter with the sacred are due to our contact with this more intense level of being and power. Stated in stimulus-response language, Eliade is saying there really is a stimulus and that it produces powerful psychological responses. In other words, Eliade is saying that the sacred is very real and that it can impact us with significant force.

Eliade's theory helps us understand the power of sacred objects, such as the sacred pole of the Achilpa clan. Since the sacred is saturated with power, when otherwise ordinary objects are associated with the sacred, they also become imbued with this power. A sacred symbol is an ordinary object that has taken on the numinosity of the sacred and has become a means to the sacred for the believer. A symbol "participates in that to which it points," as Tillich said.[5] Certain places, times, and even persons can become imbued with the sacred in this way as well. In many native cultures the chief and the shaman—the leader and healer of the tribe, respectively—are considered holy. Their power comes from their connection with the sacred.

Today, our culture still has vestiges of these notions. For example, we speak of our vocation, perhaps not realizing that the word originally meant "calling" and had to do with being called by the gods to one's task or mission. We still have holy days but now think of them in secular terms and call them holidays. We still have a few sacred places— primarily churches and temples. And many still experience a sense of awe or reverence in the presence of such spiritual leaders as the Pope or the Dalai Lama. We are still fascinated by royalty, and every election year Americans succumb to the mysterious charisma of certain political leaders seeking to be our chief. All these may be the vestiges, the faint echoes, of that ancient phenomenon of imbuing certain objects, people, times, and places with sacred power.

William James: The Sacred as the Unseen Order

William James taught at Harvard for thirty-five years. *The Varieties of Religious Experience,* published in 1902, is based on his Gifford Lectures delivered at the University of Aberdeen in Edinburgh, Scotland. *The Varieties* is a classic in the field of psychology and religion, and some regard it as the most important book written on that topic in this century.[6]

James began by dividing the religious field into two major parts— personal religion and institutional religion. He believed personal religion is the more important of the two, pointing out that churches owe their existence to the personal religion of their founders. Maintaining that "personal religion should still be the primordial thing," he devoted his book to the exploration of personal religious experience.

Early in his lectures James gave his definition of the religious attitude. He wrote:

> Were one asked to characterize the life of religion in the broadest and most general terms possible, one might say that it consists of the belief that there is an unseen order, and that our supreme good lies in harmoniously adjusting ourselves thereto. This belief and this adjustment are the religious attitude in the soul.[7]

This statement reflects James's basic model, which is that there are two worlds: the physical world and the world that he called the unseen order. While these two worlds are separate, they can make contact with each other. The unseen world sometimes breaks into our physical world in what James called invasions of consciousness, which include mystical experiences, religious conversions, and even artistic inspiration. Conversely, through such avenues as prayer and meditation, we can sometimes initiate contact with the unseen world.

According to James, the human mind or psyche is the connecting point, the bridge over which the physical and spiritual worlds have commerce with each other. The psyche is composed of the conscious self and the subconscious self. The conscious self is that part of the psyche with which we are familiar. It belongs to this physical world, and its boundaries can be quite readily defined. The subconscious self, on the other hand, is the psyche's mysterious dimension. While it begins in this world, it stretches into the unseen world, and it is not at all clear where its outer boundaries lie. James said, "Each of us is in reality an abiding psychical entity far more extensive than he knows," and "the further limits of our being plunge, it seems to me, into an altogether other dimension of existence from the sensible and merely understandable world. Name it the mystical region, or the supernatural region, whichever you choose."

Our information about this other dimension is very limited. Every formal religion, in an effort to authenticate its own faith, tries to tell us the nature of this realm. But, according to James, "Since they corroborate incompatible theological doctrines, they neutralize one another and leave no fixed result."

Therefore, what one believes about the unseen order is a matter of faith and constitutes what James called an *over-belief*, a belief to which one may be personally committed but which goes beyond the available facts. Over-beliefs can be important containers for spiritual life. James said that we should treat one another's over-beliefs "with tenderness and tolerance so long as they are not intolerant themselves" and that "the most interesting and valuable things about a man are usually his over-beliefs."

One of the features of James's model is that it can accommodate a wide range of philosophical and religious positions. For example, if one believes in God and a supernatural realm, the unseen world would be defined as the supernatural realm; prayer and meditation would be ways we contact God, while religious conversions and mystical experiences would be seen as ways God contacts us.

If one does not believe in God or a supernatural realm, one can still use James's model. In this case, the unseen order would be our own deeper nature. Prayer and meditation would be not ways to contact God, but ways to draw upon our own resources. And religious conversions and mystical experiences would be seen not as coming from God or a supernatural realm, but as originating in the deeper regions of one's own mind.

Perhaps the most important contribution of James's model is that it places psychology at the very center of spirituality and ties the two inextricably together. If, as James asserts, the human psyche is the link between the physical and spiritual worlds and participates in both, and if the very nature of the psyche itself expresses this fundamental duality, then it follows that psychology and spirituality are forever bound up together. For those who have always had an intuitive sense that the fields of psychology and spirituality are somehow connected, James's model validates that idea and articulates the connection.

This means that when we do deep explorations of the human psyche, we are doing psychological and spiritual work at the same time. Thus, the woman who seeks to grow spiritually through prayer and meditation is in fact also doing psychological work, whether she thinks so or not. And the man who goes to therapy for depth analysis is embarking on a spiritual journey as well. Depth psychotherapy takes one into the deepest regions of the psyche and, thus, by James's model, into the realm of the mystical or sacred.

Of course, many therapists think psychology should stop at the borders of the spiritual realm. And indeed, psychology has traditionally left this dimension to the care of ministers, rabbis, or priests. But if spirituality is part of the human psyche, a psychology that leaves it out is limited, and a psychotherapy that fails to explore this region is incomplete.

If James's ideas were fully accepted along with their implications, they would revolutionize the field of psychology and the nature of psychotherapy. Psychology would have to study the realm of the sacred, and therapeutic training would have to include the spiritual dimension of human experience. Never again would the psychology profession be able to separate psyche from soul and psychology from spirituality. It is unfortunate that modern psychology has ignored the spiritual domain and thus failed to explore what may be the most important dimension of the human mind.

Martin Buber: The Sacred as I-Thou Relationships

Martin Buber, probably best known for his book *I and Thou,* lived from 1878 to 1964 and devoted his life to the study of relationships.[8] He believed the sacred is found in our connections with others, with nature, and with God, the Eternal Thou, and said, "All actual life is encounter."

Buber believed that there are two basic ways of relating, which he called I-It and I-Thou. In an I-It relationship, the other is an object to us, or a means to an end. In an I-Thou encounter, the other ceases to be an object and we are drawn into a deeper kind of relationship.

When we relate to another as an It, it is not only the other that is affected, but also ourselves. The I of I-It is different from the I of I-Thou. In a sense, in an I-It relationship both the I and the It are "things." One would be quite close to Buber's meaning here if one thinks of the I-It relation as "It-It" (two objects standing in relation to each other) and the I-Thou relation as "Thou-Thou" (two "thous" standing in relation to each other).

Some have concluded that Buber was saying I-It is undesirable and I-Thou is desirable; they think that I-It means to treat another as an object and that I-Thou means to treat another with respect and kindness. But this common misunderstanding of Buber misses the depth of what he was trying to say.

I-It is not necessarily undesirable. In fact, most of our daily transactions are conducted in this mode. In a sense, we treat others as objects or means to an end all the time. And there is nothing necessarily wrong with this.

For example, at the grocery store we smile and make small talk with the woman who checks our groceries. This is an I-It interaction. On the way home we stop to buy gas for the car, and carry on a friendly conversation about our new car and its performance with the young man who assists us. This too is an I-It relation. We arrive home and our twelve-year-old needs to talk because he has just had an argument with his best friend. We listen to his hurt feelings and give him a hug. This, too, is an I-It interaction.

Two women—a therapist and her client who is feeling depressed— are quietly talking in a therapy room. As the client describes her pain, the therapist, moved by empathy and professional care, responds gently, offering suggestions that may be helpful. Even this is an I-It rather than an I-Thou encounter.

These examples should make it clear that I-It does not mean to treat others with disrespect while I-Thou means to treat them with care. In each case the other person was treated with kindness and respect. Yet none of these interactions qualifies as an I-Thou encounter.

So what is an I-Thou encounter and what is the difference between I-It and I-Thou?

An I-Thou encounter is an occurrence, a happening of intense poignancy, that interrupts our usual I-It world. I-Thou is not something we are in charge of or something we can create simply by treating another with respect. I-Thou comes by grace, a shaft of sunlight that penetrates our normal world, eternity intersecting time, the sacred suddenly manifesting in what was only moments before an ordinary relationship.

Let's go back to the example of the depressed client and her therapist. As touching as this scene may be, it is still only an I-It encounter.

But suppose that in the final moments of the therapy hour, the client pauses from her crying and looks into the eyes of her caring therapist, and in the silence of that space, love enters and both feel its presence. In that moment, roles recede and there is neither client nor therapist; there are only two women frozen in time while their souls dance for a moment on the shores of eternity. In that moment the normal structures of psychotherapy are pushed aside and the narrow boundaries of I-It open up into the boundless expanses of I-Thou. Without words the women rise in silence to end the session, and the client leaves the room.

The therapist, struck with awe, sits down to gather her thoughts before the next client. The client, now outside in her car, sits for a while behind the steering wheel, knowing that something irreversible has occurred. By whatever name they call it, and however they explain it in the weeks to come, these two women have touched the sacred. They have had an I-Thou encounter. And neither their relationship nor their individual lives will ever be quite the same.

Buber believes the sacred is all around us, always potentially present. And, like other spiritual thinkers, Buber believed that the sacred manifests in the ordinary, in the everyday events and relationships of one's life. Walter Kaufmann, one of Buber's translators, said that in Buber's writings, "one finds the central commandment to make the secular sacred."[9] At any moment I-Thou can break through into the world of I-It to touch our lives.

But how does one do this according to Buber? How does one move from I-It to I-Thou? How does one touch the sacred in everyday life?

First, it is important to remember that for Buber everything is relationship. While I-It relationships are a necessary part of life, the sacred is touched only in I-Thou relationships. Buber maintained that we are not in charge of I-Thou and that the sacred appears not by human will but by grace. But he did not mean that our will and our desire for the sacred are irrelevant. Buber said that we are often drawn into an I-Thou encounter at that moment when "grace and will are joined."

An I-Thou encounter can occur with nature, and to illustrate this Buber used the example of a tree. In an I-It relation with a tree, we might notice the size of its branches, the shape of its roots, and other physical characteristics. We might even experience its beauty and appreciate the brilliant colors of its leaves. But all this is part of I-It; the tree is still an object to us. But, Buber said, "It can also happen, if grace and will are joined, that as I contemplate the tree I am drawn into a relation, and the tree ceases to be an It." In that moment the tree becomes a Thou.

Such moments can occur not only with trees, of course, but also with mountains, oceans, sunsets, the moon and stars, a desert sunrise, and countless other events in nature. The experience is not easy to put into words, but many people have had such moments in nature and can intuitively grasp Buber's meaning here. He is talking about those special instances when the boundary between subject and object dissolves and we are caught up in a relational unity with nature. These are the times when nature opens herself up to us and draws us in. I-It becomes I-Thou, time is swallowed by eternity, mystery moves upon the breeze, and we realize we have entered the presence of the sacred.

As we have seen, I-Thou encounters also occur in human relationships. Let's suppose that a certain woman has known a certain man for many months, through work or other contacts. She may have noticed that he is attractive, has a good sense of humor, and that he is comfortable and easy to be with. But he is only another person among the many in her life. He is still an It to her, and the relationship is one of I-It.

Then one day there is a glance or a momentary pause, and in that second each catches a glint, a slight sparkle from the soul of the other. This may shake them for a moment; there may be a slight awkwardness, a stammer in the flow of words, or even a quick smile of embarrassment at the unexpectedness of what just broke through. There is a small crack, a fissure in the everyday world of I-It. I-It recedes, I-Thou opens up, and the sacred is touched. Depending on their life situations and other factors, these two people may or may not decide to develop a deeper relationship. But if they are sensitive to the sacred in human relationships, they will know that at least for that brief moment their souls touched and each glimpsed the other as a Thou.

This is more than mere personality chemistry or sexual attraction; it is soul attraction. At the same time, I would not deny the presence of Eros or the power of his arrows to pierce the world of I-It. In our society, steeped in a theology that sees the body as evil, we have dichotomized body and spirit, and separated soul from sensuality. We have boarded up the temple of Eros and cast him out of the pantheon of sacred gods. Nevertheless, Eros and sacred experience are not antithetical; Eros does not contaminate the sacred, he does not cheapen the soul. In fact, Eros often provides the initial impetus for I-Thou relationships, as well as the creative energy that nurtures and keeps them alive. For many people erotic passion is a continuing hierophany, a place where the sacred manifests again and again. Soulful energy and erotic passion, the marriage of Psyche and Eros, is one of the most powerful unions possible. Not only does it produce, as in the Greek myth, the child named Pleasure, but from this union also comes artistic inspiration, powerful creativity, and a burning passion for life. If two people are drawn together by the powers of both Eros and Psyche, they have the potential to touch the deepest and most intense regions of sacred experience.

Buber believed that life is a vast network of relationships in which we are embedded. Rather than thinking of the sacred as something "out there," Buber thought of it as potentially present in any relationship. Our task is to learn to see with sacred eyes, to see through I-It into the deeper reality of I-Thou, to know that the sacred lives in the ordinary relationships of our own life.

In his poetic way Buber summed up his belief in the omnipresence of the sacred. He wrote:

> In every sphere, through everything that becomes present to us, we gaze toward the train of the Eternal Thou; in each we perceive a breath of it; in every Thou we address the Eternal Thou; in every sphere according to its manner.[10]

Abraham Maslow: The Sacred as the Dimension of Being

Abraham Maslow, one of the founders of humanistic psychology, served for many years as chair of the psychology department at Brandeis University. Maslow spent much of his life studying what he called self-actualized individuals—exceptionally healthy and high-functioning people.[11]

Maslow found that self-actualized people reported frequent mystical experiences—times of intense bliss, joy, ecstasy, and awe. Freud had labeled such experiences pathological, saying they were signs of regression and the product of a neurotic mind. But Maslow found just the opposite to be true: the healthier and more self-actualized the individual, the more mystical experiences he or she tended to have.

Intrigued by this phenomenon, Maslow focused much of his research on these peak experiences, as he called them. In one of his early research projects, he asked 190 subjects to respond to the following instructions:

> I would like you to think of the most wonderful experience or experiences of your life; happiest moments, ecstatic moments, moments of rapture, perhaps from being in love, or from listening to music, or suddenly "being hit" by a book or a painting, or from some great creative moment. First list these. And then try to tell me how you feel in such acute moments, how you feel differently from the way you feel at other times, how you are at the moment a different person in some ways.[12]

While this approach generated some useful information, Maslow eventually found a more effective way to gather information about peak experiences. He called his new approach "rhapsodic communication." Instead of asking subjects to respond to abstract instructions like those above, Maslow would read personal accounts of peak experiences to his subjects. He also began to use more and more figures of speech, metaphors, similies, and more poetic language in general.[13] Maslow found that these personal stories and the poetic language created a resonating response in his subjects, as a tuning fork sets off a sympathetic vibration in a piano wire across the room. This new approach provided richer data. The subjects understood more clearly what Maslow meant by a peak experience and were better able to recall their own peak experiences. I believe Maslow discovered, quite by accident, what I would call soul language. Metaphors, similies, poetic images, and personal stories are the language of the soul. It is very difficult to tap into the soul using abstract and scholarly words. Those of us who wish to do research on spirituality and the sacred must invent new approaches and use language congruent with the spiritual dimension.

Maslow chose the term "peak experiences" to avoid the bias and connotations inherent in other frequently used terms. Peak experiences have occurred throughout history and in every culture, but we still know little about them. For one thing, they are different enough from our ordinary experiences that we don't have adequate categories or words to describe them. For another, the stimuli, intensity, content, effects, and interpretations of peak experiences differ from culture to culture and even from person to person. Further, people who have such experiences are reluctant to talk about them, fearing they will be thought strange or even crazy.

Nevertheless, these experiences are more common than we once thought. National polls consistently show that about one third of all Americans have had a mystical experience.[14] A national survey of psychologists carried out by one of my doctoral students showed that 50 percent of clinicians have had a mystical experience.[15] So, despite the fact that we are reluctant to talk about them, many Americans have had these intense experiences.

In *The Varieties of Religious Experience*, William James related experiences of a number of people that are recognizable as peak experiences. The subject of the following was a religious person and described his experience in religious words:

> I remember the night, and almost the very spot on the hilltop, where my soul opened out, as it were, into the Infinite, and there was a rushing together of the two worlds, the inner and the outer. It was deep calling unto deep—the deep that my own struggle had opened up within being answered by the unfathomable deep without, reaching beyond the stars. I stood alone with Him who had made me, and all the beauty of the world, and love, and sorrow, and even temptation. I did not seek Him, but felt the perfect unison of my spirit with His. The ordinary sense of things around me faded. For the moment nothing but an ineffable joy and exaltation remained. It is impossible fully to describe the experience. It was like the effect of some great orchestra when all the separate notes have melted into one swelling harmony that leaves the listener conscious of nothing save that his soul is being wafted upwards, and almost bursting with its own emotion. The perfect stillness of the night was thrilled by a more solemn silence. The darkness held a presence that was all the more felt because it was not seen. I could not any more have doubted that He was there than that I was. Indeed, I felt myself to be, if possible, the less real of the two.[16]

This story is reminiscent of the experiences of Christian mystics. The man who had this experience was overwhelmed by it. Even years later he still considered it the most important event of his life and the ground of his religious faith.

Maslow observed that peak experiences, while universal, are always interpreted within the framework of a particular cultural or personal belief system. Thus a Christian will describe the experience in Christian terms and symbols, a Hindu will use Hindu terms and symbols, and a Buddhist will use the language of the Buddhist tradition. An atheist or agnostic might describe the experience without resorting to religious concepts of any kind, perhaps using psychological or neuro-logical models to explain the experience. So peak experiences, while universal, are always dressed in the linguistic and symbolic clothing of a particular time, place, culture, and belief system.

Maslow believed that religions have their origins in the peak ex-periences of their founders. He said, "The intrinsic core, the essence, the universal nucleus of every known high religion . . . has been the private, lonely, personal illumination, revelation, or ecstasy of some acutely sensitive prophet or seer."[17] Typically, the prophet interprets the mystical experience as a revelation from God and then commu-nicates this revelation to others. If the time is right and the people listen, a religious movement is born.

Later, people in the movement attempt to codify the teachings of the founder in order to pass them on to future generations. Ironically, this institutionalization often results in a rigid orthodoxy that is then used to suppress those claiming to have direct religious experiences. As Maslow put it, "Conventional religions may even be used as defenses against and resistances to the shaking experiences of transcendence."[18] Followers of organized religion often forget that their faith was origi-nally founded on the ecstatic experiences of its prophet. The religious commitment of those associated with such an organization is no longer judged by the criteria of genuine spirituality but by the degree to which they agree with the creedal positions of the religion. Thus it becomes possible for one to be religious but not spiritual.

Maslow believed the most important function of peak experiences is that they transport us out of ordinary consciousness and bring us into contact with Being, the highest dimension of human experience. Peak experiences are windows into Being, brief glimpses of a transcen-dent reality. In these moments we touch such ultimate values as beau-ty, truth, goodness, and love, which Maslow called Being-values. This is the realm where artists, poets, writers, composers, philosophers, and spiritual leaders find their most creative insights and revelations.

Maslow did not think of Being as belonging to a supernatural sphere but as a dimension of our humanness. This dimension, which Maslow called "the farther reaches of human nature," provides a clue to the di-rection of human evolution; it is the growing edge of our becoming. Peak experiences, those brief moments of ecstasy, give us a taste of what it would be like to live at the highest level of actualization, in the presence of Being itself. William Blake said, "If the doors of perception were cleansed everything would appear to man as it is, infinite."[19] This is the way things look in the realm of Being.

Maslow believed contact with this dimension is important to psychological health. Human beings have certain needs, which he divided into basic needs and higher needs, and if these needs are not met, we become ill. Basic needs have to do with physical survival and include our need for food, water, shelter, security, and social connections. Higher needs have to do with Being-values, that is, our need for beauty, love, truth, and goodness. If we neglect these, we tend to fall into what Maslow called metapathology, a pathology which is the direct result of deprivation at the spiritual level. The best cure for this is renewed contact with the realm of Being, to which peak experiences are the "royal road."

After analyzing hundreds of peak experiences, Maslow became convinced that they are highly beneficial. People who had peak experiences reported such therapeutic benefits as the cure of addictions, the elimination of anxiety, the cure of depression, and the overcoming of fears. Others reported increased creativity, better self-integration, a greater sense of meaning, important lifestyle changes, more personal power, increased gratitude, and greater poetic gifts.

Could people be taught how to access the realm of Being and thus meet their Being-level needs? Maslow said that most people operate at the Deficiency-level and that it is not easy to teach them to perceive the world at the Being-level. One can be taught, for example, to identify the sounds of a Beethoven quartet; but, Maslow asked, how do you teach that person to hear the *beauty* of those sounds? In essence, how do you teach someone, in William Blake's words,

> To see a World in a Grain of Sand
> And a Heaven in a Wild Flower
> Hold Infinity in the palm of your hand
> And Eternity in an hour[?][20]

Obviously, this involves a different kind of education. Based on his preliminary efforts with students, Maslow believed it could be done. While we cannot teach people to have peak experiences at will, we can teach them to use what Maslow called Being-cognition, that is, seeing with sacred eyes. This is the capacity to open one's soul to the sanctity of everyday experiences, to view one's mate, children, friends, and daily activities in the light of the sacred.

A Synthesis of the Scholars

Clearly, these scholars whose work we have explored are all talking about the same thing, the sacred dimension of human experience, each using his own language. Otto called it the numinous experience, Eliade called it a hierophany, William James called it an invasion of consciousness from the unseen order, Buber called it the I-Thou relationship, and Maslow called it a peak experience that transports us into the realm of Being. They agree that the sacred dimension exists, that it is mysterious and powerful, that in all cultures and throughout history humans have had contact with it, that these contacts have a strong spiritual and psychological impact, that the results are generally beneficial, and that while we cannot control the sacred, we can learn ways to open ourselves to it.

MY VIEW OF THE SACRED

When I was growing up in the foothills of the Ozark Mountains, we had no public water system. In my father's day the country people got their water from creeks, natural springs, and hand-dug cisterns. But by the time I was born, a local man had acquired well-drilling equipment and could be hired to drill a well for so many cents per foot. He would come in his big diesel-belching truck, set up his equipment, and begin drilling into the hard Arkansas soil. Hours later, after drilling 75 to 150 feet into the ground, he would hit water. Shoring and pipes would be placed in the well, a pump installed, and cold, clear water became available at the turn of a tap. I remember as a child being struck with wonder when I first learned that underneath the dry, parched crust of those Arkansas hills was pure, refreshing water in abundance.

This story is a good metaphor for my view of the sacred. I believe that underneath the dry, parched surface of our lives there is a sacred stream that flows with life-giving water. This stream has its source in the underground fountains of Being itself, and it has the power to quench the ontological thirst of the soul.

Ontological thirst, a term first used by Eliade, refers to the longing of the soul for the sacred. The word *ontological* comes from the Greek *ontos*, which means "being." Thus, ontological thirst is the thirst for being, the longing to be truly alive, the desire to taste the passion and depths of existence.

But ontological thirst can easily become distorted and take on pathological forms. For example, in our secular society we are obsessed with the pursuit of money and material things. We run from one materialistic mirage to the next in a desperate effort to quench our thirst, but we are never satisfied because the thirst that drives us is fundamentally ontological in nature. Ontological thirst is a thirst belonging to the soul, and it can only be quenched by the cool waters that flow in the underground caverns of the sacred.

The Reality of the Sacred Stream

For me, the "underground stream" is not simply a poetic metaphor but a metaphysical premise. I believe there really is a sacred stream, a deeper dimension of reality which we can access in order to nurture and sustain our souls. This dimension is not accessible to the five senses, and we can only describe it in metaphorical and symbolic language. Nevertheless, it exists. It is part of the nature and structure of reality itself.

Metaphysics, which literally means "beyond the physical," is the branch of philosophy that deals with the ultimate nature of reality. Plato was one of the first Western thinkers to maintain that there is another dimension that lies beyond the physical plane of existence. Plato called this dimension the world of ideas and believed it to be the truly substantial world, of which this physical world, known through the five senses, is only a transient and imperfect copy. Christianity and most other world religions hold similar views. The apostle Paul, who was educated in Greek philosophy, wrote in II Corinthians 4:18, "The things which are seen are temporal; but the things which are not seen are eternal."

Long before I ever read Plato, I was a Platonist. I have always believed in another dimension—that this physical world is not all there is—though I have never had an earthshaking mystical experience or experienced any overwhelming "invasions" from this other world. And while my childhood training and my later studies in religion reinforced this belief, I have never felt they created it. Rather, they simply gave me words for something I already knew intuitively.

I realize my belief in another dimension is an over-belief in William James's sense. I cannot prove my position, and I respect those who have come to different conclusions. But they cannot prove their conclusions either. Regardless of what we believe about the ultimate nature of reality, we can never know for sure. We can only say, "This is what I believe."

My belief in another dimension comes more from my heart than my head. My knowledge of this other dimension has come primarily through what I call poignant moments—moments in which the sacred has broken through and touched my heart. In childhood, the sacred came to me through religious experiences. Later, it came through philosophy, psychology, art, and intimate relationships. The sacred once came as I stood before an original painting by Van Gogh in a museum. It has often come through my wife Sara, and my close friends. It sometimes comes through music, movies, poetry, and plays. It comes through darkness, through silence, through being in deep woods, through moonlight, through women. It comes through my sons, and through my grandchildren.

In my more rebellious days I tried to doubt the existence of the sacred, but the universe kept dancing and life kept writing poetry across my life. Just when doubt seemed to be winning, Sara would kiss me, my child would crawl on my lap, snow would fall, spring would break out, flowers would bloom, a piece of music would play, a poem would speak, a friend would call to say she loved me, or some other such thing would come out of nowhere to throw me back into total belief that life is, after all, intensely sacred.

I believe in the sacred because I simply no longer have the strength to sustain disbelief. It takes too much energy to deny the sacred, to defend against grace; too much time to block out poignancy, to explain away love. So somewhere along the way I just gave up and admitted that life is too poetic to be explained in prose and the sacred is too manifest to be denied.

And if this seems too dramatic, think of it this way: If you were told that you had only one week to live, wouldn't those last days be filled with miracles, and wouldn't they be the same things you now take for granted every day? And if the physician then called to say the diagnosis was wrong and that you were going to live after all, wouldn't you kiss the earth, dance to the sun, and celebrate the wonder and beauty of life? But because we think we are not dying and because life's wonder is a daily thing, we are blind to the miracle of existence and do not see the sacred, even though it is breaking through all around us.

The Indefinable Nature of the Sacred

While I believe in the sacred, I don't pretend to understand its nature. When I was a boy, my religion told me the nature of the sacred in exact terms. My church had it all figured out, and all I had to do was accept what I was taught. But eventually I learned that every religion has its own view of the sacred, and they all differ. A primitive shaman holds one view of the spiritual realm; a modern priest, another. Mono-theistic religions differ from polytheistic ones. Buddhism differs from Islam. Judaism differs from Christianity. Catholicism even differs from Protestantism.

The truth is, no one knows the nature of the sacred. The history of religions and spiritual systems is simply the story of how human beings, at different times and in various cultures, have struggled to understand and articulate their vague and intuitive sensings of this mysterious realm.

It seems that the sacred permeates human experience and that every discipline, in one way or another, acknowledges its reality. Religion talks about it in religious language, philosophy talks about it in philo-sophical terms, psychology describes it as the deeper regions of the psyche, artists know it as the source of their creativity, musicians say it is the place where music writes itself, and lovers touch it through intimacy and erotic passion. While their descriptions differ, all seem to know this dimension exists, and each has found a unique way to access it.

The common core of all spiritualities may be this belief in another dimension that we can draw upon to deepen and enrich our lives. As the Sufi master said, "A river passes through many countries and each claims it for its own. But there is only one river."[21]

I believe there is one river and that we need to set aside religious intolerance so that we can honor each ship that sails that river and each person who meditates upon its shores. Call this river the sacred, the supernatural, the spiritual realm, the dimension of Being, the deeper psyche, the higher self, the collective unconscious, the farther reaches of human nature, or whatever you prefer. All the names, models, metaphors, and typologies are simply our feeble efforts to grasp infinity.

Personally, I never expect to know the exact nature of the sacred. If I did know it, I suspect my brain could not contain it and my pen would explode in trying to write it. What is important, it seems, is that we are sometimes given the unspeakable gift of touching this domain. And what we need are not arguments about the nature of the sacred, but rather, an open heart and a willingness to wait in those places where the sacred might appear. The sacred is not closed to our long-ings nor deaf to our entreaties. It has a peculiar way of opening itself up to the soul that seeks it, and those openings, those moments of com-munion, are the times when our souls are nurtured and our lives are filled with meaning and depth.

THE CONTINUUM OF SACRED EXPERIENCE

Since many people think sacred experience is a strange, esoteric event that has nothing to do with their lives, it is important to em-phasize that sacred experience exists on a continuum of intensity, the lower end of which is experiences we all have. The following diagram illustrates these degrees of intensity.

Intensity Levels of Sacred Experience

Poignant Moments	Peak Experiences	Mystical Encounters
(Low Intensity)	(Average Intensity)	(High Intensity)
1 2 3	4 5 6	7 8 9

Poignant moments are the most common sacred experiences. These are the times when our soul is gently stirred, when the sacred brushes against us. They may occur when we listen to music, watch a sunset, play with our child, or take a walk by the ocean. Poignant moments are not earthshaking or life-changing, but they certainly touch our hearts and nourish our souls.

The following story from Abraham Maslow's files is a good example of what I would call a poignant moment:

> A young mother was scurrying around her kitchen and getting break-fast for her husband and young children. The sun was streaming in, the children, clean and nicely dressed, were chattering as they ate. The husband was casually playing with the children; but, as she looked at them she was suddenly so overwhelmed with their beauty and her great love for them, and her feeling of good fortune, that she went into a peak experience.[22]

This was not an overwhelming event that forever changed this young woman. It was simply one of those special moments in life when the soul is touched and a sense of gratitude and well-being rise up in the heart.

I experienced such a moment last spring. On my way to work I stopped at a traffic light. On my right was a bed of brilliant, multi-colored flowers. The California sun was shining overhead and the intense colors of the flowers almost took my breath away. Suddenly, tears from some unknown place came to my eyes. When the light changed, I drove on. But for a few seconds I had touched the beauty and wonder of life. I had experienced a poignant moment.

Peak Experiences, as I use the term, are more intense than poignant moments. Maslow used the term peak experiences to refer to the entire range of mystical experiences; I use the term to refer only to the middle range of the continuum. Compared to poignant moments, peak experiences tend to last longer, touch us more deeply, and produce more lasting changes in our lives. Yet these experiences lack the overwhelming power of a full-blown mystical encounter.

A graduate student told me the following peak experience: She had gone for a walk on the beach in the late afternoon. As the sun was setting, she climbed onto a boulder at the water's edge. Gazing out to sea, she felt herself slowly becoming one with nature—with the sun descending toward the horizon, the waves crashing at her feet, the pastel colors that streaked the western sky. She said, "In that moment I felt eternity. I knew these things had gone on for millions of years before I came and that they would go on for millions of years after I'm gone. It felt good to be alive, to be part of all this. I was deeply moved and began to cry."

This experience had a profound impact on this young woman. It stayed with her for days afterwards and prompted her to make some important decisions about her life.

Mystical encounters are the most intense forms of sacred experience. They are sometimes so powerful that they produce temporary psychological disorganization. Mystical encounters are often "border events," events that mark a transition from one way of life to another. Prophets and seers have been called to their missions by such events. Among indigenous people these experiences often manifest as a state of being possessed, and in traditional religion they sometimes occur as overwhelming conversions or calls to a new way of life.

The religious literature of Western culture is filled with accounts of mystical encounters. Two of the most famous are the story of Moses and the burning bush, and the conversion of the apostle Paul. When Moses approached the site of the burning bush, he heard a voice say, "Take off your shoes because the ground where you are standing is holy ground." This was a border event, God's call to Moses to lead the children of Israel out of Egypt to the Promised Land.

Saul—Paul's name before he became a Christian—was on his way to Damascus to persecute Christians when he was overcome by a blinding light. A voice said, "Saul, Saul, why are you persecuting me?" Saul asked, "Who are you?" And the voice answered, "I am Jesus whom you are persecuting." Overwhelmed, Saul had a complete reversal of heart. He became a Christian, changed his name to Paul, and eventually became the foremost missionary of the early church, spreading Christianity across the Roman Empire and writing almost half of the books in the New Testament. His story is a dramatic example of a mystical encounter and the radical changes such events can produce.

A number of the mystical experiences recorded in *The Varieties of Religious Experience* were reported by well-known and highly respected people of the day. The following story, which I would classify as a mystical encounter, is from a Dr. R. M. Brucke, a Canadian psychiatrist.

> I had spent the evening in a great city, with two friends, reading and discussing poetry and philosophy. We parted at midnight. I had a long drive in a hansom to my lodging. My mind, deeply under the influence of the ideas, images, and emotions called up by the reading and talk, was calm and peaceful. I was in a state of quiet, almost passive enjoyment, not actually thinking, but letting ideas, images, and emotions flow of themselves, as it were, through my mind. All at once, without warning of any kind, I found myself wrapped in a flame-colored cloud. For an instant I thought of fire, an immense conflagration somewhere close by in that great city; the next, I knew that the fire was within myself. Directly afterward there came upon me a sense of exultation, of immense joyousness accompanied or immediately followed by an intellectual illumination impossible to describe. Among other things, I did not merely come to believe, but I saw that the universe is not composed of dead matter, but is, on the contrary, a living Presence; I became conscious in myself of eternal life. It was not a conviction that I would have eternal life, but a consciousness that I possessed eternal life then; I saw that all men are

immortal; that the cosmic order is such that without any peradventure all things work together for the good of each and all; that the foundation principle of the world, of all the worlds, is what we call love, and that the happiness of each and all is in the long run absolutely certain. The vision lasted a few seconds and was gone; but the memory of it and the sense of the reality of what it taught has remained during the quarter of a century which has since elapsed. I knew that what the vision showed was true. I had attained a point of view from which I saw that it must be true. That view, that conviction, I may say that consciousness, has never, even during periods of the deepest depression, been lost."[23]

Poignant moments, peak experiences, and mystical encounters are cut from the same cloth and all qualify as sacred experiences. While differing in intensity, each touches the soul and leaves us with a sense of awe, wonder, and reverence.

Several years ago I made a trip to Egypt. While shopping in Cairo, we decided to visit a perfume factory. Our guide led us up some narrow, winding streets toward the factory. As we approached, I could smell a trace of perfume in the air. At the entrance the aroma was much stronger. Once inside, the fragrance was almost overwhelming. Sacred experiences are like this. Poignant moments are the traces of the sacred that come to us on the daily breezes of life; peak experiences are the stronger aromas near the entrance to the sacred; and mystical encounters are like being inside the house, potent with the very presence of the sacred itself.

MODELS FOR UNDERSTANDING THE SACRED

While we can never know the exact nature of the sacred, there are certain ways of approaching this mysterious force that can illumine its nature and help us connect with its power. This section will explore some of these approaches to the sacred.

The Sacred as Mode of Consciousness

The poet Rumi would sometimes stay up all night with his community of dervishes. They would dance and write poetry, waiting for the sacred to appear. At the end of one night, as dawn was breaking, they found themselves in the presence of the sacred. In this ecstatic state Rumi wrote the following poem:

This we have now
is not imagination.

This is not
grief or joy.

Not a judging state,
or an elation,
or sadness.

Those come
and go.

This is the presence
that doesn't.

It's dawn, Husam,
here in the splendor of coral,
inside the Friend, the simple truth
of what Hallaj said.

What else could human beings want?

When grapes turn to wine,
they're wanting
this.

When the night sky pours by,
it's really a crowd of beggars,
and they all want some of this!

This
that we are now
created the body, cell by cell,
Like bees building a honeycomb.

The human body and the universe
grew from this, not this
from the universe and the human body.[24]

There is a certain state of consciousness that facilitates the appear-
ance of the sacred. Rumi and his community used dancing and poetry
to reach this state; the Christian mystics used prayer and meditation;
Native American shamans reach it through peyote and ritual; and

many indigenous peoples chant and dance to exhaustion to reach this ecstatic state.

I call this state sacred consciousness. Sacred consciousness is that state of mind in which we are more attuned to the spiritual dimension of life. Today, we live primarily in profane or secular consciousness, but for thousands of years human beings lived in sacred consciousness. Fortunately, we still have this capacity. It is an archetypal ability, part of the soul's heritage, a deeply imprinted gift from our ancestors.

Charles Tart, a psychologist at the University of California in Davis, believes that what we call normal consciousness is only one of several states available to us.[25] Dream, meditation, and drug-induced states are examples of what Tart called altered states of consciousness, and each of these states has its own characteristics and functions.

William James also believed we have other states of consciousness available to us. At the turn of the century, long before Tart did his work, James wrote:

> Our normal waking consciousness, rational consciousness as we call it, is but one special type of consciousness, whilst all about it, parted from it by the filmiest of screens, there lie potential forms of con-sciousness entirely different. We may go through life without sus-pecting their existence; but apply the requisite stimulus, and at a touch they are there in all their completeness, definite types of men-tality which probably somewhere have their field of application and adaptation.[26]

Applying these ideas, I would say that sacred consciousness is an altered state in which we are more attuned to the sacred. In this state our souls are open and we are sensitive to spiritual things. Sacred con-sciousness allows us to feel, experience, and know things we cannot access in the secular mode of consciousness. This is why people who are stuck in the secular mode have so much difficulty understanding matters of the soul. They are, as it were, tuned in to only one station. In fact, they may not even realize other stations exist.

There is a distinct difference between the secular and sacred modes of consciousness. The following stories will help make this difference clear.

Several years ago I had a client who was very attuned to the sacred. Her father, however, did not share his daughter's spiritual sensitivities. Once, while on vacation in France, her father visited Notre Dame

Cathedral. As he looked at the majestic architecture that has inspired millions of souls to soar, his only comment was, "It sure is a lot dirtier than I expected." Obviously, this man was not in the sacred mode!

Some people visit the Grand Canyon in Northern Arizona and see only a great hole in the ground. Others, more intellectually inclined, chatter away about the historical periods represented by the various layers of rock. But a few stand in awed silence before the grandeur and beauty of this marvel of nature and touch for a moment the heart of eternity. They are in the sacred mode.

In the 1800s, as the pioneers pressed westward across America, they found rich plains, virgin timberlands, sparkling rivers, and fish and game in abundance. But the pioneers pursued an agenda inspired by secular consciousness. Soon the buffalo were killed by the millions, the timberlands were raped, the plains ploughed to dust, the rivers polluted, and the fish and animals almost decimated. All this destruction was wrought in less than a century. By contrast, Native Americans, who regard nature as sacred, had lived in harmony with the land and the animals for thousands of years.

Far too often, secular consciousness leads to the desacralization of life. This attitude has even entered the healing professions, as the following story from Abraham Maslow shows.

> The first operation I saw was almost a representative example of the effort to desacralize, i.e., to remove the sense of awe, privacy, fear, and shyness before the sacred and of humility before the tremendous. A woman's breast was to be amputated with an electric scalpel that cut by burning through. As a delicious aroma of grilling steak filled the air, the surgeon made carelessly "cool" and casual remarks about the pattern of his cutting, paying no attention to the freshmen rushing out in distress, and finally tossing this object through the air onto the counter where it landed with a plop. It had changed from a sacred object to a discarded lump of fat. There were, of course, no tears, prayers, rituals, or ceremonies of any kind, as there would certainly have been in most preliterate societies. This was all handled in purely technological fashion—emotionless, calm, even with a slight tinge of swagger.[27]

When I first read this story, I was reminded of a young man, a good friend, who once came to my office very upset. His wife had just had a hysterectomy and was in the hospital recovering. When I asked him what was wrong, he said, "I don't really know, but I'm really angry at the doctor." He went on to tell me that his wife's surgeon had come by the hospital room on his morning rounds. My friend had asked a question about his wife's condition. In answer, the doctor had abruptly thrown back the sheet, pushed up her gown, and begun to poke her vaginal area, describing the procedures of the operation. After the doctor left, my friend felt angry and upset. But because the doctor had not actually harmed his wife physically, he couldn't understand the intensity of his own reaction.

My friend was experiencing the desacralization that is far too common in modern medicine. This doctor had at that moment entered the private, sacred world of this woman's body with neither permission nor respect. He was a profane man trespassing on sacred ground. And while my friend's intellect could not understand his own reaction, his soul had known and registered this violation of the sacred.

I do not wish to leave the impression that secular consciousness is always bad and sacred consciousness is always good. Obviously, both are important to our lives. But we are so permeated by the secular attitude today that we have forgotten the value of sacredness. We need more men and women, including those in science and medicine, who can rise above the desacralizing forces inherent in their professions and maintain a sacred vision of life. In short, we need more people who know how to access and honor the sacred mode of consciousness.

The Sacred as Place

Since ancient times the earth has been full of places that are imbued with numinous energy and mysterious power, places such as Stonehenge, Delphi, Jerusalem, Mecca, the Himalayas, the Ganges, Ayers Rock in Australia, the Mountains of the Moon in Africa. Even today mysterious energies hover about these places, and the sacred seems only a whisper away.

It seems that sacred places are openings in the secular world, clearings where the sacred can manifest. For example, the ancient pillars of Stonehenge stand on the barren plains of England like sentries guarding some cosmic mystery. In that place we sense the presence of something so old that we have forgotten its name. The soul loves such places. It vibrates, resonates, and comes alive. At some deep, primordial level it knows that this is home.

From a logical point of view, the consecration of space makes no sense. Yet the soul seems driven to create sacred places and has done so for thousands of years in every culture of the world. Even today, each community has its holy places—temples, churches, altars, groves, cemeteries, shrines, or sacred lands. Even private homes seem to have sacred areas. I have seen coffee tables that looked like religious altars, complete with Bible, family album, wedding pictures, and other sacred objects of the clan. A few years ago, when fire swept through some areas of Southern California and people had to evacuate their homes immediately, these were the items they took with them on their way out.

On the Big Island of Hawaii there is a sacred place called the Place of Refuge. Centuries ago it was the home of the old Hawaiian kings, who were thought to be divine. Today, black stone walls still line the perimeter, and rock foundations mark where the temple and other buildings once stood. There are petroglyphs carved into the rocks by ancient hands, hand-dug pools where fish were kept for the king, and natural tide pools in the black lava rock that stretches out to meet the sea. Walking among these ancient ruins, one can almost feel the presence of the old Hawaiian gods, hear chanting in the distance, and see the fires that lit the night. The place has a mysterious, almost numinous atmosphere. To use Eliade's words, it seems saturated with power.

Sara, my wife, loves the Place of Refuge. In 1990, when we made our third visit to the Big Island, she was going through a difficult time in her life and felt strangely drawn to visit there again. When we arrived at the sacred grounds, Sara took off her sandals and began to walk wherever her intuition led her. I followed quietly behind, watching her. At one point she sat for several minutes on a large black rock facing out to sea. The rock had been the favorite meditation spot of one of the old Hawaiian kings. Then she walked to the beach and sat under a palm tree for a long time, watching the ocean and listening to the eternal rhythm of the waves. Finally, she said, "I'm ready to go now."

That experience had a profound effect on Sara, which she described:

> I don't consider myself a mystical type of woman, so that experience
> was very unusual for me. Even before we flew to Hawaii I knew I had
> to go to the Place of Refuge; the pull was very strong. That day, as I
> walked around the grounds, I was almost in a trance. It seemed that
> I could feel sacred energies in some places, not in others. When I felt
> the energy, I would stop and open my soul. I know this makes no
> sense logically, but my soul seemed to know what it needed. Finally,

there came a point at which I felt finished. The experience was very healing; it left me feeling centered and more in tune with life.

We have much to learn about sacred places and the healing energies associated with them. Much like music, poetry, and other things of the soul, sacred places touch the deeper layers of the psyche and have a centering, anchoring, and realigning effect on the soul. How this occurs is not clear, but it seems that certain configurations of space and the atmosphere they create have the ability to reach us at a profound level. They promote healing and contribute significantly to our spiritual development.

The Sacred As the Source of Personal Passion and Power

There is a strange, mysterious energy associated with the sacred which can infuse us with passion and power. We know little about this energy, but it manifests in all cultures and in many different forms.

For example, when the sociologist Emile Durkheim studied native cultures, he discovered a special power called *mana* that was associated with the sacred domain. When a tribesman went away to commune with the sacred, he would return to the village filled with this mysterious power. This led Durkheim to say, "The believer who has communicated with his god is . . . stronger. He feels within him more force, either to endure the trials of existence, or to conquer them."[28]

Francine, one of my doctoral students, was born on a small island in the South Seas. For the first eight years of her life she lived in a hut with a dirt floor, spoke the language of her people, and participated in the beliefs, rituals, and daily activities of her village. One day in class I was struggling to describe the sacred and how it fills us with passion and power. Francine kept nodding her head and seemed to understand exactly what I was trying to say. She said, "That's what my people call *pakaramdam*."

Never having heard this word, I asked her to say it again. She spelled it and then pronounced it slowly—"pahk-ah-rahm-dahm." She said, "In my village when people spoke from down here (pointing to her solar plexus), it was said that they were speaking with pakaramdam. This meant that they were speaking with deep emotion, power, and passion—very different from ordinary speech."

In his *Havana Lectures*, the Spanish poet and playwright Federico Garcia Lorca called this mysterious power *duende*. He said:

Everything that has black tones has duende. And there is no truth greater. These black tones are mystery itself whose roots are held fast in the mulch we all know and ignore, but whence we arrive at all that is substantial in art. Black tones . . . are "a mysterious power which everyone feels but which no philosopher can explain." So then, the duende is a power and not a method, a struggle and not a thought. I have heard an old guitar teacher say that "the duende is not in the singer's throat, the duende rises inside from the very soles of one's feet." That is to say, it is not a question of ability or aptitude but a matter of possessing an authentic living style; that is to say of blood, of culture most ancient, of creation in art. This "mysterious power which everyone feels and no philosopher can explain" is in short, the spirit of the earth. The true struggle is with the duende.

The arrival of the duende always presupposes a radical transformation on every plane. It produces a feeling of totally unedited freshness. It bears the quality of a newly created rose, of a miracle that produces an almost religious enthusiasm. All art is capable of duende. But the place that it naturally occurs is in music, dance, or spoken poetry because they require a living body for interpretation and because they are forms that perpetually live and die, their contours are raised upon an exact presence.[29]

As Lorca indicates, artists know this mysterious power as the source of their creativity. One of my students, a black woman, grew up in a family of jazz musicians. When she read Abraham Maslow's description of peak experiences and the realm of Being, she was convinced that jazz musicians often tap into this dimension when they jam together. For a research project, she interviewed several world-class jazz musicians to ask them about this. Every one of them, without exception, knew immediately what she was talking about. Using their own words, they described those special moments when an entire band is caught up in the universal. They become one with the music they are creating; there is an intense sense of flow and connection. Each player knows intuitively what the others are going to do before they do it. In those moments they become servants to the creative process, instruments through which the duende creates the new.

Even as a professor, I know this force. On some days my lectures lack life. My notes lie there dead in front of me and no matter how hard I try to breathe life into them, nothing happens. My students feel the deadness and dutifully take their notes. Yet on other days the duende breaks in. A deep, authentic force wells up and my words seem to flow of their own accord. The students come alive. Pakaramdam fills the classroom, and we talk from our hearts with power and passion. These are the special moments in education, perhaps the only times when real learning occurs.

Carl Rogers, in his famous conversation with Paul Tillich, talked about the occurrence of this in psychotherapy: "I feel as though I am somehow in tune with the forces of the universe or that forces are operating through me in regard to this helping relationship."[30]

As a writer, I depend on the duende. I work for hours on a few paragraphs; my work is mechanical, laborious, uninspired. Then suddenly the duende breaks in, and the words come so fast I can hardly keep up with them. Every writer knows these moments and thanks God for the duende!

The duende is portrayed for us in literature and film. Zorba, the hero of the book and the film *Zorba the Greek*, lives with intense passion. He loves women, wine, food, song, dance, and sensuality. Serving as mentor to his uptight young friend from England, he teaches him about life and the passions of the soul.

In the movie *Like Water for Chocolate*, we are artfully introduced to the passion, power, blood, and romance of the Latino culture. And in the movie *The Postman*, we see the opening of a young man's soul to the power of poetry and romantic love. As he discovers the passion of life, he comes to believe anything is possible and finds the courage to live his destiny.

What is this mysterious power that everyone feels but no philosopher can explain? I believe it is the mystery of life itself, the powerful energies of the sacred. When we touch this domain, we are filled with the cosmic force of life itself; we sink our roots deep into the black soil and draw power and being up into ourselves. We know the energy of the numen and are saturated with power and being. We feel grounded, centered, in touch with the ancient and eternal rhythms of life. Power and passion well up like an artesian spring and creativity dances in celebration of life.

Federico Garcia Lorca was right. The true struggle, and the only one that really matters, is with the duende.

The Sacred as Transcendent Perception

Finally, the sacred is associated with what I call transcendent perception, or the ability to see with sacred eyes.

We human beings have the capacity to experience ordinary things in extraordinary ways. For example, when I was a young man, I had a friend who was in love with a very ordinary looking woman, but he continually rhapsodized about her beauty. When he looked at her, he obviously saw things the rest of us simply could not see.

For another example, most of us agree that a baby is a wonderful thing; but in one sense, a baby is just a small organism that does little except eat, sleep, and mess its diapers. Yet through the eyes of love, parents see their baby with transcendent perception and believe it to be the most beautiful thing in the world.

Or to use a different example, when we look into the night sky, we see the moon and stars. In one sense, the moon is nothing but a desolate, uninhabited satellite endlessly circling the earth, and the stars are simply distant suns, millions of light years away. But when we gaze into the sky on a clear winter night, we are struck by its beauty and are filled with wonder and awe. This is transcendent perception—the capacity to see ordinary things in an extraordinary way.

I think transcendent perception is often at work even with regard to things we consider to be intrinsically beautiful. For example, in one sense a painting by Van Gogh is really nothing but a bunch of multi-colored smudges on an old piece of canvas. Similarly, music is nothing but the sounds that come from plucking strings, beating drums, and blowing air through hollow objects. Yet, when those smudges or sounds are arranged in a certain pattern, our soul goes forth to meet a Van Gogh masterpiece or the sounds of a symphony, and in that meeting something happens, and we are transported into realms of exquisite beauty.

Transcendent perception is related to our human capacity for exaggeration, dramatization, idealization, and romanticization. It is the ability to see with the eyes of the heart and the imagination. It is similar to what Maslow called Being-cognition, the ability to view life "under the aspect of eternity."[31]

Miguel de Cervantes wrote his book Don Quixote, Man of La Mancha to poke fun at chivalry and romantic idealism, but his literary goal backfired.[32] The main character is a romantic fool who sees all of life with transcendent perception. In spite of his tilting at windmills and his overdone idealism, we fall in love with this crazy man. And we are left a bit confused: Is this man who sees life through the eyes of passion, romance, and honor simply a romantic fool? Or is it we who are the fools, we who have lost our ability to see the world as enchanted?

The troubadours, who flourished in France and Italy from the eleventh to the thirteenth centuries, may have been the first true romantics of the West. These minstrels fell devotedly in love with women they could never have and traveled across Europe pouring out their romantic idealizations in poetry and song. Fanning the flames of their own unrequited love, the troubadours lived on romance, passion, melancholy, and love.

In the eighteenth century, the spirit of the troubadours broke out again in the form of the Romantic Movement. This movement, which spread across Europe, was characterized by romanticism, idealization, imagination, and passion. The movement focused on the personal, the natural, the primitive, the emotional. In literature it took the form of aesthetic sensibility, emphasizing feelings, poetic sensitivity, and even the pleasures of melancholic reflection. The Romantics viewed life with transcendent perception and focused their creative energies on expressing the deepest passions of the soul.

Of course, it is easy to see these movements as extreme and to make fun of romantics. In our cynical age, which prides itself on being realistic, we feel uncomfortable and even a bit embarrassed by the sensitivities of the romantic soul. But we have these sensitivities within us too, and in those unguarded moments when our hearts are tender, we are also swept along by the feelings of the heart and the passions of the soul. In such moments we see that our cynicism is a defense against wonder, a wall we build around our hearts to protect ourselves from the power of awe. Realism and cynicism are the dark goggles that protect us from the brilliant sun of transcendent perception. But the romantics—whether Don Quixote, the troubadours, or perhaps our own daughter as she falls in love—blow our cover. They force us, at least for a few moments, to remove our dark glasses, tear down the walls around our heart, and open our eyes to the miracle of life.

The opposite of transcendent perception is reductionism, the tendency to make life less than it is. Reductionism is a "nothing but" way of seeing. Reductionistic people are the realists of the world, and in our cynical age they rule the day.

Viktor Frankl, best known for his book *Man's Search for Meaning*, was one of my graduate professors.[33] Frankl had survived the concentration camps of Hitler and was deeply concerned about reductionistic science and the desacralization of human life. One day in class, to show us the limitations of operational definitions, he defined a kiss as nothing but the affixing of the upper ends of two gastrointestinal tubes. When we laughed at this, he said, "You are right to laugh because intuitively you know that, while this definition is technically and operationally correct, a kiss is more than that. And it is the "more," the very part that reductionism leaves out, that makes a kiss human and gives it its true meaning."

Transcendent perception is the ability to see the "more." It is poetics applied to everyday life, a way of looking at one's experience through sacred eyes. Certainly there are dangers in transcendent perception. We can over-idealize and fail to see the reality of a situation. But in our present culture, steeped as it is in desacralization and reductionistic thinking, I believe the greater and often unrecognized danger lies in the other direction—in being so realistic that we fail to see the beauty and wonder of life.

Henry David Thoreau said it well:

> I fear chiefly lest my expression may not be *extra-vagant* enough, may not wander far enough beyond the narrow limits of my daily experience, so as to be adequate to the truth of which I have been convinced. . . . I am convinced that I cannot exaggerate enough even to lay the foundations of a true expression. . . . Why level downward to our dullest perception always, and praise that as common sense? The commonest sense is the sense of men asleep, which they express by snoring. . . .[34]

THE ETERNAL SACRED

We are moving into a postmodern age. Our sacred pole has broken and the old structures of meaning are giving way to new and multiple realities. Past societies built their lives around a common belief system, a sacred pole that stood at the center of their culture. But today in our shrinking world there are dozens of sacred poles, each vying for our allegiance. The spiritual diversity that has always existed globally is now in our own village.

As we move into this new age, we will no longer be able to equate spirituality with a particular set of religious beliefs and symbols. We will be forced to acknowledge that spirituality manifests in hundreds of different ways across all cultures. It will become increasingly difficult to convince ourselves that one religious system is necessarily better than another simply because it is ours. Perhaps the day will come when the validity of one's spirituality will be judged not by the correctness of one's theology but by the authenticity of one's spiritual life. When that day comes, an authentically spiritual Buddhist and an authentically spiritual Christian may find that they have more in common with each other than they do with those in their respective religions who have failed to develop their spirituality. And there may even come a time, perhaps centuries from now, when religion itself will fade away, leaving only the universal wisdom that has proven effective in the development of our spiritual nature.

Durkheim said, "There is something eternal in religion which is destined to survive all the particular symbols in which religious thought has successfully enveloped itself."[35] I believe that something is the sacred, that primordial region of human experience that has always fed the human soul. Sacred poles break and symbols change. But the sacred can provide an anchoring point on this sea of endless spiritual forms and possibilities.

The poet Rainer Maria Rilke said it best in his poem, "Buddha in Glory":

> Center of all centers, core of cores,
> almond self-enclosed and growing sweet—
> all this universe, to the furthest stars
> and beyond them, is your flesh, your fruit. . . .
>
> a billion stars go spinning through the night,
> blazing high above your head.
> But in you is the presence that
> will be, when all the stars are dead.[36]

A MODEL FOR NONRELIGIOUS SPIRITUALITY

In this first part of the book I have defined spirituality, the soul, and the sacred in nonreligious terms and emphasized that these terms belong to humanity, that they are not the exclusive property of organized religion. These three constructs and their dynamic relationship to one another provide the foundations for a new nonreligious vision of spiritual development.

When the soul is nurtured through contact with the sacred, the result is spiritual growth or spirituality. The soul is not a religious entity, but the deepest core of our own being. The sacred is not a force available only to those in religion, but a powerful dimension of life available to all through poignant moments, peak experiences, and, sometimes, mystical encounters. When one's soul is nourished on a regular basis by these sacred experiences, spiritual growth is the inevitable result. Thus, one might say that the sacred provides the nourishing energy that feeds the soul and thereby produces spiritual growth.

Thus, the idea of a nonreligious spirituality is really quite simple. All human beings, whether religious or not, have a soul. All human beings, whether religious or not, have access to the sacred. Therefore, it follows that all human beings, whether religious or not, can learn to access the sacred, nurture their souls, and develop their spirituality.

PART II

Part II describes eight alternative paths to the sacred and shows you how to use these paths to develop your spirituality. The symbols of traditional religion, which serve as cultural access codes to the sacred, are breaking down in Western culture. Therefore, we must find new paths to the sacred, alternative ways to access the spiritual dimension. These eight paths will show you how to nurture your soul and build a spiritual life outside the walls of traditional religion.

The final chapter of the book presents step-by-step instructions on how to develop a personal program for spiritual growth. It will help you pinpoint the activities and experiences that nurture your soul and then show you how to design a three-month pilot program for spiritual development.

Know the male, yet keep to the female.
—Lao-tzu

THE FEMININE
The Path of the Anima

One of the most powerful paths to spiritual development is the path of the anima. In this culture we tend to honor the masculine and neglect, or even betray, the feminine. At the societal level this betrayal enthrones masculine biases and maintains the patriarchal power structures of society. At the personal level those who neglect the feminine side of their personalities cut themselves off from their souls and impede their spiritual growth. Yet both men and women can reclaim the feminine and use the path of the anima to deepen and enrich their spiritual lives.

THE ANIMA, THE FEMININE, AND THE SOUL

The words *anima, feminine,* and *soul* all point to the same phenomenological reality. As noted earlier, *anima,* a feminine noun, is the Latin word for soul. Thus, even language reflects the fact that the anima, the feminine, and the soul are closely connected.

Spiritual growth depends on our learning to honor the feminine. While it may seem strange to link spirituality with the development of the feminine, if we remember that the word *anima* is simply another word for soul, then to develop the anima is to develop the soul. Thus, the path of the anima is the path of the soul and the road to a deeper, richer spiritual life.

Carl Jung agreed with this perspective. He used the terms *anima* and *soul* interchangeably, and in his psychological theory the anima is the major feminine archetype of the male psyche—the unconscious and often undeveloped female aspect of the male.[1] Jung believed the corresponding archetype in women is the animus, the male aspect of the female psyche. Later Jungian scholars, however, have pointed out that all of us, whether male or female, carry both archetypes in our psyche.[2] In other words, both women and men have both a masculine and a feminine side, which they may or may not have developed.

As was pointed out earlier, when I use the term *feminine*, I am referring to that side of ourselves, whether we are male or female, which is more relational, intuitive, mystical, imaginative, artistic, creative, emotional, flowing, and right-brained. It can be contrasted with the *masculine* side, which is more logical, rational, analytical, sequential, organized, structured, and left-brained. While the terms *masculine* and *feminine* are not ideal because they can be used in sexist ways, they are useful as long as we remember that these terms point to two sides of the personality which exist, at least potentially, in both women and men.

MEN WHO FLEE THE FEMININE

In this culture most men are taught to flee the feminine. From the time they are little boys, they are encouraged to develop their masculine traits but discouraged from developing their feminine qualities. This emphasis on the masculine and the corresponding neglect of the feminine seriously impacts men's spiritual development. Thus, Carl Jung believed the central task of psychotherapy with male clients is to introduce them to their anima, to the neglected feminine side of their personality. For many men, this is the beginning of their spiritual journey as well as an important step in their psychological growth.

The Oedipal Phase: First Betrayal of the Feminine?

According to classical Freudian theory, the first real denial of the feminine occurs at the time of Oedipal resolution. Simply put, this theory says that sometime around four years of age the little boy begins to want his Mom sexually, but since Dad is much stronger and might cut his penis off or even kill him, the little guy has a dilemma. Eventually, if all goes well, he resolves this conflict by identifying with his masculine Dad and spiritualizing his erotic interest in Mom. According to the theory, this is how little boys solidify their gender identity and become "little men." So Freudian theory sanctions an early denial of the feminine, seeing it as a necessary step in the healthy development of the male child.

But I wonder if the Oedipal resolution is not, in fact, the first betrayal of the feminine for a male child growing up in a patriarchal society. I wonder how these Oedipal dynamics between a boy and his parents would differ in a matriarchal or a partnership society, where feminine traits would be as highly valued as masculine. In such a society, would it still be necessary for a young boy to make so decisive a break from the feminine and establish so strong an identification with the masculine? Or would he remain more connected with his mother and the feminine while still affirming his gender identification with his father?

Carol Gilligan has suggested that children's identities are established primarily in relation to their mothers. Thus, girls establish their identity through affiliation with the same-gender parent, while boys, being of the opposite gender from the mother, must establish their identity by separation. And therefore, girls grow up to fear individuation, which threatens their identity founded on affiliation, while boys grow up to fear intimacy, which threatens their identity based on separation.[3]

In general, Gilligan's theory seems useful, and most of us probably do go through the process of identity formation she describes, as well as the classical Oedipal conflict and resolution described by Freud. But are these processes the expression of some biologically based inevitability, or are they rather an early manifestation of a patriarchal society's interest in grooming young boys to betray the feminine and to identify with those masculine traits that will eventually allow them to take their "rightful" place in the masculine power structures? Is the separation from the mother and the identification with the father, described by both Gilligan and Freud, a healthy process of identity formation for the young boy, or is it a pathological betrayal of the feminine?

Today I often see young men who were raised in families where gender boundaries and stereotypes were not so rigid, and I am touched by their ability to acknowledge and express their more feminine qualities.

These young men are clearly different from the men, often of my generation, who describe to me in psychotherapy how their fathers could never hug them or say, "I love you." These men tell me, "I know my dad loved me, but I just wish he could have said so." Even as adults, men often long for this kind of affirmation from their fathers. This is one reason the betrayal of the feminine is such a tragedy for males. This betrayal leaves men emotionally mute and prevents them from giving to one another the masculine nurturance they all need as little boys and even as grown men. This betrayal creates chasms between each other as males—between father and son, brother and brother, friend and friend, man and man.

Adolescence: The Second Betrayal of the Feminine?

From age six to age twelve most boys develop friendships with other boys and make it clear that girls are not part of their inner circle. Boys fear being called a "sissy" or other names that might suggest they are feminine. During this latency period, as Freud called it, boys often pretend, at least in the presence of their male friends, that they have no interest whatsoever in girls.

Then, at puberty, something happens. As they stand on the threshold of adolescence, boys begin to show interest in girls, but at the same time the denial of the feminine in themselves becomes even more pronounced. Ironically, while it is now acceptable to like girls, masculine posturing tends to increase, apparently as a masculine-devised way to impress and attract girls. Such male posturing may continue into young adulthood; indeed, for some men it continues throughout life.

Thus, the entire period from childhood through adolescence seems to be a training ground where boys learn to deny the feminine side of themselves and develop the masculine. Certainly there is nothing wrong with boys honoring their masculinity and feeling good about the fact that they are boys. But the extreme way in which many boys focus on the masculine and ignore, or even denigrate, the feminine side of their personalities raises serious questions about the way we socialize boys in this society. Is this a healthy process of male development, or is it an apprenticeship in patriarchal attitudes and values which are destructive to the boy's soul and, eventually, to those who share his life? Does this extreme training in the masculine traits produce men who are unable to express their feelings, empathize with others, or sustain intimate relationships? Or, perhaps the most disturbing question of all, does this one-sided training tend to produce men who are angry, aggressive, and even violent?

Male Rites of Passage: Yet Another Betrayal of the Feminine?

Many indigenous tribes have rituals or rites of passage for boys to mark the transition from childhood to young manhood. I once viewed these tribal rituals with Rousseau-like innocence, seeing them as expressions of a natural order that our more complex society had lost.

But there is something about these rituals, imposed by patriarchal men, that increasingly troubles me. Typically, the ritual involves adult males taking the boys into a secret place and putting them through a frightening, painful initiation. A boy is deemed to have become a man when he has endured all the initiation trials without showing fear or pain. The initiates are then instructed as to how they must treat—*mistreat* would be more accurate—the women in the tribe. This often involves such "manly" actions as rejecting former female playmates, not addressing females, or speaking only to give orders to them—and this includes the boy's own mother—as though manhood were somehow synonymous with subjugating women.

I now see such "natural" rites of passage as contaminated by patriarchal values designed to insure that young men will deny the feminine and identify with a tribal system founded on male power and dominance over women. Such subjugation of women is no more appealing among primitives than it is among Ivy League graduates.

This is not, however, to deny the need for rites of passage. Our society presents such confusing images of manhood that most young men are never quite certain what marks their passage to that status—whether it is their Bar Mitzvah, their confirmation, their first sexual experience, getting drunk, joining a gang, joining the army, turning eighteen, turning twenty-one, getting married, having a child, becoming a grandfather, or retiring!

Since our society provides no clear demarcation for this passage, I think it might be meaningful if parents created a ritual to mark this important turning point in their son's life. However, instead of confirming the boy's masculine side and denying the feminine, as so many rites of passage do, it seems to me that such a ritual should confirm both his masculine and feminine sides. This would be an opportune time for a mother to confirm her son's masculinity, including his emerging sexuality, and for a father to show him that manhood involves gentleness and care. I suspect that a ritual integrated in this way would provide a young boy with an indelible definition and map of what it means to be a man.

Men and Masculinity

It is ironic that in our patriarchal society, which encourages males to betray the feminine, men are frequently insecure about their masculinity. As the growing number of books on masculinity and men's gatherings attests, many men are now seeking to reclaim their masculinity. The men's movement has been instrumental in this task by helping men reclaim and express the positive aspects of their masculinity. I feel in deep accord with these men, but I also believe, somewhat paradoxically, that the recovery of the feminine is a major step toward a deeper masculinity.

As contradictory as it may seem, I am suggesting that part of every man's journey to reclaim his masculinity is the development of his feminine side. Every woman of depth knows that the feminine is a significant part of a man's masculine appeal. Men also recognize the importance of this dimension when they cease competing and reach out in gentle caring to one another. Just as the truly feminine woman is one who has moved beyond effeminacy to her deepest power and strength, so a truly masculine man is one who has moved beyond machismo to the deeper, gentler regions of his soul. A whole person, whether man or woman, is one whose feminine and masculine sides are well-developed and integrated, supporting and strengthening each other.

One of my doctoral students recently provided empirical support for this point of view. For his doctoral thesis he conducted in-depth interviews with several highly developed men, who were selected because of their exceptional levels of leadership and personal development. The goal of the study was to determine the values and characteristics of these men. One of the major findings of the study was that each of them, without exception, had a highly developed feminine side as well as a highly developed masculine side. This suggests that ideal masculine development goes hand-in-hand with the development of the feminine. It seems that self-actualized, highly developed men are those who have achieved an integrated balance between their masculine and feminine sides.[4]

The Masculine in Religion

One reason it is so hard for men to develop their feminine side is that our culture is permeated by masculine assumptions. Conservative religion in particular, which exercises considerable influence in this culture, is a major haven of patriarchal attitudes and masculine biases. By promoting these attitudes as "the will of God," these churches perpetuate attitudes in our society that are destructive to the soul and to the feminine side of the personality.

This is not always easy to see because, in some ways, conservative religion does honor the feminine. When I was a boy growing up in rural Arkansas, my conservative church was one of the few places I could hear adults talk openly about love, kindness, and forgiveness. Even crusty old farmers sometimes found the courage to express their gentler emotions at church. And the worship services, with their music, prayers, and sermons, were often nourishing to the soul. So in this sense feminine values were honored, and both men and women were encouraged to nurture and develop their souls.

Yet, like many conservative churches, mine was ultimately no haven for the feminine. For all its gentle and loving aspects, it was highly masculinized in its theology and outward forms. God was definitely male, and the public worship was conducted entirely by men. Women were required to keep silent in the public assembly lest they "usurp the authority" of the men. Our hyper-masculine "God the Father" was judgmental, intolerant, and punitive. If one wanted God's love and grace, one had to toe the line and do nothing to displease him. Above all, one had to be theologically and morally "right." In one's personal life, one had to be continually on guard lest one's words, actions, or thoughts became tinged with sin. In short, in order to enjoy God's love and acceptance, one had to risk the hell of his wrath and endure his exacting demands. At the time, this male God did not seem strange or pathological at all; in fact, he seemed like most of the men I knew.

I know that my experience is similar to that of thousands of other men who grow up in conservative religions. Patriarchal attitudes—which include dogmatism, legalism, intolerance, and sexist attitudes—tend to permeate these institutions. We sometimes blind ourselves to the spiritual destructiveness of these attitudes because we have been taught that the church is a refuge of righteousness and spirituality. But on closer analysis, it becomes clear that many churches promote beliefs, attitudes, and moral perspectives that are damaging to the human spirit and antithetical to authentic spirituality.

I believe the betrayal of the feminine is often at the heart of this destructiveness. As Riane Eisler has pointed out, it is difficult for a male God, as well as for those who follow him, to tolerate the feminine. As ancient patriarchal gods subjugated the goddess, so modern religious men, also threatened by the feminine, tend to perpetuate patriarchal assumptions and subjugate the feminine principle.[5]

And women hardly have a chance in patriarchal religion. The sexism that pervades conservative religion would result in multimillion-dollar lawsuits in any other societal institution. The theology of most conservative churches is blatantly sexist, and the submission of women to men is praised as godliness. Single and divorced women are second-class citizens; working mothers are made to feel guilty; little girls are taught in Sunday school to submit to God first and to their husbands second. And all this violence to the female spirit is sanctioned by a patriarchal theology that disguises it as the will of God.

I believe in God, but not in a God who crushes the spirit of little girls and grooms little boys to become sexist. I cannot believe in a God who tells women they must bow in submission to a man. I cannot believe in a God who condemns assertive women but approves violent men. I cannot believe in a God so threatened in his own masculinity that he cannot even hear the voice of the feminine if it dares question his authority. Such a God is too ancient and too savage for those of us who long for a society in which women and men respect each other as equals and celebrate each other's dignity and strength.

I would like to make it clear, however, that there are exceptions. There are churches, even some conservative churches, that are working hard to overcome their patriarchal attitudes; and many churches on the more liberal end of the continuum are open, tolerant, and dedicated to compassionate action in the world. These groups are trying to dismantle sexism in both their theology and their practice. Morality is defined in the context of compassion instead of by legalistic mandate. The feminine is honored, and women are respected as a vital part of the religion in both its private and public aspects. Such religious groups deserve our deepest respect; they serve as models of what institutional religion, at its best, can be.

Reclaiming the Feminine: Women Who Awaken Men's Souls

Carl Jung believed that one of the best ways for men to learn about their anima or feminine side is through their relationships with women. Because the feminine side is unconscious in most men, they tend to project it onto the women in their lives. Jung believed, for example, that when a man feels romantically drawn to a woman, the energy of this infatuation comes from the fact that his underdeveloped anima is being constellated by this particular woman. In other words, she is awakening and enlivening his feminine side, the "woman" within himself. The man then projects all the positive aspects of his own anima onto this woman and insists, in his romantic fervor, that she is the embodiment of all heavenly qualities. The truth is, as he will undoubtedly discover in time, she is only a woman; and while she may be a wonderful woman in her own right, the qualities he projects onto her in his romantic ecstasy actually belong to him, to his own unconscious anima, which she has simply awakened from its dormant state. Just as a projection screen allows one to see what is on the film, such a woman allows a man to see his own anima through the characteristics he projects onto her. In these situations, the therapeutic task for the man is to understand and "own back" or reclaim his projections. Through this process he will come to know his anima and incorporate into his own conscious personality the feminine qualities he had attributed to the woman. This may be the most effective way for a man to develop his soul, his feminine side.

My own story is relevant here. Soon after I began Jungian therapy in 1976, I had a dream of a beautiful woman in a flowing, white dress dancing by herself. She moved gracefully, lost in her own mysteries, her dress floating gently on the air as she moved. Between me and this numinous woman was a thick glass wall. I could see her clearly through the wall; but I could not talk to her, touch her, or dance with her.

"That," my analyst said, "is your anima."

He explained that the anima is the female aspect of the male and that she often appears in men's dreams. He said that my therapeutic task over the next several months was to remove the wall, come to know my anima more deeply, and learn to "dance" with her in my life.

At that time I had a close female friend, whom I will call Rachel, who in many ways was the embodiment of my anima archetype. Interestingly, Rachel was not my wife. In fact, one of the reasons I had begun therapy was that I felt so drawn to this woman that I was confused about what this meant for my marriage. While our relationship was not a sexual affair, it was an affair of the soul. I cared for this woman and seemed to know myself better in the intimacy of our friendship. Fortunately, I had an accepting wife who stuck with me through this confusing period. All my cultural, religious, and parental training had told me that it was impossible to love two women. But my experience was that I deeply loved Sara, my wife, and I had also come to love Rachel.

From a Jungian perspective, I had projected my anima onto Rachel, and my relationship with her therefore provided an opportunity for me to know this side of myself more fully. So for several months she was the focus of my therapy. Encouraged by my analyst to deal with my "Rachel side," as he called it, I talked about her in therapy, wrote letters never mailed to her, even wrote poetry to her.

Gradually I began to realize that my intense feelings about Rachel were really about a lost feminine side of myself that was struggling to be born. As this awareness dawned, Rachel as a person became less central to my therapy, and what she represented in me became the focus. I began to see that while Rachel was a special person in her own right, what she had constellated in me was uniquely me and mine. I slowly began to reclaim the feelings, stirrings, and qualities I had projected onto her. I began to appreciate my own feminine side and the increasing depth it was bringing into my life. Instead of feeling embarrassed about my gentleness, kindness, and empathic qualities and wondering, in typical male fashion, if these somehow made me less a man, I began to embrace these neglected parts of myself and integrate them into my life.

Earlier, my analyst had told me that the soul can be nurtured in nonreligious ways, but I had no idea that my feelings for Rachel were in any way related to spirituality. I was amazed that a woman could awaken my soul and deepen my spirituality far better than the rituals of religion. This is what the path of the anima can do.

When my therapy came to an end, my analyst said that I should always have female friends, women of depth, in my life. Unwaveringly supportive of Sara and my marriage throughout the therapy and always insisting that I take responsibility for my projections, he nevertheless recognized the value of female friends and the capacity of certain women to nurture a man's soul.

It has now been more than twenty years since my Jungian therapy ended, and my therapist's advice has proved to be one of the wisest prescriptions I have ever received. I have several female friends in my life; and today, after more than thirty years of marriage, Sara is still my best friend, as well as my wife. I am pleased that she chose, and continues to choose, to share her life with me. She is my church; her presence and being nurture my soul.

I feel sad for men who have no intimate friendships with women. Male friends can be wonderful, and nothing I say here is meant to disparage the deep relationships men are sometimes able to forge with one another. Still, for a man there is something unique about friendship with a woman, and there are some things about himself and life and nurturing the soul that a man can never learn until he has a female friend. In my opinion, there is no better way for a man to develop his anima, his feminine side, than through intimate relationships with women.

Midlife: Coming Home to the Feminine

Most men flee the feminine again and again, especially in the first half of life. But as they enter midlife, many men for the first time begin to pay more attention to the soul. The midlife years are a time of reevaluation, and men often discover that their lives have been one-sided—too devoted to masculine pursuits and negligent of the more soulful and feminine dimensions of life. Thus, for those who have failed to develop the anima in their younger years, midlife often represents a call for them to reconnect with their souls, to come home to the feminine.

Stan was in his late forties when he came to therapy. He was a successful executive with a major corporation but was feeling depressed. In our first session he said, "In my twenties and thirties, I was excited about my job; I worked long hours to prove myself and to get the promotions I wanted. But in the last few years, the excitement has gone. I've achieved most of my goals, but now I wonder if it was worth it. There's got to be more to life."

Paul, a factory worker in his late thirties, had a similar complaint. He said, "My dad taught me that a man's job is to provide for his family, and I always tried to do that. But last year, after sixteen years of marriage, my wife left me and took the kids with her. She tells me that I don't know how to have a relationship, that I was never there for her or the kids emotionally. And I think she's right. I always thought that by working hard I was being a good husband and father, but I guess there's more to it than that."

Stan and Paul are typical of many men in the midlife years. In psychotherapy I have heard so many middle-aged men speak of the emptiness in their lives. Often they are good men who truly love their families, but their lives have been dedicated to making money or advancing their careers, sometimes to the neglect of their families. At midlife, some of these men see that something is missing, and they want to re-order their priorities to spend more time with their wives and children. They begin to recognize that a wife needs a husband who listens to her, empathizes with her feelings, and shares his own feelings with her. They see that children need a dad who supports them not just financially but personally and emotionally, loving and nurturing them each day.

Having seen the need to change, many men nevertheless remain trapped by habits, uncertain how to make changes that seem to mean spending hours with their families on top of long hours spent at work. But when they begin to develop their feminine side, many of these things begin to change automatically. When a man reconnects with his soul, talking with his wife is no longer a chore or an obligation; it becomes a satisfying exchange of ideas, feelings, dreams—an opportunity to truly know the deepest thoughts and hopes of this woman one loves. And when a man's soul comes alive, his children flourish and thrive in the presence of a father who is filled with passion. He easily feels their joy and pain and is there for them because they are part of his very soul.

I, too, was one of those men who spent the first half of life working long hours and building my career, sometimes to the neglect of my family. But at midlife, with the help of a good therapist, I saw how much I had neglected the people and the things that really mattered to me. So I quit working such long hours and rearranged my priorities. I began to spend more time with my wife; I got in touch with friends and made sure I saw them more frequently; I began to listen to music, write creatively, read poetry, spend more time at my cabin in the mountains. In short, at midlife I finally began to take care of my soul and reclaim my passion.

As a result, the last ten years of my life have been the best I have known. I am happier, more creative, and more passionate than ever before, and my spirituality has deepened in ways I could not have imagined in earlier years.

When I see men whose lives are passionless and dead, I want to say to them, "It doesn't have to be that way. You can reclaim your soul and rediscover your passion. But to do this, you must let go of your masculine defenses, rearrange your priorities, and open yourself to your anima—that lost, neglected, and betrayed feminine side that you forsook so long ago."

WOMEN WHO DEVALUE THE FEMININE

Men are not the only ones who neglect the soul. Many women also devalue the feminine and eventually find themselves confused and unhappy as a result.

Lonnie, a businesswoman in her late thirties, came to therapy because she knew something was missing in her life and that she needed to make some changes. In our early sessions, Lonnie's behavior was quite masculine, and our interactions sometimes had almost a man-to-man quality to them. By contrast, her dreams were full of women and feminine themes. When first I suggested that we explore her feminine side, Lonnie was a bit defensive. Because of her background, she associated the feminine with weakness, dependency, and powerlessness. I explained that the deep feminine was different, that it has its own inherent power and strength, and that her dreams were telling her that she needed to know more about it.

Gradually, Lonnie began to open up to her feminine side. She read several books that honored the feminine and was especially drawn to mythology, goddess cultures, and Jungian psychology. As time went on, she explored shamanism, the sacred, and the soul. She was drawn to the moon, to wolves, to the desert, and to the dark. She kept a journal in which she wrote about her dreams and about the feminine energies she was discovering in herself. Having starved this side of herself for years, she discovered that she was ravenously hungry for anything having to do with the soul.

As she nurtured her soul, Lonnie became more sensuous, more attuned to others, to nature, and to the sacred. She began to pay more attention to her intuition and her inner rhythms. Near the end of her therapy she decided to leave her job, and she began making plans to move to New Mexico, a place she believed would better support her emerging spirituality.

At Lonnie's request, we held her final therapy session at the beach. I am quite traditional in the way I conduct therapy, so this was unusual for me. When I arrived, she had already prepared a sacred circle of rocks and invited me inside it. For an hour we listened to music she had selected for the occasion and engaged in various rituals that marked the end of her therapy and expressed her hopes for the future. It was a deeply moving experience, created entirely out of Lonnie's awakening soul.

As part of the ritual, she read a poetic summary of her therapy which she gave me permission to share. It depicts the beauty and power of a woman who has reconnected with her soul. She wrote:

> We have spoken of soul, the sacred, following your bliss, of beauty, of honoring the primitive, wild women, wolves, the deep feminine, and of the night, the dark, and leaning toward the light.
>
> We have spoken of love, eros, sensuality, Manon of the Spring, gods and goddesses, ceremonies and rituals, convention, boxes, caging and uncaging.
>
> We have spoken of dreams, fantasies, imagination, of flying, the journey, the edge, nature, and of flowers blooming as an old man walks past. And of shamans, artists, fire, passion, of women and men, of utopian communities, relationships, friendships, of creativity, and of Being.
>
> These ideas, symbols, and ways of being represent my rebirth into the living. This sacred circle that embraces us today symbolizes the new life that has been created through my relationship with you.
>
> Now, I am learning to do these things for myself and am discovering that everything is sacred, everything has meaning.
>
> I have also discovered an eternal source of strength and energy deep within that I am progressively learning how to access and care for. My soul speaks to me and I am continually looking for ways to feed, nurture, and communicate with her.
>
> The path is in front of me and there is no turning back.

Lonnie was a special client, but her story is all too typical. Thousands of women in the business world have denied their feminine side and lost contact with their souls. Maureen Murdock has worked with many such women. In her book *The Heroine's Journey* she wrote:

> Working as a therapist with women, particularly between the ages of thirty and fifty, I have heard a resounding cry of dissatisfaction with the successes won in the marketplace. This dissatisfaction is de-

scribed as a sense of sterility, emptiness, and dismemberment, even a sense of betrayal. These women have embraced the stereotypical male heroic journey and have attained academic, artistic, or financial success; yet for many the question remains, "What is it all for?" The boon of success leaves these women overscheduled, exhausted, suffering from stress-related ailments, and wondering how they got off track. This was not what they had bargained for when they first pursued achievement and recognition. The image they held of the view from the top did not include sacrifice of body and soul. In noticing the physical and emotional damage incurred by women on this heroic quest, I have concluded that the reason they are experiencing so much pain is that they chose a model that denies who they are.[6]

I believe Murdock's analysis is correct. However, we must not blame the victim. In order to gain power and economic status, women of the previous generation had no choice but to learn how to compete with men on their own terms. There was no shortage of books with titles like *Games Mother Never Taught You* and *Hardball for Women* that instructed women in the masculine skills required to succeed at this game,[7] and over the past twenty-five years or so, increasingly greater numbers of women have ascended to positions of power in formerly male bastions of business, politics, and the professions. These modern pioneers demonstrated that women can be just as assertive, logical, hardworking, and competitive as men, and, what is more, can match men's performances, even in the face of salary inequities, sexual harassment, and a pervasive attitude that women who seek advancement are encroaching on the natural habitat of the male. Despite this lack of a level playing field, these women opened the doors and made it easier for the current generation of young women to succeed in the marketplace.

Yet, as honorable and admirable as their achievements may be, in order to pursue them many of these women had to sacrifice their souls. And while opportunities are greater for women today than ever before, our society still devalues the feminine and often insists that the only success worthy of respect depends on playing masculine games. In addition, many women go home from work to husbands who still assume that child care and household chores are ultimately the wife's responsibility. No wonder so many American women are anxious, depressed, and suffering from stress-related ailments!

But the grimmest result of all is the death of something inside these women. When they sacrifice their souls to the masculine gods, they risk losing touch with their intuition, imagination, spirituality, and creativity, as well as with their body-awareness, passion, and sensuality. Working for years in an environment unfriendly to the soul, women may lose contact with the natural rhythms of life, with other women, with their own mother and daughters, and with themselves. When women betray the feminine, a chasm of emptiness and despair yawns before them. Whether male or female, we cannot find a satisfying life if we betray our soul.

Carol, a successful thirty-five-year-old businesswoman, is a case in point. She found that the more attention she gave to her soul, the more difficult it was to remain at her job, which was heavily oriented to masculine values. With tears in her eyes, she described her dilemma: "Sometimes I go to a weekend workshop or some other activity that really nurtures my soul. Then when I go back to work, my job is hard to take, hard to stomach. It is so head-oriented that in order to do it, I have to put my soul on the back burner. If I try to stay in contact with my soul, I become aware of how much I hate my job, and of course I can't do it well, feeling that way. I don't know what to do. I make good money, but my soul is dying inside."

Reclaiming the Feminine in the Workplace

What can a woman do about this kind of situation? Most women do not have the luxury of being able to quit their jobs. Besides, retreating from the office to the home is no solution; that would simply set women back and perpetuate the reign of patriarchal values in the workplace.

The women's movement has recently begun to struggle with this issue. While some women feel that the feminine is merely a social construct designed to keep women subservient, others are coming to believe that the feminine is a life-giving force that women must embrace if they are to develop their full powers and authentic selves. In an article in Ms. Magazine, Madeleine L'Engle wrote: "My role as a feminist is not to compete with men in their world—that's too easy and ultimately unproductive. My job is to live fully as a woman, enjoying the whole of myself and my place in the universe."[8]

Riane Eisler has described the life-affirming nature of the feminine principle in ancient agrarian cultures and has painted a picture of what our society could be if the feminine were deeply honored.[9] Carol Gilligan has also emphasized the importance of embracing the feminine voice and has shown how important the feminine perspective is in areas such as morality and values.[10] Writers such as Jungian analyst Jean Shinoda Bolen have talked about goddess mythology, encouraging women to access the deep feminine by working with these archetypal symbols.[11]

Many women in various walks of life are seeking to reclaim the feminine and create new forms and structures that are more sympathetic to the soul. Some women in positions of power are experimenting with management styles, work schedules, employee benefits, and work environments that allow more room for feminine values. Women are tired of playing men's games by men's rules and are no longer willing to deny their own natural strengths in order to have power, position, and equality in the workplace. Many of them are coming to see that the feminine is a dynamic power, radically different from masculine power.

The stereotype of a feminist as a loud, aggressive, masculinized woman who views all men as the enemy is unfair but persistent, and many women, rightly or wrongly, cannot relate to that model. But a feminist perspective that emphasizes the deep feminine has the potential to capture the imagination of the thousands of women who are put off by the other image. If the stereotype of the aggressive feminist could give way to a feminist image of a strong, confident woman who is deeply in contact with her feminine power, all women would benefit greatly. In both the women's movement and the men's movement we need role models who are highly developed and integrated, who contain the best masculine and feminine qualities.

Anaïs Nin, who spoke for women's freedom long before it was politically correct to do so, was once asked what she thought of the women's movement. She replied:

> There is far too much imitation of man in the women's movement. That is merely a displacement of power. Woman's definition of power should be different. It should be based on relationships to others. The women who truly identify with their oppressors, as the cliché phrase goes, are the women who are acting like men, masculinizing themselves, not those who seek to convert or transform man. There is no liberation of one group at the expense of another. Liberation can only come totally and in unison.[12]

The danger in imitating men is that women may fail to actualize the deep feminine power that lies within themselves. It would be tragic if the women's movement failed to seize this historical opportunity to assist in the rebirth of the feminine principle.

But it is not easy to actualize the feminine in this culture. As Murdock says, "When a woman decides not to play by patriarchal rules anymore, she has no guidelines telling her how to act or how to feel."[13] In addition, she will find that the old patriarchal structures and attitudes do not give way simply because she has seen through them.

But there is hope. Something is moving beneath the surface of our culture, and it has a feminine name. The Goddess has been in exile a long time, but there's evidence that she is now coming home. As Marianne Williamson says:

> There is a collective force rising up on the earth today, an energy of reborn feminine. She is peeking around corners, taking over businesses, tucking in children, and making men go wild in every way. She knows us at our source. She is not, as we are not, lacking in virtue. She remembers our function on earth: that we should love one another. She has come to reclaim us. She has come to take us home.[14]

And what can women do to help with this transformation? Williamson provides some clues:

> Many women I know are already living attuned to their feminine radar while fully involved in worldly careers. They are forging new paths of feminine participation in the worldly dance. They know the ultimate purpose of their careers, which is the same as the purpose of our bodies and our relationships: to do the Goddess's work, to do what we can to give birth to a new world. It ultimately doesn't matter whether we start a company, nurse a child, produce a movie, or make a soup. What really matters is that we do it with love.[15]

It is not easy for either women or men to integrate the feminine into their lives. Those who follow the path of the anima will often feel at odds with a society that discounts the soul. Nevertheless, for both women and men the key to life is the recovery and nurturance of the soul, our feminine side.

*Art washes away from the soul the dust
of everyday life.*
—Picasso

PATH TWO

THE ARTS
The Path of the Muses

Willa Cather was one of the great writers of our time. In her short story *Eric Hermannson's Soul*, Cather told the story of a son who loves to play the violin and of a mother who, along with a fundamentalist preacher, believes that Eric's violin is the one thing that stands between him and God. Describing this conflict, Cather wrote,

> The final barrier between Eric and his mother's faith was his violin, and to that he clung as a man sometimes will cling to his dearest sin, to the weakness more precious to him than all his strength. In the great world beauty comes to men in many guises, and art in a hundred forms, but for Eric there was only his violin. It stood, to him, for all the manifestations of art; it was his only bridge into the kingdom of the soul.[1]

A dramatic scene occurs when the preacher, Asa Skinner, in the midst of a hallelujah-shouting congregation, begins to preach directly to Eric, pleading with him to save his soul and come home to God— meaning, to give up his violin. Wanting to please God yet loving his violin, Eric lets out "a groan of ultimate anguish." As the preacher's intense pleading continues, there comes a point where Eric can no longer hold his ground. In her dramatic climax to this scene, Cather wrote, "Eric Hermannson rose to his feet; his lips were set and the lightning was in his eyes. He took his violin by the neck and crushed it to splinters across his knee, and to Asa Skinner the sound was like the shackles of sin broken audibly asunder."

This heartbreaking story reveals both the destructiveness of fundamentalist religion and the power of art—even for a poor, uneducated boy like Eric Hermannson—to be what Cather so beautifully called a "bridge into the kingdom of the soul."

Art is the natural and universal language of the human soul. When the soul speaks, she does so through image and symbol; and when she needs nurturance, art is the language she understands best. So whether we are viewing a prehistoric painting on a cave wall in Southern France, listening to a symphony in a modern amphitheater, or playing a violin like Eric Hermannson, we are in the kingdom of the soul. Art is the most direct route to this realm; it is an ancient and universal path to the sacred.

DEFINING ART

The word art refers to the entire spectrum of creative expression, including music, poetry, painting, dance, literature, sculpture, and theater. Matthew Fox suggests that we should expand our traditional definition of art to include what he calls the personal arts. He writes:

> What are the personal arts that we all need to start birthing anew? They include the art of friendship, the art of making beauty where we dwell, the art of conversation, of massage, of laughter, of preparing food, of hospitality, of the sharing of ideas, of growing food and flowers, of singing songs, of making love, of telling stories, of uniting generations, of putting on skits, of satirizing human folly. The personal arts include the arts of listening and of healing, of enjoying oneself with others in simple ways; the art of creating our lifestyles and our communities; the art of conviviality; the art of parenting and of forgiving.[2]

In The Sane Society, Erich Fromm takes a similar view, pointing out that in Western culture art has become the domain of professional artists, and most of the rest of us have lost our sense of art as a dimension of everyday life.[3] By contrast, in some societies art permeates daily life. I understand, for example, that in the Balinese language there is no word for artist. Image, ritual, beauty, and artistic creativity are part of the daily life of the Balinese. In a culture where everyone is an artist, there is no need for "artist" to be a separate category.

To use art as a path to the sacred, we need to be more than simply consumers of art and must learn how to access our own creativity. At the same time, I believe professional artists serve an important function in society. Every culture produces individuals who are especially gifted in the arts. Where would the world be without Shakespeare, Michelangelo, Beethoven, Mozart, Van Gogh, Rilke, Rumi, and others of their stature? While each of us may have some creative ability, these gifted artists tower above the rest us like mountains and enrich the entire world with their art. Great artists deserve societal support, and we need to provide arenas where the talent of promising artists can be nurtured and where mature artists can do their work. While art should never become exclusionary and elitist, any culture which fails to support its artists is only contributing to its own impoverishment.

Art and Truth

What is art? At first glance, this seems like a simple question; but some of the greatest minds have struggled to define art. In his book *Poetry, Language, and Thought,* the philosopher Heidegger addressed this question.[4] He said that all works of art have what he called a thingly character. He wrote, "There is something stony in a work of architecture, wooden in a carving, colored in a painting, spoken in a linguistic work, sonorous in a musical composition." But, "the art work is something else over and above the thingly element, and this something else in the work constitutes its artistic nature." In other words, while art's medium or tangible character is an important element, something else must be present for it to be truly art. In his efforts to define the "something else," Heidegger came to the conclusion that true art is always a revelation of truth. However, for Heidegger truth meant something quite different from our usual definitions of the term. Most of us think of truth in propositional terms: if a statement corresponds with reality or with the facts, we say it is true. But Heidegger's understanding of truth is something deeper. He referred to an ancient Greek word for truth, *aleitheia,* which refers to the kind of truth one sees when something reveals its essence or true nature. Heidegger argued that authentic art is an opening for *aleitheia;* it is a place where a deeper kind of truth can shine forth.

Art and Being

Art not only has to do with truth; it also has to do with Being. While this word has various philosophical meanings, I use the word here to refer to that deeper dimension of human experience where potential and possibility lie. Being is the "underground river" that we access in creativity; it is the source of the images and symbols that become part of the artistic work. Being is the smithy of the soul, as James Joyce called it, where new visions and realities are forged. In psychology, Being is the source of what Carl Rogers and other humanistic psychologists have called the actualizing tendency, the motivating force that pushes us toward higher levels of becoming and toward more authentic self-realization. From an evolutionary perspective, Being is the creative life force that moves all creation toward higher and higher levels of complexity and continually opens up new vistas of possibility. In human consciousness, Being has become aware of itself, perhaps for the first time in evolutionary history. As Heidegger said, "Being's poem, just begun, is man."[5]

Artists, poets, shamans, mystics, and prophets live in direct contact with Being. They have a special sensitivity to this dimension, an ability to access its creative energy and shape it into new forms and possibilities for humankind. This is what James Joyce meant when he said, "I go to encounter for the millionth time the reality of experience and to forge in the smithy of my soul the uncreated conscience of my race."[6]

But this is not easy. Being does not lie there just below the surface of consciousness like a vein of gold, ready to be brought out in huge, brilliant chunks by anyone who shows up with pick and shovel. In the gold mines of Being there are dark, bottomless shafts of non-Being into which artists can fall. The same sensitivity that opens artists to Being also makes them vulnerable to the dark powers of non-Being. It is no accident that many creative people—including Dante, Pascal, Goethe, Nietzsche, Kierkegaard, Beethoven, Rilke, Blake, and Van Gogh—struggled with depression, anxiety, and despair. They paid a heavy price to wrest their gifts from the clutches of non-Being. But this is what true artists do: they make their own frayed lives the cable for the surges of power generated in the creative force fields of Being and non-Being.

In addition to their inner struggle, artists often have to deal with a society that is ignorant of the value and purpose of art. Throughout history artists have been ostracized, imprisoned, or even killed because those in power could not tolerate the truths they portrayed or face the darkness they unveiled. Hitler despised Germany's artists, and in that dark period many of those in the lower middle classes who followed Hitler would go to the museums to mock the works of the artists. It is well known that Russia imprisoned some of its greatest artists in an effort to quell their influence. And in America we have politicians who would like to censor art by refusing to fund endowments for artists who create images which the politicians find disturbing or express ideas with which they disagree. Many great artists have lived without honor in their own time, not living to see how their art was eventually honored by the world. For example, Van Gogh could not sell his paintings even with the help of his brother, who was an art dealer. No one recognized the value of his work and the depth of his genius and spirituality. Emotionally troubled and distraught, Van Gogh killed himself, never knowing how future generations would bow before "The Starry Night" and gaze with belated understanding at "Crows Over a Cornfield."

It is sad but true: we stone our greatest prophets and crucify our most compassionate saviors. Culture has a fierce homeostasis that fends off or destroys anyone who is different or who challenges the status quo. To dabble in oils or watercolors on weekends is one thing; but to be a true artist, one who descends into the depths of Being and brings back that which may shake the foundations of society and create a new vision of reality, is a fearsome task. No wonder Rollo May titled his book on artistic creativity *The Courage to Create*.[7] And while most individual artists do not create a cultural revolution with their art, each one contributes to this end by chipping away at the foundations of old values and structures that no longer serve humanity and by presenting visions of more humane possibilities. Every true artist, no matter how compassionate, is an iconoclast who razes the old to make place for the new. Pablo Picasso said, "Every act of creativity is first an act of destruction." Yet the world they destroy is their own world, which they love and with which they often feel deep kinship. Most artists are not angry rebels; rather they are, as Robert Frost said, lovers of the world who happen to have a quarrel with it.[8] And they know, like Samson of the Old Testament, that when they pull down the temple, they pull it down upon themselves.

This struggle begins in the heart of the artist. Working with the forces of Being and non-Being, the artist must find the courage to forge the gift and lay it before his or her contemporaries regardless of their capacity to understand or accept it.

Art and Eternity

Some have said that art is motivated by a desire for immortality, that artists create because they want to live on in their artistic work. While there is some truth to this, I would suggest something more: art is not so much an attempt at immortality as it is an effort to touch eternity now. Some think of eternity in linear or quantitative terms, that is, as unlimited time. But there is another view that says eternity is a qualitative dimension of experience which can be accessed in the present. As Joseph Campbell said, "Eternity is a dimension of here and now."[9] The Gospel of John, the most philosophical of the four Gospels, speaks of eternal life as a present reality, not as a future reward. There are certain experiences in life in which eternity intersects time; time stands still, as it were, and we find ourselves in an eternal now. Art touches this eternal dimension that lies just beyond linear time. Immersed in the fires of creativity, time ceases for the artist. And for us, when we stand before a painting or listen to a beautiful piece of music, sometimes eternity breaks in, limitedness falls away, and we find ourselves in an eternal present. Eternity ceases to be a question, for now we know; we have touched it in our own souls. This is what William Blake meant when he said, "Hold Infinity in the palm of your hand / And Eternity in an hour."[10]

Art and Death

There is a poignancy in beauty that sometimes causes us to weep. The weeping does not come from sadness but from a deep, existential longing characterized by an awareness of life's limitedness and our own mortality. The poignancy of beauty opens up a profound gratitude for life, mixed with an awareness that life will not last. For example, when loving parents look at their beautiful toddler, they are filled with love yet are also keenly aware that the child will not always be little. He will grow up, leave home, and establish his own life. Of course, loving parents would have it no other way; but there is an almost overwhelming poignancy in such realizations. We are mortal. Life moves on. Everything changes and passes away.

When I saw my first painting by Van Gogh, I felt as though an invisible shaft of light emanating from the painting had stabbed my heart. I stood there impaled, brushing away tears, overcome with the thought that Van Gogh's own hands had touched this painting. I felt a deep sense of joy mixed with a profound sadness. The joy came from the affirmation of life that flowed from the painting. The sadness had to do with death and mortality, with the "bitter" of life's bitter-sweetness. I was also weeping for Van Gogh, who embodied this paradox of life, who, in the midst of despair, nevertheless found the courage to affirm life again and again.

There is something existentially nourishing about such experiences. In *Amphitryon 38*, a play by Jean Giraudoux, the god Jupiter describes his love for a mortal woman to Mercury:

> She will use little expressions that widen the abyss between us. . . . She will say, "When I was a child"—or "When I am old"—or "Never in all my life"—This stabs me, Mercury. . . . We miss something, Mercury—the poignance of the transient—the intimations of mortality—that sweet sadness of grasping at something you cannot hold.[11]

We know that we are mortal, that each day we are drawing closer to our own demise, that someday we will be only a memory, and after that we will fade completely into oblivion; no one will know or tell the story of our lives. Yet, in spite of this knowing, with tremendous courage and existential resilience we choose to live—even to dance—until the flame sputters out in eternal silence and darkness.

Art in its beauty and poignancy somehow touches this same existential domain of the soul. This is why we leave museums, concerts, poetry readings, plays, and other artistic events with tears in our eyes and gratitude in our hearts. Despair and joy, bitterness and sweetness, life and death—these are the great paradoxes of life and the essence of the human condition.

Art and Soul

Everything that has been said about art to this point is really an explication of how soul operates through art. Art "bodies forth" from the creative depths of the artist's soul and takes form in time and space to touch the souls of others. Art speaks the nonrational language of the soul, using image, symbol, color, sound, shape, and form. But, as we have seen, art is more than her medium; she is also truth, being, eternity, death, and soul. Art gently holds all our ultimate concerns; she is the symbol of those things that make us human.

THE POWER OF CREATIVITY

The ancient Greeks were committed to art. They honored their artists, filled their cities with art, and included in their mythology the nine muses, who were believed to inspire creativity in various arts. These nine muses provide an early taxonomy of art, a classification system which covers the various types of artistic expression. It is interesting that astronomy and history were considered arts. We view astronomy as a science, but the ancients, responding to the awe-inspiring wonder of the universe, placed it among the arts. And history, which we see as an effort to report the facts of the past, was seen by the Greeks as an opportunity for creative myth-making around heroic figures and historical events, somewhat the way Hollywood creates a dramatic film based on actual people and events.

Creativity and the Muses of Ancient Greece

The following is a list of the muses and the arts for which each was responsible:

1. Calliope   Her name means "beautiful voice," and she was the muse of heroic poetry and eloquence.

2. Terpsichore   She was the muse of dance and the mother of the sirens. Her name means "rejoicing in the dance."

3. Melpomene   Her name means "singing." She was the muse of tragedy, and the tragic mask of drama is one of her symbols.

4. Urania   Her name means "heavenly," and she was the muse of astronomy.

5. Pollyhymnia   She was the muse of sacred songs, heroic hymns, oratory, and mime. Her name means "many hymns."

6. Erato   She was the muse of love poetry and marriage songs. Her name means "passionate," and lovers believed themselves to be under her spell.

7. Thalia   Her name means "flourishing," and she was the
                 muse of comedy and pastoral poetry.

8. Euterpe   She was the muse of music and lyric poetry.
                 She was believed to be the inventor of wind
                 instruments such as the flute. Her name means
                 "charming" and refers to her ability to charm with
                 music and lyrics.

9. Clio   Her name means "celebrating fame." She is the
                 muse of history.

The Mystery of Creativity

The muses are personifications of the forces an artist feels in creative moments. This energy seems to come from outside of him. And
whether we call it the power of the muse or some other name, the artist
feels inspired in the original meaning of that term—that a spirit has
entered him. Sometimes, in a flash of creativity, artists are given an
entire poem, book, or musical composition by this mysterious power.
A friend of mine, author of several books of poetry, told me how an
epic poem, several pages in length, was given to him in a matter of
minutes. The creative flash came while he was driving, so he pulled to
the side of the road and began to write as fast as he could. When he
was finished, he had before him one of his best poems.

This is the secret of authentic art: it comes not from oneself but
from the creative fire that blazes in the depths of the soul. Whether we
locate this force within ourselves or say that it comes from the gods, as
the ancient Greeks did, it is the same creative power.

Creativity and *Ex Nihilo*

The artist creates *ex nihilo*, out of nothing. Art is the bringing into
existence of something that did not exist before. This is the god-like
quality of the creative act. The book of Genesis tells how God created
the universe *ex nihilo*. The first two verses state: "In the beginning God
created the heaven and the earth. And the earth was without form,
and void; and darkness was upon the face of the deep. And the Spirit
of God moved upon the face of the waters. And God said, Let there
be light, and there was light."

Creative artists can identify with the process described in these
verses. In the beginning, before creation, an image or intuition stirs the

soul of the artist. At this point the image exists only in imagination; it has no tangible habitation; there is no heaven and earth. When the artist approaches that which is to become, she finds that it is void and without form. Certainly she has an intuition, perhaps even a burning sense, of what is to be; but its form is still vague, unclear. Darkness is upon the face of the deep. Then the artist begins to work with the void. Moving upon the face of nothingness, she works the invisible clay, first this way, then that. Suddenly, in the midst of this creative experimentation, something is hit upon, and that which is trying to become says, "Yes, that's it. You're on the right track. Stay with that." And in time the nothingness begins to yield somethingness. The image that is trying to become begins to take shape. As the dialectic continues, artist shaping art and art shaping artist, the image comes into being. Its form grows clearer, stronger, more vibrant. And at some point, there is the declaration "Let there be light," and suddenly the image shines forth in its own being. The object of art steps, as it were, through the door of existence, and enters the world. The void has become form; the darkness has been dispelled by light; non-being has yielded to being. *Ex nihilo*, out of nothing, something new has come into the world. That which was once only an image in the soul of the artist now has a tangible existence.

We live in worlds that have been created *ex nihilo*. Because we are symbolic creatures, we probably live more in imagination than we do in objective reality. And art has provided many of the rooms in our imaginal house. When I was a boy, my favorite book was *The Adventures of Huckleberry Finn*. My imagination was stirred by Huck and his friend Jim leaving civilization and going down the Mississippi River on a small raft in search of adventure. That book is part of my imaginal world. Although I read the book forty years ago, I can still see Huck there under the night skies, floating gently along on the currents and eddies of that mighty river. And when I cross the Mississippi in my travels, I usually think of Huck, and part of me wants to scan those muddy currents to see if I can spot him. *Huckleberry Finn* is also part of America's heritage. With that book Mark Twain captured the romance of the Mississippi, the dreams of boys, and the hopes of a young nation. It is almost a shock to remember that Huck never really existed and that the events of that book never took place. They all came from the rich imagination of Samuel Clemens. *Ex nihilo*, out of nothing, Clemens created this masterpiece of American literature.

Shakespeare understood how the artist creates out of nothing. Speaking of poetry, he wrote:

> The poet's eye, in a fine frenzy rolling
> Doth glance from heaven to earth,
> from earth to heaven; And as imagination bodies forth
> The form of things unknown, the poet's pen
> Turns them to shapes and gives to airy nothing
> A local habitation and a name.[12]

Evolution's most important achievement may not be the logical mind, as we so often think, but the quantum leap required for the simple act of creativity. Creativity represents a complexity of neurological functions—and perhaps even something beyond neural explanation—that logical thought simply cannot trace or duplicate. Every theory of creativity pales before the thing itself. In the act of creation, the artist becomes the instrument for an energy, almost tangible, that surges in the body and mind like the tides in the sea. In the most intense experiences of creativity, there is no sense of an "I" that is in control, an "I" that is responsible for the variegated images that flash spontaneously through the mind. Rather, in these moments artists feel that they have tapped into the source, the "underground river," and that their job is to capture this energy in some form before it goes away. So they paint, write, sculpt, or compose furiously, losing track of time, staying up for hours, forgetting to eat, exhausting their bodies—anything to be the conduit for this new entity that wants to come into the world. Creativity is the great mysterious overwhelmingness out of which comes some of life's greatest gifts. In the moment of creative inspiration, something within us surges beyond the stable point of human evolution and opens up what Maslow called the farther reaches of human nature. In its most intense forms, creativity is a window into the future, and the artist is a scout who returns with stories and images of worlds waiting to be born.

THE HEALING POWER OF ART

Shaun McNiff is an art therapist who has helped hundreds of psychiatric patients find their way back to emotional health. He has worked in hospital and clinic settings for years and is a specialist in the healing power of art. His book, *Art As Medicine*, is rich with wisdom and insight.[13]

McNiff believes that when the soul is in pain, she automatically turns to art for healing. He writes, "Whenever illness is associated with loss of soul, the arts emerge spontaneously as remedies, soul medicine." In his work, McNiff found that even patients who had no artistic interest prior to their illness turned to creative expression in the healing process. McNiff believes the soul has the power to heal herself and that art is the key that unlocks this power and releases the soul's own therapeutic forms. As a young therapist searching for guidance in the artistic care of the soul, McNiff came upon the work of Hans Prinzhorn, an art historian who had become a psychiatrist. Like McNiff, Prinzhorn had discovered the healing power of art in his work with psychiatric patients. Commenting on Prinzhorn, McNiff writes:

> He proves that when the soul is lost, art comes spontaneously to its assistance. When the soul is depressed, isolated, mad, and distraught, artistic images appear. Prinzhorn noted . . . that people without a background in art began to create in response to their suffering. The creative imagination acts spontaneously as it own savior.[14]

According to McNiff, art heals because of the power of image to bypass the logical mind and reach into the imaginal depths of the soul. He said that image has the ability "to expand communication and offer insight outside the scope of the reasoning mind." Further, "the medicine offered by meditation on art is generally an infusion of imagination and awareness rather than a specific answer. 'Messages' may ultimately be less significant than the engagement of images." Thus, art is a way of "treating disorders of imagination through the constructive workings of imagination."

McNiff believes that patients should be free to express whatever emerges, and that this creative expression should be honored as a production of soul, rather than as a manifestation of pathology. McNiff does not deny the existence of pathology, but he believes healing involves allowing patients to embrace and work with their pathology through art. He writes, "Creative expression of the soul's aberrations gives them the opportunity to affirm rather than threaten life."

Early in his career, McNiff ran into the pathologizing tendencies of modern psychology and psychiatry. He found that practitioners used patient's art as a way to diagnose and pathologize the patient instead of viewing it as an attempt of the soul to heal itself. He commented:

The psychiatric and psychological traditions of analyzing paintings and drawings on the basis of theories of psychopathology made as little sense then as they do now. I was amazed that eminent professionals could say that little boys who make pictures of lawnmowers suffer from castration fears and that girls who draw vacuum cleaners experience oral deprivation.[15]

McNiff believed that such interpretations, based on a single, Freudian analytic view, are reductionistic and betray a profound misunderstanding of the multiple motivations involved in the mystery of art. This led him to say:

> As a beginning art therapist I rejected Freudian analytic psychology and its diagnostic industry's assumption that the works of artists can be reduced to facts about a person's past. These judgements were based on a single, psychosexual theory of behavior. Years of studying the artistic motivations of children and adults have shown me that there are multiple motives for creative expression. . . . Attempts to unravel the labyrinthian dynamics of art's propulsion according to the categories of the reasoning mind—mine and those of the reductionists—will never replace the mystery with an explanation. . . . All of my reflections on the source of art confirm the inability of the mind to "explain" its origins. The phenomenon simply exists. Art cannot be isolated from its context and then used to support a foreign system of concepts.[16]

I would like to add my own voice to McNiff's concerns. In my own training I saw professors pore over every detail of a patient's drawing in an effort to detect pathology and help assign a diagnosis. Yet in six years of graduate training there was never a course, nor even a single lecture, on the healing power of art. I now find it ironic that my professors could believe that art provides valuable insights into the patient's pathology but apparently saw no value in using art as a way to work with this inner material in therapy. Today, psychologists continue to use art for diagnostic purposes, but few take the next logical step and use it in treatment.

When McNiff saw how well his patients responded to art, he wondered why this approach was not being used in all areas of psychological healing. When he pursued this question, he found that the healing professions had no interest in the soul and thus no interest in art as a way to heal the soul. This led him to conclude:

> Although there are occasional and distinguished exceptions, we
> have given over the care of the soul to medications, institutions, and
> a host of procedures that continuously undermines its dignity. The
> suffering soul, the basis of our Western religious traditions, has been
> abandoned.[17]

This disparagement of art and soul is to be expected in a profession
dominated by reductionistic thinking and mechanistic techniques.
Western medicine has a deep-seated prejudice against anything which
does not fit its own philosophical assumptions and preconceived ideas
about healing. And because of the way psychotherapists are trained,
most of them have no idea how to assist clients from an imaginative
framework. Nevertheless, art may be the most potent medicine available for healing the wounded soul.

ART AND JUNGIAN PSYCHOLOGY

Carl Jung knew the power of art to nurture and heal the soul. In his
therapeutic work he encouraged clients to paint, sculpt, write poetry,
and engage in other forms of imaginal activity. And in his own life
Jung constantly engaged in artistic activities. Among other things, he
helped quarry the stones for his house at Bollingen and later carved
figures and symbols on the stones.

In his work with clients, Jung used an approach called active imagination. Active imagination involves drawing on one's creativity to
amplify images or feelings that arise in the course of psychotherapy.
For example, if a client has a dream about a beautiful swan, a Jungian
therapist might instruct the client to go home and paint the swan or
write poetic prose describing the feelings associated with this image.
Jung believed such artistic elaboration allowed time for the images to
have their full impact on the psyche and to do their nurturing and
healing work.

Another artistic technique derived from Jungian psychology is the
sand tray. The sand tray is literally a tray or box of sand. Typically, the
therapist provides the client with a wide array of small objects and
toys, such as trees, flowers, grass, rocks, people, animals, houses, cars,
and countless other bits and pieces of life. The client, following his intuition, chooses some of the objects and places them in the sand, slowly constructing an imaginative world from his own creative depths.
The finished sand tray often reflects some new perspective, inner con-

flict, or emerging dimension of the client. Even clients who think of themselves as having no artistic abilities frequently find the sand tray a powerful path to the inner workings of the soul.

Melanie, a good friend and fellow therapist, uses sand trays in her therapeutic work and also as a way to enhance her own psychological growth. I asked her to describe her experience.

> I did my first sand tray at a workshop when I was an intern and was overwhelmed by the experience. My sand tray picture seemed to create itself, and when I was finished, I was deeply moved. The picture seemed to know me better than I knew myself. I remember feeling vulnerable and exposed, not only to the other interns, but to myself. When the leader asked me to describe my sand tray, my voice quivered and tears came to my eyes. That first sand tray had a profound impact; it touched a deep place in my soul. That experience was a sacred moment for me.
>
> Immediately, I began collecting objects for my own sand tray. Since then I have done sand trays on a regular basis. I do them when I feel angry, sad, or afraid; and I notice that my emotions soften as the feelings are released through this tactile and visual process. I also do them when I feel "stuck" in my life, and I find that they "loosen the clay" around my feet so that I can move forward again. I do them during periods of confusion and find that they shed enough light for me to regain faith in my process. Sometimes I do the sand tray with a particular issue in mind; at other times I simply let the images call to me and allow my unconscious free rein in the evolution of the sand tray picture.
>
> One of my most unusual experiences involved a certain object I chose—or perhaps it chose me. The object was a wooden, bearded monk-like figure wearing a long robe with a key dangling from his folded hands. While other objects often represented masculine or feminine aspects of my psyche, this figure was neither. Nor was it ever placed inside the primary areas of my sand trays. It was always off to one side or in a corner, standing patiently, looking on with a sense of compassion and wisdom. It often stood in a peaceful nature setting and was associated with the future direction of my life. I felt no judgment, no pressure, no criticism from this Wise Being. I felt protected and unconditionally accepted by the gentle strength and wisdom of this shaman-like figure. Its caring detachment from the stages and crises that arose during my journey increased my own patience and acceptance of my process. This Wise Being embodied wisdom, understanding, compassion, patience, peace, caring kind-

ness, and unconditional acceptance—qualities which, I understand, are associated with healers or shamans in many cultures.

This figure, which appeared early in my sand tray activities, stood by me through a long period of struggle, pain, grief, and letting go. One day, near the end of my crisis, I found myself placing the key, which had been in its hands, in front of another figure that represented my true Self, which was kneeling in gratitude and humility for the new life I had finally found. I felt at peace, surrounded by beauty and possibilities. I felt that the whole world was available to me, that I belonged to the universe, and that I was finally free to create a life that is mine.

I have come to believe that the Wise Being was a shamanic figure that came to help me through my crisis. I know how strange that sounds; but I have found that artistic images have a life of their own and, if worked with over time, they have a powerful effect on the psyche. As one who has been very "head-oriented" most of my life, perhaps the greatest value of the sand tray for me is its ability to bypass the cognitive processes and go straight to my soul. Its symbols and images allow me to access my inner wisdom without getting entangled with the verbal and intellectual web of my brain. The creative process involved in doing a sand tray allows me to connect with a deep place in my soul. After doing a sand tray, I usually feel as though something inside me has shifted and I am ready to move on. For me the sand tray has become a sacred time, a time to commune with my soul. I recommend it to anyone who is looking for an artistic, creative way to nurture the soul.

THE SHAMANIC IMAGE

Melanie mentions how strange it sounds that the shamanic image helped her through a crisis. Unfortunately, she is right. In our culture the healing professions have made almost no place for the healing power of such images. This is unfortunate because artistic images, perhaps better than anything else, are able to minister to the soul. When Western psychology decided to follow the medical model, it disowned the soul and rejected approaches to healing that were associated with the soul, including the shamanic image.

In ancient cultures, as well as in many parts of the world today, the shaman was the healer or the official medicine man or woman of the tribe. The underlying assumption of animistic cultures is that spirits are everywhere and that they determine practically everything that happens. Thus when one falls ill, the illness has to do with the spirit world in one way or another. Because of his special connection to the spiritual world, the shaman is able to discern the nature of the problem and prescribe the proper remedy. A rather unusual skill of the shaman is soul retrieval. Many animistic cultures believe it is literally possible to lose one's soul. In such situations, the shaman must engage in appropriate healing ceremonies to retrieve the soul and facilitate its return to the one who has lost it.

Modern psychology, of course, has rejected shamanism and the ideas of healing associated with it. Yet I am convinced that shamanism, understood metaphorically rather than literally, is exactly what modern psychology most desperately needs for revitalization, for the shaman is an expert at accessing the archetypal world. Through art, symbol, ritual, and ceremony he is able to stimulate the natural healing processes of the soul.

In a metaphorical sense, we could say that psychologists work with clients who have lost their souls and that part of their task is to help them retrieve their souls and set their lives on a more solid spiritual basis. I am not suggesting that therapists should dress like medicine men, burn herbs in their offices, or chant with their clients. But I am suggesting that Western psychology needs a radical shift in paradigm to give the spiritual dimension priority in psychological healing. Ironically, modern psychology has lost its own soul, and the entire profession could use a shamanic healing of soul retrieval. Modern psychology must expand beyond the narrow perspectives of Western medicine and rediscover models of healing that draw upon the imaginal capacities of the soul. In other words, we need ways to help our clients reconnect with their souls and rediscover the power of the sacred.

McNiff made use of the metaphor of shamanistic ideas in his writing. He said, "Psychic illness is an alienation of soul and a possession of the psyche by preoccupations, obsessions, fears, anxieties, and other distractive conditions that are contemporary equivalents of the aboriginal 'evil spirits.'" On the one hand, "the soul cannot be lost in a literal sense because it is always present with us. However, we do lose contact with its movements within our daily lives, and this loss of relationship results in bodily and mental illness, rigidification, the absence of passion, and the estrangement from nature." McNiff noted that the imagination has always been the working terrain of shamans. Further, each of us has an inner shaman that can guide us through the healing process. He wrote, "Shamanic images and patterns emerge whenever we engage ourselves in the therapeutic rituals of the arts in painting, dance, dream, song, and other media." And, "images and the artistic process are the shamans and familiar spirits who come to help people regain the lost soul."[18]

If shamanism still seems too remote as a metaphor for expanding modern psychology, perhaps it will help to remember that Mircea Eliade, one of the most brilliant minds of our time, said, "The shaman is indispensable in any ceremony that concerns the experiences of the human soul."[19] I would hope that psychotherapy would be included in that category.

Perhaps because I am a psychologist, I have emphasized the power of art in psychotherapy. But I would like to make it clear that the healing power of art extends beyond the therapeutic arena. When author William Styron was in a suicidal depression, art was part of his healing. Describing Styron's experience, David Rosen wrote that music had "pierced his heart" and helped save him from suicide.[20] And when Rosen himself was in a deep depression, he found his way out of it by painting. Rosen also tells us that when former minister and best-selling author Robert Fulghum feels depressed, he plays Beethoven on his piano.[21] And Beethoven himself once said, "He who understands my music will be released from the misery of this world."[22]

THE NURTURING POWER OF ART

Art not only heals the wounded soul; it also nourishes our spiritual life. Art and symbols are the language of the soul. She will tell us who she is, what is wrong, and what we need to do about it, but she needs artistic media to do this. The soul communicates very poorly in linear language; she speaks best through image, symbol, metaphor, and simile. So if you want to hear what your soul has to say, you must put a pencil in her hand and let her draw, or set an easel in front of her and let her paint, or place some clay in her hand and let her mold, sculpt, and shape.

Art, like nothing else, opens the door to the imaginal world and introduces us to our own soul. As we decipher her language, it becomes increasingly clear who we are, what our mission is, and what our life is about. As James Hillman said, the soul contains the code for our unique existence. And art is the best way to unlock that code and to open our lives to becoming who we are meant to be.

There are many ways to nurture the soul through art and creative expression. I have a friend who expresses his artistic nature through a flower garden that blooms in vivid colors across his back yard. Recently, a client who loves computers told me how she uses computer graphics to draw three-dimensional images. This woman has the soul of an artist, and tears came to her eyes as she described the elegance and beauty of the designs she is able to create. In *Art and Artist* Otto Rank pointed out that creativity can be turned toward the exploration and development of one's personality.[23] In other words, one can become an artist of life, making one's very way of being in the world an expression of the soul's artistic and creative capacities.

In recent years many people have discovered the value of keeping a journal. I am convinced that journaling is helpful primarily because it is a creative way of communing with one's own soul. Journaling has little impact if it is simply a record of facts and observations. But when it becomes a creative process in which we listen to our depths and say new things to ourselves, journaling is transformed into an artistic medium that accesses and expresses the soul.

Artistic opportunities abound. There are countless way to access and express our creativity, thereby nurturing our souls. So if you cannot paint, dance, or sing, do not be dismayed. As every person has a soul, so every person is an artist; it is simply a matter of discovering your particular medium.

In the meantime, we can nourish our souls from the art and beauty that are all around us. Simply turn on your radio and you will hear the beauty of classical and contemporary music. Pick up a poetry book and you will find the soul-nurturing words of Rilke, Machado, Yeats, Neruda, Rumi, Blake, Shakespeare, or any one of a hundred other poets. Go to a good play and see how this ancient art form penetrates and enlivens your heart. Visit a museum and see paintings that have nourished the souls of countless millions. Buy a CD of your favorite artist and spend a few hours letting the music roll over your soul and fill your heart. Look up at the night sky and gaze in wonder at the moon and stars shining there on their dark, cosmic canvas. Take a walk in nature and see the woods, the fields, the wildflowers, the meadows, the streams, the mountains, the oceans. Surely, first and foremost God is an artist!

If you wish to nurture your soul, turn to the arts. Whether you immerse yourself in the creations of others or engage in your own artistic pursuits, you will find that art is one of the most immediate and rewarding paths to the sacred.

Except in the modern world, sexuality has everywhere and always been a hierophany.
—Mircea Eliade

PATH THREE

THE BODY
The Path of Eros, Sex, and Sensuality

It may seem strange to speak of eros, sex, and sensuality as a path to the sacred. In Western culture we have separated "flesh" and "spirit" and have difficulty imagining that erotic pleasure could be connected with spiritual experience.

Yet, when we survey world history, it becomes apparent that our view is a deviation. The vast majority of cultures have regarded sexuality and spirituality as intimately connected. Early primitive religions, for example, were profoundly sexual; they celebrated fertility and had elaborate rituals involving the pleasures of the flesh. This combination of sex and religion continued in ancient Greece, where certain gods and goddesses, such as Aphrodite, Eros, and Dionysus, were specifically dedicated to love, sexuality, and the passions of the body. Even today, indigenous religions throughout the world continue to regard sexuality as sacred.

Typically, we tend to dismiss these religions as unevolved, pagan, and immoral. We like to think that our cultural views are more sophisticated. But does this attitude blind us to a truth these other cultures discovered—that eros, sex, and sensuality are indeed paths to the sacred? Perhaps we need to reexamine our own attitudes toward sexuality. For example, why do our religions moralize about sexual sins but say little about sexual joys? Why do so many people raised in Christian churches grow up to think of sex as shameful or even "dirty?" Why do so many parents find it difficult to talk to their children about sex? Why do some put their children at risk for pregnancy or sexual disease rather than give them information about birth control and protection? Why do fundamentalists continue to hold judgmental attitudes toward gays and lesbians? Why does the Catholic Church continue to insist that sex between a husband and wife is wrong if artificial birth control is used instead of acknowledging that eroticism is a gift in itself? Are we really more enlightened than primitive cultures? Are our religions really more evolved than those which celebrated sexuality as a divine gift?

Ancient religions remind us of something our religions have forgotten—that authentic spirituality is grounded in the body. Spirituality is not a pristine, "up-in-the-clouds" quality that only virgins and celibates possess; it is the natural bouquet of an earthy, lusty involvement with life. The Christian Church, with its historical emphasis on celibacy, virginity, and sexlessness as morally superior states has done a great disservice to Western culture. Jerome, one of the early church fathers, went so far as to say that sex was only tolerable because it produced virgins for God's service! Such religious attitudes have produced a bland, de-eroticized spirituality more appropriate to sexless eunuchs and cloistered nuns than to men and women immersed in life. "Sexless spirituality" should be an oxymoron; unfortunately, the church has sold us this brand of spirituality for two thousand years. Matthew Fox, an outspoken Catholic priest, said,

> When I listen to what religion in the West teaches us about sexuality, I hear two things: The first, paradoxically, is silence: no puberty rites, no effective rites of passage for our young to celebrate the immense news that they are now fit and able to pass on the mystery of human life. . . . A second response to sexuality from our religions is moralizing. Telling us all the sins we are capable of performing with our sexual organs does not enlighten us about our sexuality.[1]

While religion has failed the West in this area, there are other voices that have given hope. Carl Jung, speaking of sexuality, said, "It is, in truth, a genuine and incontestable experience of the Divine, whose transcendent force obliterates and consumes everything individual."[2] Georg Feuerstein, after extensive research on sexuality, said, "My investigations . . . have convinced me that sex can be an important gateway to mystical experiences or encounters with the sacred."[3] And Walt Whitman wrote, "If life and the soul are sacred, the human body is sacred."[4]

Eros, sex, and sensuality are an authentic path to the sacred, but the path is in great disrepair, overgrown with thorns and briars and covered by the piled-up debris of centuries of religious repression. To walk this path, we must clear the debris. Underneath we will find an ancient path that leads to the presence of the divine.

SEXUALITY AND SACRED EXPERIENCE

The thesis of this chapter is that passionate sexuality is a path to transcendence. In her book *Ecstasy in Secular and Religious Experiences*, Marghanita Laski said that 33 percent of the subjects in her research group named sexual love as a trigger to ecstatic experience.[5] Sexuality can be a hierophany, an encounter with the sacred. There are those special moments when sexual passion is so intense that lovers break into another dimension. Those who have had this experience know that sexuality is indeed a path to the sacred.

In his book *Sacred Sexuality*, Georg Feuerstein gives several accounts of people who touched the sacred through sexual love. The following is from a thirty-four-year-old man:

> We were making love, and while I was kissing her, I felt a strong desire to be a part of her, and for her to be a part of me. Our kissing intensified, and I began to experience the sensation that my physical senses were falling away. My body was disappearing, as was the sensation of her body against mine. I began sensing energy swelling and flowing toward her, and in my mind's eye I saw a white shapeless form, moving and growing. As the form grew, the energy grew and intensified.
>
> This lasted just a few seconds, before I pulled away from her lips. I was as startled by this as she was. We both gasped in surprise and looked at each other for a few seconds, not knowing what had happened and not knowing what to say. She then told me that she had never been kissed like that before, and I confessed the same to her.[6]

Another account is that of a twenty-five-year-old woman who fell in love with a man she deeply respected. She had never had a spiritual experience before, but making love with this man took her to a transcendent place. Later, she described her experience:

My first memory of that incident is of awakening one morning after a night of lovemaking and feeling as if I had not been asleep. I felt as though I was conscious or constantly awake on some higher plane. That entire day I remember feeling totally and perfectly relaxed.

In this perfect relaxation I stood outside of time. It was as if time normally flowed in a horizontal plane, and I had somehow stepped out of this horizontal flow into a timeless state. There was absolutely no sense of the passage of time. To say there was no beginning or ending of time would seem irrelevant. There was simply no time. . . .

This particular moment remains, seventeen years later, the single most significant moment of my life. It was also the most ordinary, simple, happy, normal, neurosis-free moment of my life.[7]

If religious devotees were flooded by such ecstatic feelings in a religious setting, they would immediately identify them as spiritual. But when these same feelings of ecstasy occur in the bedroom, we are reluctant to call them spiritual and to classify them as sacred experiences. In Western culture we tend to leave God at the church building and forget that the sacred permeates all of life—including the sexual realm. In ancient religions it was exactly this kind of sexual ecstasy that was seen as a hierophany, a manifestation of the sacred.

Sexual love in itself can take us to the sacred. But it also fuels the fires of romantic passion, which has spiritual possibilities of its own. Romantic love is a powerful force that can open the soul and cleanse the doors of perception so that we see the beauty and depth of life. When a man falls in love with a woman who stirs both his soul and his deepest erotic desires, the possibility of transcendence is near. And when a woman finds a man whose very being awakens her body and touches her soul, she is on the brink of sacred experience.

Thus, passionate lovemaking and romantic ecstasy go hand in hand. When two people are immersed in these wonderful energies, they discover that sexuality and romantic love are paths to transcendent experience.

SEXUALITY IN ANCIENT CULTURES

Western religion has separated sex and spirituality, but there was a time, thousands of years ago, when human beings saw no contradiction between religion and sexuality. Georg Feuerstein points out that our early ancestors ascribed sacred power to fertility and sexuality. As they learned to plant and harvest crops, they looked to the earth as the Great Mother. Through magical and analogous thinking, they believed that rituals involving sex and fertility would please the Goddess and ensure her continued blessing on their agrarian lives. Throughout the emerging civilizations of the ancient world the Goddess, appearing under various names, was a dominant force. As Feuerstein says:

> We do not know her earliest names, but later, after writing had been invented, she was celebrated as Inanna in Sumer, Ishtar in Babylon, Anaith in Canaan, Astarte in Phoenicia, Isis in Egypt, Nu Kua in China, Freya in Scandinavia, and Kunapipi in aboriginal Australia.[8]

Marija Gimbutas, a scholar of prehistoric cultures, was one of the first to bring our attention to the gods and goddesses of the ancient world.[9] Her careful research amassed mountains of data showing that the Goddess religions dominated early civilizations, including those of Old Europe. Unlike our own patriarchal religions, the Goddess religions celebrated women, the body, and sexuality. Fertility was at the heart of these religions, and sexuality was seen as a path to the Goddess.

In her book *When God Was a Woman*, Merlin Stone says the archaeological evidence shows that the Goddess religions began about 7000 B.C. and continued until the closing of the last Goddess temples, about A.D. 500. Stone goes on to say that some authorities would place the beginnings of Goddess worship as early as 25,000 B.C. Echoing Gimbutas, Stone says that in these early religions sexuality was central, and women and female sexuality were highly revered. Stone writes, "In the worship of the female deity, sex was Her gift to humanity. It was sacred and holy. She was the Goddess of Sexual Love and Procreation."[10]

Riane Eisler, in *The Chalice and the Blade*, argues that the civilizations of the early Goddess religions, while permeated by the feminine principle, were not matriarchies. Rather, they were partnership societies in which women and men lived together as equals, with neither sex dominating the other. While women held most of the positions of power, they did not use this power to domineer over the men. As Eisler says, "Despite such evidence of the preeminence of women in both religion and life, there are no indications of glaring inequality between women and men. Nor are there any signs that women subjugated or oppressed men."[11]

According to Eisler, this mutual respect also extended to sexual attitudes. Art from these early cultures shows a genuine appreciation of both male and female sexuality. Describing one of these ancient societies, Eisler wrote,

> In Minoan Crete the entire relationship between the sexes—not only definitions and valuations of gender roles but also attitudes toward sensuality and sex—was obviously very different from ours. For example, the bare-breasted style of dress for women and the skimpy clothes emphasizing the genitals for men demonstrate a frank appreciation of sexual differences and the pleasure made possible by these differences.[12]

In her book *The Sacred Prostitute*, Nancy Qualls-Corbett, a Jungian analyst, calls attention to a central figure in the Goddess religions, the sacred prostitute.[13] Temples were built to the Goddess in various cities, and thousands of sacred prostitutes served in the temples, offering their bodies as sexual gateways to communion with the divine. In Corinth, for example, the temple of Aphrodite had more than a thousand sacred priestesses, and the temples of some cities may have had as many as six thousand. These women, unlike prostitutes in our own society, held a position of honor as servants of the Goddess. They were seen as spiritual women deeply committed to the service of their god.

According to Qualls-Corbet, in some cultures each woman was expected to serve at least some time in the temple as a sacred prostitute. Women did not see this as a distasteful obligation but as an opportunity to express their sexual passions in the service of the Goddess. Maidens often took on the role of the sacred prostitute in order to be initiated into womanhood. Other women stayed at the temple for years, dedicating their bodies and their lives to the Goddess. Men went to these sacred prostitutes not simply to have sex, but to worship the Goddess and ask her blessing on their families and crops. By having sex with the sacred prostitute, who symbolized the Goddess herself, men were able to commune with their god.

THE RISE OF PATRIARCHAL RELIGIONS

The Goddess religions which dominated the ancient Near East and Europe for thousands of years have now faded from the earth. Whether from within the agrarian cultures themselves or as a result of patriarchal invaders, male gods and masculine power eventually replaced the

Goddess and feminine power. Women, who had held prominent positions in the Goddess cultures, were forced into a subordinate role. The female body and female sexuality, so honored in the Goddess religions, were now debased. Women came to be viewed as men's property and were often used, controlled, and exploited as men saw fit. Among the ancient Hebrews, the Goddess was considered an abomination and her worship was abolished. Judaism and Christianity, which have roots in ancient Hebraic culture, have likewise always portrayed God as male and would consider it blasphemous to worship the Goddess. Historically, both Judaism and Christianity have subjugated women and surrounded female sexuality with male-initiated taboos. Women who openly expressed their sexuality or were simply disobedient to their husbands, have been stoned, hanged, burned, branded, imprisoned, or publicly humiliated, depending on what the times allowed.

Patriarchal religions, including Judaism and Christianity, have not yet owned up to their responsibility in creating a sexually repressed culture in which women have often been considered of little more value than property or animals. We may criticize the Goddess religions for their pagan sexuality; but I suspect such sexuality is far more forgivable than the subjugation of hundreds of thousands of women by patriarchal religions in the name of God. I do not romanticize the Goddess religions, as some do; I suspect they had their flaws as well. But in those ancient religions it is unlikely that women, made in the Goddess's own image, would have been treated in the barbarous ways our patriarchal religions have treated them.

The Church and Sexual Repression

The Christian Church has been one of the major instruments of sexual repression. Because the Church has dichotomized sex and spirituality, millions of Christians have grown up associating sex with sin instead of seeing it as a path to the sacred.

Church History and Sexual Repression

Throughout its history, the Catholic Church has regarded the body and sexuality as obstacles on the path to spiritual perfection. Fasting, deprivation, exposure, self-flagellation, and other forms of asceticism were associated with higher spiritual states. Celibacy, virginity, and control of one's sexual thoughts and feelings were considered signs of an evolved spiritual nature. When these extreme measures failed to bring the body and sexuality under control, some men even submitted to castration in an attempt to achieve a state of spiritual purity. Priests, nuns, and the Virgin Mary were the spiritual ideals, and sexuality was seen not as a path but as an obstruction to the sacred.

When the Protestant Reformation spread across Europe, its leaders rejected celibacy as a requirement for its clergy, but they did little to improve attitudes toward sexuality. Most Protestant groups continued to associate sexuality with evil and to warn parishioners of its dangers. They made sure that people got the message that bodily pleasures and heavenly aspirations do not mix.

Fundamentalist Religion

This religious repression continues today, especially in fundamentalist and conservative religion. Many churches continue to teach that "lust" is evil and that sex is a temptation of the devil. These messages turn people against their own bodies and make them feel that in order to be spiritual they must repress their erotic feelings.

When I was a minister, I found that the majority of spiritual problems of men in my congregation had to do with lust and what they considered to be impure thoughts. It was not that these men were having affairs or doing anything harmful to others. But because the church taught that lust is a sin, equivalent to committing adultery in one's heart, these men were constantly struggling to keep their minds pure. Even young men, bursting with hormones, were not supposed to have any lustful thoughts; and if they did have one, they were immediately to put it out of their minds. Women were told that they must not wear shorts, halter tops, bikinis, or any other skimpy or sexually-revealing clothing that might incite a man's lust, causing him to have an impure thought. In such cases God would hold the woman just as responsible as the man. So, in their own way, women also got the message that lust was a sin and that a Christian woman must never look sexy except by accident.

This repressive attitude toward erotic feelings is characteristic of conservative Christian groups. From the time they reach puberty until they are old men, most Christian males struggle with "the sin of lust." Even President Jimmy Carter, a Baptist, admitted that he had committed the sin of lust.

A friend of mine who grew up in a fundamentalist church put into words what many men, raised in conservative churches, go through. He wrote:

> The only thing my church ever taught me about sex was that it was one of the "temptations of the devil." Our minister said that if we lusted in our hearts, it was the same as committing adultery. As a teenager, when I saw a pretty girl or a suggestive picture, I couldn't help but look, but then I'd feel guilty, thinking I had sinned. When I was eighteen, I starting dating Janet. After several months we knew we were in love. One night we began kissing and things got really intense. At some point I touched her breast. Being a "good Christian girl," she gently moved my hand. I was flooded with guilt and told her I was sorry. She wasn't upset but said she knew we had to wait until we got married. But that night opened the gate, and for the next two years we were on this endless merry-go-round of petting, feeling guilty, "repenting," and then doing it all over again. For both of us, trying so hard to be "good Christians," this experience was pure torture. Janet and I have now been married twenty-two years. When I look back at our experience, I can sometimes see humor in it: two kids trying to stop a cycle as old as life itself. But mainly I feel angry. My religion made my sexual awakening a shameful thing. It said that those wonderful feelings that flowed through my young body were evil. My religion made me feel guilty every time I felt attracted to a girl or had a sexual thought. It even made me feel guilty for touching the girl I was coming to love more than life itself. Frankly, any religion that does that to two good, decent kids is sick!

I think William Blake would have agreed with my friend. In his poem "The Garden of Love," he wrote:

> I went to the Garden of Love.
> And saw what I never had seen:
> A Chapel was built in the midst,
> Where I used to play on the green.
>
> And the gates of this Chapel were shut,
> And Thou shalt not writ over the door;
> So I turn'd to the Garden of Love,
> That so many sweet flowers bore.
>
> And I saw it was filled with graves,
> And tomb-stones where flowers should be:

> And priests in black gowns,
>   were walking their rounds,
> And binding with briars, my joys & desires.[14]

It is ironic that fundamentalist religion, which tries so hard to squash sexuality, also seems obsessed with it. Of course, this is not hard to understand. Repression and denial are not effective ways to deal with sexuality, and pretending that our erotic feelings do not exist does not make them go away. Fundamentalist religion needs to rethink its position on lust. It might discover that its own repressive attitudes help create and maintain our culture's obsession with sexuality. It might find that erotic feelings, instead of being sinful, are actually a gift. It might realize that erotic energy, the same energy it calls lust, is actually part of the formula for a spiritual energy that can take us into the presence of the sacred.

SEXUALITY IN AMERICA

While conservative religion continues to preach sexually repressive messages, our culture itself has made some rather dramatic changes. Over the past thirty years two major forces have helped shape the sexual landscape of America.

The Sexual Revolution

The first was the sexual revolution. Beginning in the 1950s and really getting underway in the 60s and 70s, this revolution had a major impact on sexual attitudes in America. Thousands of baby boomers, rejecting the sexual values of their parents, experimented with love-ins, communes, living together, open marriage, multiple partners, and alternative life styles. Pornography was legalized, Broadway plays featured nude scenes, adult movies went mainstream, and nude dancing establishments sprang up in most major cities. The birth control pill became available and courts legalized abortion, giving women greater sexual freedom by removing the fear of an unwanted pregnancy. During this period, people read Masters and Johnson's report on sexual behavior, reread the Kinsey reports, and poured over a steady stream of new books, magazines, and surveys that gave us sexual information and told us how to enhance our own erotic lives. As time went on, Americans became increasingly comfortable with nudity in the movies, rented X-rated movies at the video store, read books on women's sexual fantasies, learned that homosexuality was not a perversion after all, and found out that masturbation not only would not make one go blind or insane but was being encouraged by sex therapists as a way for nonorgasmic women to become familiar with their body's sexual response.

While fundamentalist preachers and a few conservative politicians condemned these trends, most Americans seemed to take this new sexual world in stride. And when several scandals broke out, it appeared that some of those fundamentalist preachers and conservative politicians were more involved in the sexual revolution than we had thought. While not endorsing the extremes, most Americans seemed pleased that the repressive attitudes of the 40s and 50s no longer prevailed and that we could finally get information and talk more openly about our sexual attitudes, values, and practices.

Then came the 1980s and the advent of AIDS. When this deadly disease broke out in the gay community, some quickly proclaimed it as God's punishment for homosexuality; but when it spread to heterosexuals and we realized we had a national epidemic on our hands, people became scared. While some apparently were not scared enough and continued to practice unsafe sex, millions of others cooled their sexual activity and settled into monogamous relationships. Tantra workshops, "hot monogamy," and other approaches to sexual enhancement became major themes as couples looked for ways to increase their sexual enjoyment within the boundaries of their dyadic relationship.

Today, as we near the end of the 1990s, there is another blip on the sexual screen. An increasing number of straight women are having sexual relationships with other women. *The Janus Report on Sexual Behavior,* published in 1993, reported the results of a national survey which found that 23 percent of career women have had a homosexual experience and 63 percent of these women reported that they continue to do so occasionally.[15] If one statistically eliminates lesbians from this group, this means that about 16 percent of career women have had a homosexual experience and 10 percent continue to have such experiences occasionally. Keep in mind that these are not closet lesbians finally coming out and acting on their homosexuality; these are heterosexual women making love with other women.

Nancy Friday, one of the leading popular writers on women's sexuality, says that women's fantasies about other women is now one of the major themes in her research. She says this fantasy, which was hardly mentioned twenty years ago, began gathering steam in the early 1980s and is now a favorite fantasy that shows no signs of going away. In her 1991 book *Women on Top*, Friday devotes over one hundred pages to the topic of women with women.[16] She said, "Judging from my research, there are far more of these women today than ever before in modern history." She goes on to say that since the trend began, "women have never stopped the emotional and sexual turning to one another that began twenty years ago."

Friday speculates that one reason women are turning to women is that they are not finding with men the kind of tender sexuality they desire. She writes, "All fantasies with other women begin and end with tenderness. When women are with women, they do not rush sex. However aggressive the sex may become later, it begins with a slow and loving seduction."

A historical perspective may shed some light on this phenomenon. Women's sexuality has been repressed for centuries. Women have been forced, often under threat of humiliation or death, to express their sexuality within the narrow confines of a patriarchal society where men's vision of sexuality, not women's, has been the cultural norm. Trained to deny their sexuality, most women followed the man's lead and did sex his way. But today, as American women gain greater freedom, they are exploring their own sexual needs and developing their own vision of sexuality. As Nancy Friday suggests, most women prefer a sexuality that is more tender, nurturing, and relational. Not finding this kind of sexuality with men, who are often stuck in a more "phallic" and orgasm-dominated sexuality, women are turning to other women for a more "feminine" and sensual experience.

But the deeper meaning of this trend may extend far beyond the personal desires of the women involved. From the perspective of cultural history, this trend may reflect an unconscious effort on the part of modern women to recover something that was lost long ago: female energy, female power, and female sexuality—all of which died with the Goddess religions. Thus, archetypally speaking, we may be seeing a resurrection of the Goddess in the awakening sexuality of American women, just as we have seen an increase of female energy and power in other domains of our society.

In *The Erotic Silence of the American Wife*, Dalma Heyn opens up another taboo area—married women having sexual affairs.[17] She points out that American wives, especially younger ones, are having more affairs today than ever before. Heyn knows how disturbing her book is to most Americans. She says that while most cultures have always tolerated men's affairs, a wife's infidelity has been regarded as one of the most heinous sins a woman can commit. Throughout history, women have been humiliated, beaten, and put to death for adultery. Even today, in some countries a man can kill his wife with impunity if he discovers that she has been unfaithful. Heyn points out that even Western literature makes sure that wives get the patriarchal message. From *Madame Bovary* to *Anna Karenina* to *Tess of the D'urbervilles* to *The Scarlet Letter*, women who commit adultery die, are killed, or lead a life of public humiliation.

In stark contrast to these negative messages, Heyn found that many of the women she interviewed felt revitalized by their affairs. I do not wish to romanticize affairs—for either women or men. As a therapist, I have seen the pain that an affair can cause to the betrayed spouse, to children, and to other family members. But I do believe Heyn's book is an important chapter in the story of women's emerging sexuality. If more married women are having affairs and even finding them fulfilling, this flies in the face of the patriarchal message about wifely infidelity. It also says that, whether men like it or not, women are taking charge of their own sexuality and claiming for themselves the sexual freedoms that most societies have accorded men for centuries.

Thus, today it seems the sexual revolution is primarily centered in young women, the daughters of the baby boomers. These young women are a new breed: they are less inhibited, more sexually experimental, and more demanding of freedom in the sexual arena. After thousands of years of repression, women are finally reclaiming their sexuality. The goddess archetype, it seems, is stirring in the souls of American women.

The Feminist Movement

The second major force in recent history for lifting sexual repression and freeing both women and men to embrace their sexuality has been the feminist movement. When women have their own careers, make their own money, and are no longer controlled by men, they almost invariably become freer in the sexual arena as well. Many men, though at first intimidated by the idea of women's freedom, have come to realize that a strong, sexually aware woman is far more appealing than the dependent, sexually naive woman who was once the patriarchal ideal. In countless ways the feminist movement has contributed to the sexual liberation of both women and men.

However, all is not well on the feminist front, at least according to Rene Denfeld. In her book *The New Victorians: A Young Woman's Challenge to the Old Feminist Order,* Denfeld charges that in recent years the feminist movement has become sexually repressive. She says that in their zeal to expose men's sexual abuse, harrassment, and exploitation of women, some feminists have gone too far and are now attacking sexuality, and especially heterosexuality, itself.[18]

Denfeld, a woman in her late twenties, says the women of her generation are turning away from the feminist movement, not because they oppose equal rights, but because the movement is promoting extremist views that alienate young women. Denfeld quotes a 1986 Department of Education survey of over ten thousand young adults which showed that well over 95 percent of young women believe that women should have the same educational opportunities as men, be paid the same money for the same work, and be given the same consideration for jobs as executives and politicians. In other words, they support the basic feminist agenda of equality. Yet these same young women overwhelmingly rejected the feminist label. Denfeld says that older feminists usually explain such survey results by saying that young women just don't understand or that they have been influenced by a male-inspired backlash against feminism. Rejecting these explanations as patronizing, Denfeld suggests another reason: the feminist movement itself with its extreme anti-male and anti-sex views.

Denfeld points out that feminist leaders are now attacking male sexuality and even heterosexuality itself as the root cause of women's oppression. She writes:

> While this may sound absurd—and is—leading feminists have developed a theory that labels male sexuality and the practice of heterosexuality as the foundation of sexism and virtually all other forms of oppression. Feminist theorists have gone beyond blaming male-dictated law for sexual inequality and now blame what they term the "institution" of heterosexuality, or heterosexual sex."[19]

Denfeld says that such extremist views alienate young women, most of whom like men and do not feel sexually dominated, possessed, or exploited.

Denfeld also criticizes the new, sweeping definitions of sexual harrassment, saying that today's hypersensitive woman is reminiscent of Victorian women who fainted at the mention of sex. She even explores the issue of date rape, a topic of serious concern to her generation. She points out that the expanded way in which it is sometimes defined—painting all men as predatory animals and all women as innocent victims with no complicity or responsibility in the sexual encounter—is a Victorian view of women and sexuality.

Relentless in her critique, Denfeld goes on to say that some feminists have even joined hands with religious fundamentalists in an effort to censor sexually explicit materials, including *Playboy* and even erotic lesbian publications. Viewing such efforts as misguided and repressive, Denfeld says, "By blaming sexual material for sexual violence, current feminists invoke the Victorian-era belief that sexuality is inherently evil and any display of it must be squashed."

Denfeld's basic message is that the current feminist movement, led by a few extremists, is creating a sexually repressive Victorian culture. This is why she calls her book *The New Victorians*. She believes these extremists would take us back to a Victorian mentality where women were viewed as pure, chaste, sexless creatures whose only value seemed to be that they could bear children and that they were morally superior to men.

As a feminist myself, I am pleased that Denfeld and other young women are speaking up and giving balance to a movement that does seem to be alienating many people. In my work as a graduate professor, I am in contact with many bright, sophisticated young women in their twenties and early thirties. In confirmation of Denfield's view, I have found that most of them, while supporting equality, nevertheless reject the feminist label because of its negative connotations. Most of them do not like the anti-male and anti-sex messages that they often heard in their undergraduate women's studies courses and that they continue to hear coming from the movement. I also know several older feminists who agree with Denfeld's basic thesis. One recently told me, somewhat facetiously, that the feminist movement needs a new branch called "Feminists Who Love Men and Sex." She believes thousands of American women, turned off by the current rhetoric of the movement, would join up!

Of course, the feminist movement is broad and contains many different perspectives. It would certainly be unfair to characterize all feminists as "anti-male" and "anti-sex." Nevertheless, I believe Denfeld's point is important. If it is true, as she charges, that leading feminists are invoking Victorian attitudes and becoming sexually repressive, this is unfortunate. Historically, the feminist movement has been at the fore-front of sexual liberation. It would be a shame to see it become a re-pressive force simply because a few extremists have managed to grab the spotlight and microphone. No pun is intended when I say that feminists, Victorians, and religious fundamentalists make strange bed-fellows indeed!

TOWARD AN EROTIC SPIRITUALITY

Despite religious repression, gender politics, and other cultural prob-lems related to sexuality, I believe it is possible for us to create an erotic spirituality that can serve as a path to the sacred.

Definition of Erotic Spirituality

The term *erotic spirituality* refers to the union of flesh and spirit, the integration of sexuality and spirituality. One might say that erotic spir-ituality is a spirituality based in sexuality and a sexuality based in spirituality. In erotic spirituality, these two powerful energies come together, combining sexual ecstasy with spiritual energy and thereby opening the doors to sacred experience.

If one imagines a continuum of human energies with sexuality at one end and spirituality at the other, then erotic spirituality brings both ends of the continuum together. It integrates the earthy, lusty, primal dimension of sexuality with the ethereal energies of the spiri-tual. Those who leave out the earthy dimension tend to produce an other-worldly spirituality that is not grounded in the body, similar to what happened in the medieval church and what seems to happen even in some Eastern sexual practices. Conversely, if we eliminate the spiritual dimension, we end up with an empty, shallow sexuality that has few transcendent possibilities. But when we combine the two ele-ments—integrating flesh and spirit, body and soul, earth and heaven, sexuality and spirituality—we create a powerful amalgam, an erotic spirituality that can take us into the presence of the sacred.

Reclaiming Eroticism

To create erotic spirituality for our own lives, we must first reclaim our eroticism. Eroticism refers to the sexual feelings that flow through our bodies when we are sexually attracted or aroused, the same energies that religion often denigrates as lust and associates with the sins of the flesh.

In contrast to such repressive messages, I would suggest that erotic energies are wonderful, God-given feelings that we should embrace and celebrate. Erotic energy or lust, if you please, can renew our lives, fill us with passion, and help us on our journey toward the sacred.

Peggy Kleinplatz is a Canadian psychologist who specializes in sex therapy. In an article "The Erotic Encounter," she said that one of the most pervasive problems seen by sex therapists over the past decade is "Inhibited Sexual Desire" (ISD).[20] ISD is a condition in which the client feels little or no sexual desire or arousal. Clients with ISD may be sexually sophisticated, proficient in sexual technique, and have no sexual dysfunctions. Their problem is simply that they have lost their sexual desire; they have no interest in making love.

Kleinplatz, after spending a great deal of time trying to understand this problem, came to the conclusion that our culture's repression of eroticism, or sexual pleasure for its own sake, is at fault. She writes:

> Whereas the need for sexual interaction, particularly intercourse, has been acknowledged and tolerated, albeit reluctantly, within this society, the seeking of arousal for its own sake or for the enhancing of sexual pleasure has been denigrated, denied, and suppressed; it has been condemned as sinful by the Christian church; declared illegal when sexually explicit materials serve to inflame sexual desire without any other "redeeming" social value; it has been obscured in sex education. . . .
>
> Although progressive parents and schools tell children about the mechanics of sex and reproduction, they are conspicuous in their failure to say aloud what every young child, immersed in genital exploration, already knows: It feels good."[21]

Kleinplatz advocated a frank and full-hearted embrace of eroticism in the context of a caring relationship. Defining eroticism as "the intent to contact and arouse another" she went on to say that "the erotic experience is to be found with a partner who values enhancing sexual pleasure for its own sake rather than as a means to a goal, for example, en route to coitus, tension release, orgasm."

Kleinplatz is stating for modern Westerners what spiritual traditions focused on enhancing sexuality have always said: orgasm must be moved out of the center of sexuality. The focus must shift from "coming" to giving and receiving erotic pleasure. Immersion in sensuality rather than a linear progression to orgasm opens the path to sacred experience.

Noting the mechanistic, depersonalizing emphasis on sexual technique in our culture, Kleinplatz writes, "One of the best ways to ruin a potentially satisfying relationship is to do what works—relentlessly." She points out that many of us, after learning what pleases a partner, tend to rely on these "successful" sexual routines instead of seeking new and creative ways to make love. Kleinplatz says, "This approach reduces the potentially erotic experience to masturbation. Technical proficiency (for its own sake), no matter how skillful and adroit, reduces the experience to one of a mechanical nature. One becomes an object to be manipulated." Indeed, "There is quite a contrast between the lover who seeks the formula for how to bring his or her partner to orgasm versus a lover whose goal is arousal and providing a pleasureful, erotic experience for a partner."

Kleinplatz advocates an eroticism that involves deep sharing of both body and soul. She says, "Eroticism is about the exploration and exposure of the other's wounds, dreams, passions, desires, hopes, and so on in a sexual context. It is about allowing the vulnerability that one (or both) experiences in this endeavor to be exposed in the hope that whatever is discovered will be accepted, valued, cherished, and regarded as precious." Quoting Califia, another writer who has addressed these issues, Kleinplatz says, "A good scene doesn't end with orgasm—it ends with catharsis."

This is a powerful vision of sexuality. It is a celebration of erotic energy and a view of sexual pleasure as wholesome and life-enhancing. While Kleinplatz does not use spiritual terms, she articulates with power and precision exactly what I am trying to say here: reclaiming our eroticism is the first step on the road to an erotic spirituality.

From an evolutionary perspective, sexual energy is simply nature's way of guaranteeing the continuation of the species. But because we are human beings and for us this energy is not sex-bound, it can be transformed into passion for living. Freud called this energy libido and, following his Darwinian bias, limited it to sexual energy. Jung, while acknowledging its sexual dimension, saw this energy in broader terms and called it life force. Georg Feuerstein, in agreement with Jung, referred to it as the universal life force and said that our early ancestors saw sexuality as the focal point for this power. Feuerstein pointed out that the Melanesians call this energy mana, and added:

> This cosmic power is what the ancient Germans called Od, or what the Hindus have for millennia named *prana*. It corresponds to the *orenda* of the Iroquois, the *oki* of the Hurons, the *ton* of the Dakotas, the *wakonda* of the Sioux, and the *megbe* of the Pygmies."[22]

This is the same energy I called duende and pakaramdam in chapter 4. By whatever name, this energy is recognized throughout the world for its ability to infuse life with passion and power. While sexuality is not the only source of this energy, it is certainly one of the major wells where we can fill our water jars with this life-enhancing power.

Here we begin to see the connection between sexuality and spirituality. Erotic energy, which is generated by sexual passion, can be transformed into spiritual life force. The early church fathers sensed this connection but got it wrong. They knew sexual energy was a powerful force but then decided that by being celibate, one could conserve this energy and sublimate it to higher spiritual purposes. The ancient Goddess religions, by contrast, got the formula right. They recognized sexuality as the force field in which spiritual energy is generated. Thus, the more emphasis on sexual passion, the more energy available for spiritual life. Shutting down the generators, as one attempts to do in celibacy, may give one more time to focus on spiritual things, but the spirituality produced is likely to be sterile and de-eroticized, lacking the earthy, life-giving power that characterizes a spirituality rooted in a full-bodied sexuality. Thus eroticism, the stone that Christianity rejected and called lust, becomes a major foundation stone of authentic spirituality. And sexuality, which the church saw as an obstacle on the road to spiritual growth, turns out to be a gateway to the sacred.

Soul Work: Images of Transformation

Once we can embrace and celebrate our erotic feelings, the next step toward an erotic spirituality involves soul work. The integration of sexual and spiritual energies is a mystical process that takes place in the deep recesses of the soul. This integration does not occur simply by conscious effort or by following a linear program. Rather, it requires images of transformation that can activate archetypal processes related to the union of sexuality and spirituality.

Unfortunately, in Western culture we have almost no images that can help us with this transformative work. Our images of spirituality tend to be sexless, and our images of sexuality tend to lack a spiritual dimension. We have dichotomized spirituality and sexuality; the madonna-whore complex is the symbol of our pathology. This is where the ancient Goddess religions can be helpful to modern consciousness, for they can provide us with the archetypal images we need.

The Sacred Prostitute. The image of the sacred prostitute, drawn from the Goddess religions, speaks to our own efforts to integrate sexuality and spirituality. Here, united in one image, is a passionate sexuality integrated with a deep spiritual devotion. Where in Western culture do we find such an image? The Virgin Mary, the most revered female image in Western religion, holds the spiritual part of the image but not the sexual. In fact, the Church would consider it blasphemy if someone described the Virgin as lusty, sexual, and erotic. Yet the very fact that we cannot view Mary in this way points to the pathology at the heart of Western religion. Reflecting on these repressive sexual attitudes, Merlin Stone suggested that future historians and scholars may call our religions "sterility cults!"[23]

Qualls-Corbett believes the sacred prostitute is a powerful archetypal image that still resides in the depths of our soul and is capable of bringing renewal to our lives. She originally became interested in the sacred prostitute because she wondered why women's sexuality, which was revered in these ancient cultures, is now so exploited and debased. She also wondered why sexuality and spirituality, united in the Goddess religions, are now considered opposites. In her work as a Jungian analyst she found that many clients complained of feeling empty, unloved, and unfulfilled. They told her, "My body is dead" or even, "My soul is dead." As she studied the ancient Goddess cultures, Qualls-Corbett became convinced that there was a link between her clients' feelings of emptiness and the loss of the spiritual-sexual energies that were part of the Goddess religions. She wrote:

> I began to see that the pervasive emptiness people complained of could be explained in terms of the loss of the goddess—the one who renews life, brings love, passion, fertility—and the sensuous priestess—the human woman who brought the attributes of the goddess into the lives of human beings. The connection to an important layer of instinctual life—joy, beauty, a creative energy that unites sexuality and spirituality—had been lost.[24]

For most of us, this requires a major theoretical leap. In Western culture we have no place for this ancient priestess or for the erotic spirituality she symbolizes. As Qualls-Corbett said:

> Indeed, the term "sacred prostitute" presents a paradox to our logical minds, for, as I have indicated, we are disinclined to associate that which is sexual with that which is consecrated to the gods. Thus the significance of this temple priestess escapes us, and we remain disconnected from an image that represents the vital full-bodied nature of the feminine. Without this image, modern men and women continue to live out contemporary persona roles, never fully realizing the depth of emotion and fullness of life inherent in the feeling tone which surrounds the image of the sacred prostitute.[25]

Qualls-Corbett invites us to imagine that we are in the temple of the Goddess, observing one of these ancient rituals. She writes,

> A figure moves gracefully before the altar, illuminating it by bringing fire to the clay oil lamps all around. Behold the priestess of the temple of Venus, the goddess of love. She is the sacred prostitute. . . .
>
> As the sacred prostitute moves through the open temple doors she begins to dance to the music of the flute, tambourine and cymbals. Her gestures, her facial expressions and the movements of her supple body all speak to the welcoming of passion. There is no false modesty regarding her body, and as she dances the contours of her feminine form are revealed under an almost transparent saffron robe. Her movements are graceful, as she is well aware of her beauty. She is full of love, and as she dances her passion grows. In her ecstasy she forgets all restraint and gives herself to the deity and to the stranger. . . .
>
> The sacred prostitute leads the stranger to the couch prepared with white linens and aromatic myrtle leaves. She has rubbed sweet smelling wild thyme on her thighs. Her faint smile and glistening eyes tell the stranger that she is full of desire for him. The gentle touch of her embrace sparks a fiery response—he feels the quickening of his body. He is keenly aware of the passion within this votary to the goddess of love and fertility, and is fulfilled.

Qualls-Corbett then describes the meaning of this ritual for both the priestess and the man:

> The woman and the stranger know that the consummation of the love act is consecrated by the deity through which they are renewed. The ritual itself, due to the presence of the divine, is transforming. The sacred prostitute, now no longer a maiden, is initiated into the

fullness of womanhood, the beauty of her body and her sexuality. Her true feminine nature is awakened to life. The divine element of love resides in her.

The stranger too is transformed. The qualities of the receptive feminine nature, so opposite from his own, are embedded deep within his soul; the image of the sacred prostitute is viable within him. He is fully aware of the deep emotions within the sanctuary of his heart. He makes no specific claims on the woman herself, but carries her image, the personification of love and sexual joy, into the world. His experience of the mysteries of sex and religion opens the door to the potential of on-going life; it accompanies the regeneration of the soul.[26]

The Hieros Gamos. Another image from the Goddess religions is the *hieros gamos*, the sacred marriage. In this ritual, apparently common in ancient religions, a specially selected woman and man engaged in sexual intercourse at the beginning of the new year as a way to ensure fertility for the people and the land. Their coupling was considered a sacred marriage that symbolized the Great Goddess making love with her consort. This ritual contained the two essential ingredients of erotic spirituality—a primal earthiness combined with spiritual energy. As Carl Jung said, the *hieros gamos* involved "the 'earthing' of the spirit and the spiritualizing of the earth."[27]

In *The Sacred Prostitute* Qualls-Corbett imagines what this ritual was like. She writes:

> After much feasting and merriment, the bridal couple retires to the sacred chambers of the ziggurat, the tower of the temple. There the nuptial bed is perfumed with myrrh, cloves and cinnamon. The waiting masses sing hymns and love songs to enhance the rapture and the fertilizing power of the goddess and her lover, the sacred prostitute and the king.[28]

We cannot imagine such explicit sexuality as part of a religious service. But for these ancient people reverence for the Goddess meant reverence for sexuality, fertility, the earth, and the body. They saw no contradiction between spirituality and passionate sex. Thus, the *hieros gamos* was the perfect ritual for uniting spiritual devotion with erotic energy.

This image, like that of the sacred prostitute, has transformative possibilities for us today. This does not mean that we should take these images literally and attempt to reinstate goddess worship and sacred prostitution. Those who get stuck in debates about the morality and literal value of such practices miss the point. Rather, we must see the symbolic value of these images—the fact that they are symbols of sexual and spiritual integration—and allow the images to awaken our own soul and constellate our own energies in ways that are appropriate to our contemporary cultural situation. In other words, the message of both the sacred prostitute and the *hieros gamos* is that we, too, need to experience within our own archetypal depths the marriage of the sacred and the sexual. Properly understood, the sacred prostitute and the *hieros gamos* are images that can help us unite erotic and spiritual energies in the depths of our own psyche.

The Black Madonna

While Christianity is almost devoid of images that unite sexuality and spirituality, there is one that has such possibilities. In certain cathedrals across Europe, there is a figure known as the Black Madonna.[29] These icons are deeply venerated and are believed to have special powers. While the Black Madonna is now associated with Christianity, this image of a dark female deity predates Christianity by thousands of years. The Black Venus of Lespugue, for example, now in a Paris museum, dates back to 24,000 B.C.

What is the symbolic meaning of the Black Madonna? *Madonna*, of course, is associated with spirituality; but *black* brings in another dimension. Blackness is associated with the night, with rich, dark soil, and with the earthy, fertile, feminine nature. Carl Jung spoke of the shadow archetype, which has to do with the dark side of our nature. This archetype, once activated, contains powerful, creative energies capable of opening the gateways of passion and bringing renewal to our lives. Blackness and the energy it evokes reminds one of Federico Garcia Lorca's statement, "Everything that has black tones has duende." The Broadway play *The Phantom of the Opera* is a contemporary exploration of the archetypal theme of darkness, and this, I am convinced, is its power. "The Music of the Night," the most haunting song of the play, touches the regions of the soul where our own darkness resides.

The Black Madonna, too, is an image that has the power to activate archetypal energies much older than Christianity that reside in the depths of our souls. The image invites us to find our own darkness so that we can bring substance and "grounding" to our spiritual nature.

Opening to Erotic Spirituality

In addition to the above, there are other practical steps you can take to help open your life to an erotic spirituality.

Reexamining Your Values. Every culture surrounds sexuality with values and taboos. This is, at least in part, a tribute to the importance and sacred nature of sexuality. But sometimes the values become so rigid and oppressive that they shut down the flow of erotic energy and prevent us from enjoying ourselves as sexual beings. Therefore, as adults, it is important to reexamine the sexual attitudes and values we were taught as children.

In my therapeutic work, I have seen couples whose values were so rigid that all sexual passion had died. By exploring their values and "opening a few windows," some of these couples were able to renew their sexual relationship. Religious clients have sometimes found help by talking to a caring, open-minded minister, priest, or rabbi. They often discover that even from a religious perspective they have been far too hard on themselves. I have a minister friend who tells his parishioners, "Look, God made your body and gave you those erotic feelings. He certainly didn't mean for you to shut them away in the basement as though they don't exist. So if your values are killing your sexuality, then there's something wrong with your values."

Reowning the Body. Most of us are out of contact with our bodies, unable to feel and trust the deep sensuality that is our birthright. For many, the body is an object to be shaped, sculpted, lipo-suctioned, and exercised into shape. For others it is a machine to be finely tuned so that it will run efficiently and not break down. Few of us live "embodied" lives, truly immersed in the sensual, sexual, and passionate energies of the body. To reown the body means to reestablish contact, to truly indwell the body, to attune ourselves to the sensations, feelings, and ecstasies of bodily existence.

This cannot be accomplished with the mind. In fact, living in our heads is part of the problem. The way back to the body is through the body itself. Whether one uses massage, hot baths, hatha yoga, aerobics, walking, running, bioenergetic therapy, tai chi, the martial arts, or any of a dozen other routes, one must directly reawaken the body, relight the passion, and clear the pathways for erotic energy.

Perhaps the most powerful way to reown the body and open up the channels for erotic energy is through pleasuring, or what Masters and Johnson called "sensate focus."[30] As part of their sex therapy, Masters and Johnson would ask couples to participate in extended pleasuring sessions. The couple was told not to have sexual intercourse but simply to touch and give sensual pleasure to each other. This was intended primarily as a desensitizing exercise to reduce anxiety concerning sex, but it can be used to generate erotic energy and connect with the life force that flows in deep sexuality. Couples who engage in pleasuring often find that it gets them back in contact with their bodies and changes lovemaking from a performance focused on orgasm to a deeply erotic and sensual experience.

GIFTS OF AN EROTIC SPIRITUALITY

Those who learn to use eros, sex, and sensuality as a path to the sacred will find that they bring many gifts into their lives.

One of those gifts is sexual healing. In a loving, erotic relationship souls touch, soothe, and affirm each other. In familiar arms, we find the cares of the day melting away and a renewed strength to carry on. If old wounds come to the surface, a knowing partner who understands us better than anyone else can help soothe and heal the pain. As Kleinplatz said, "The erotic encounter is empathy in motion."[31]

Another gift is creative inspiration. Theologian Nicolas Berdyaev said, "Erotic energy is the eternal source of creativity."[32] Throughout history, creative artists have found their inspiration in erotic lovers who acted as their muses, filling them with passion and connecting them to the creative stream.

A few years ago one of my doctoral students interviewed a well-known artist in her eighties. At one point the student asked how she kept her creativity alive. The old woman abruptly got up, went to the back door, and called to her seventy-seven-year-old husband. When he appeared at the door, she pointed to him and said, "Younger men!"

Sexuality taps into the "underground river." It stirs our creative passion and opens the floodgates of the soul. Erotic energy and creative energy are the same. It is no accident that so many artists have been intensely sexual; how else could they sustain the creative fire?

Another gift of erotic spirituality is passion. Sexual energy, when combined with spirituality, revitalizes one's existence. Once immersed in erotic energy, we find that it infuses everything we do. Work, friend-ships, food, and play may take on sensual aspects. Even the way we think, move, touch, and talk are affected. Eros is a powerful energy, a life-enhancing river that brings passion and new life wherever it flows.

Finally, another gift of erotic spirituality is a deeper relationship with the person we love. Matthew Fox said, "Two people riding the great horse of lust can indeed ride more deeply and swiftly into one another's souls."[33] Erotic spirituality is a way of "knowing into" the one we love. Passionate lovemaking takes us to new places in ourselves and opens up new vistas in our knowledge of our partner. Bodies interwine, souls mix, and deep relationship is forged in the fires of spiritual sex.

Orthodox Western psychology has dealt very poorly with
the spiritual side of man's nature, choosing either to ignore
its existence or to label it pathological. Yet much of the agony
of our time stems from a spiritual vacuum. Our culture, our
psychology, has ruled out man's spiritual nature, but the
cost of this attempted suppression is enormous.
—Charles Tart

PATH FOUR

PSYCHOLOGY
The Path of Counseling and Psychotherapy

Psychology is a powerful path to the sacred. At their best, counseling and psychotherapy are ways to nurture the soul, roads to a deeper spiritual life. Unfortunately, in today's world of HMOs and managed care, psychotherapy is becoming a medical, mechanistic enterprise that has little to do with the soul. Therefore, this chapter is a critique of modern psychology as well as an exploration of what a deeper, more mature therapy can be.

I have been a psychologist for twenty years, and I have been training counselors and psychotherapists for more than fifteen years at my university. Therefore, this chapter is addressed not only to the general reader but also to all students, counselors, and therapists who were drawn to this field because they wanted to be healers of the human soul.

HOW PSYCHOLOGY LOST ITS SOUL

The word *psychology* comes from two Greek words, *psyche* and *logos*. Psyche means "soul" and logos, in this context, means "study."

Thus, the word *psychology* literally means "the study of the soul." In the same way, other key words in the field also point to the soul. For example, the word *therapist* originally meant "servant" or "attendant."[1] Thus, etymologically, a psychotherapist is a "servant or attendant of the soul." Even the word *psychopathology* refers to the soul. It comes from the Greek words *psyche* and *pathos* and literally means "the suffering of the soul."

Based on this rich etymology, one would think that modern psychology would at least be interested in the soul. But this is not the case. Instead, modern psychology chose to cut itself off from its etymological roots and to graft itself onto the tree of medicine and the physical sciences. Freud, the founder of therapeutic psychology, wanted psychoanalysis to be a medical specialty dedicated to the cure of mental diseases. Thus, from the beginning, psychotherapy was cast in the mold of the medical model. Words such as *doctor, patient, illness, diagnosis, treatment,* and *cure* were used to describe and structure the therapeutic process. The medical model so permeated the field of therapeutic psychology that today it is almost impossible to discuss psychotherapy in any other terms. Although several major schools of psychotherapy, along with thousands of individual therapists, have opposed the medical model, saying that it does not describe what actually occurs in therapy, the model—backed by the American Psychiatric Association, the drug companies, the insurance industry, and now the entire HMO/managed care complex—remains securely entrenched. Against such monolithic power structures, those who suggest that psychology is the study of the soul or that therapy is a spiritual, existential, and creative process are viewed as modern Don Quixotes tilting at windmills.

Further, from its inception psychology has been permeated by the assumptions and methods of the physical sciences. After the Renaissance, science increasingly turned its attention to the study of the physical world, developing methods and procedures appropriate to that inquiry. Early thinkers in the field of psychology, desperately wanting psychology to be a science, followed the path of the physical sciences, failing to realize that psychological phenomena often cannot be translated into the categories of physical reality. The methods and statistical procedures which work so well in the physical sciences are often ineffectual and reductionistic when applied to psychological phenomena. In other words, studying a human being is simply not the same as studying a rock—or an electron or a nebula or a bacterium or a piece of DNA. When we study a rock, a "subjectivity" is studying an "objectivity." But when we study another human being, a "subjectivity" is studying another "subjectivity." And this makes all the difference in the world. Human beings are not objects; they have awareness and they react to the way they are treated. Therefore one cannot disregard the human relationship inherent in psychological research. As a researcher I may try, in the name of neutrality and scientific objectivity, to be distant and aloof, but I am still giving a relational message: I am saying that the nature of my relationship with my subject is one of distance and aloofness. Now if my subject were a rock, she might not pick this up. But since she is a human being with awareness and feelings, she will not only pick this up, but will probably think, feel, and act differently in the experiment than she would otherwise. On the other hand, if I relate to her as another human being, with warmth and respect, she will also notice this and respond accordingly. And in each case she will give me data that reflects the relationship I have created with her.

Because there is no such thing as a neutral or objective relationship between a researcher and a human subject, it is difficult, if not impossible, to get objective psychological data on human beings. Our data must always be interpreted in light of the relationship and context. Sören Kierkegaard once said that he was against any calculation that leaves out the relationship. So am I. This is one reason I believe psychology can never be a science in the manner of the physical sciences.

Amedeo Giorgi and Abraham Maslow are among those who have emphasized that psychology is a human science and should not, therefore, be forced into the mold of the physical sciences.[2] Rather, psychology should have its own epistemological assumptions and methods. What we study should determine how we study it. If we choose to study such distinctly human phenomena as love, values, or spirituality, we will probably find that the traditional methods of the physical sciences are not phenomenon-friendly; that is, these methods may not be able to capture and may actually damage the phenomenon we are trying to study. A hammer is a great tool for driving nails but is not very useful for catching butterflies. And if I insist on using a hammer to catch a butterfly, I will probably do great damage to the butterfly. In fact, I may have nothing left to study but a blob of protoplasm. If I wish to study butterflies, I have to use a butterfly net, which is "butterfly-friendly."

Hopefully, the metaphor is obvious. The traditional methods of the physical sciences, while elegant and effective in studying material phenomena, are often inappropriate, ineffective, reductionistic, and damaging in the study of humanness. To study human beings, other methods—phenomenological, ethnographic, historical, literary, narrative, theoretical, hermeneutic—will have to serve as "butterfly nets" for the subtle and exquisite human phenomena that cannot be caught and handled by traditional scientific methods. *Science* is the pursuit of knowledge. *Scientism,* on the other hand, is the narrow philosophical position that the methods of the natural sciences should be used in all investigative endeavors. In psychology we need more science and less scientism.

And what does this have to do with psychology as a path to the sacred? As long as the medical model dominates the field, our research, training, and practice will focus on the diagnosis, treatment, and cure of mental illness and will give little or no attention to the soul or to alternative ways of conceptualizing the therapeutic process. Similarly, as long as psychology continues to cast itself in the mold of the physical sciences, we will marginalize, or even denigrate, those dimensions of therapy that do not fit our scientific assumptions and procedures. Because the soul is a "butterfly" which does not lend itself to the methods of the physical sciences, it will be ignored. And if it should happen to fly into one of our training programs or research centers, or be smuggled in by some soulful student, it will be summarily smashed by the elegant hammers of those committed to the "science" of psychology.

A great tragedy has occurred in modern psychology: the soul has been shut out of its own house and exiled from its own kingdom. Psychology has lost its soul.

TOWARD A PSYCHOLOGY OF THE SOUL

Fortunately, there is a growing number of psychologists who believe that the banishment of the soul was a major historical mistake and that it is now time for psychology to return to its roots, as the discipline that studies the soul.

Carl Jung was the first psychologist to recognize the importance of the soul and make it a major psychological construct. Jung made spirituality the center of his therapeutic work and believed the recovery of the soul was essential for both the individual and Western society.

In the 1960s, the humanistic-existential movement in psychology, which arose as a reaction against the reductionism of classical behaviorism and psychoanalysis, placed great emphasis on the spiritual dimension, and people such as Abraham Maslow tried to bring this topic into mainstream psychology. Then, in the late 1960s, with the support of Maslow, the transpersonal psychology movement was launched. Transpersonal psychology was an outgrowth of the humanistic movement and was dedicated to the transpersonal or spiritual dimensions of human experience. In 1969, in the first issue of the *Journal of Transpersonal Psychology,* editor Anthony Sutich defined transpersonal psychology as "an emerging force in the psychology field by a group of psychologists and professional men and women from other fields who are interested in those ultimate human capacities and potentialities that have no systematic place in positivistic or behavioristic theory ("first force"), classical psychoanalytic theory ("second force"), or humanistic psychology ("third force")."[3] Calling this new movement the "fourth force" in psychology, Sutich went on to list a host of topics with which transpersonal psychology was concerned. The list included such things as ultimate values, unitive consciousness, ecstasy, mystical experience, awe, bliss, wonder, ultimate meaning, transcendence of the self, cosmic awareness, and the sacralization of everyday life.

Over the past thirty years, transpersonal psychologists such as Ken Wilber, Frances Vaughan, Roger Walsh, Stanley Grof, Christina Grof, and others have written extensively on spirituality, showing how it can be incorporated into psychological theory and practice.[4] Transpersonal thinkers tend to be acquainted with the spiritual traditions of other cultures and often combine Eastern thought with their theories and approaches. Unfortunately, mainstream American psychology, with its medical and materialistic assumptions, has tended to ignore transpersonal psychology and to marginalize its contributions. Nevertheless, the movement continues to attract students, clients, and practitioners.

In recent years, James Hillman has probably done more than any other psychologist to call us back to psychology as the study of the soul. Hillman believes that by abandoning its roots as the study of the soul, psychology has lost its identity and can no longer define its borders. He sees the soul as the one central, organizing construct that can give focus and boundaries to our profession. In his book *Re-Visioning Psy-*

chology, which was based on a series of lectures he gave at Yale University, he challenged psychology to return to its roots and to make the soul the center of its work and the measure of the discipline. Differentiating what he considers to be true psychology from that which is often called psychology, Hillman said, "Where there is connection to soul, there is psychology; where not, what is taking place is better called statistics, physical anthropology, cultural journalism, or animal breeding."[5]

I believe there are some very good reasons to follow Hillman's advice and "re-vision" psychology from the perspective of soul. I also believe that, from a historical perspective, this could be the *kairos*, the exactly right time, to create a psychology that pays more attention to the spiritual dimension of human beings. Several observations have led me to this conclusion.

First: Several surveys have shown that the majority of practicing psychologists, while not involved with organized religion, consider spirituality important to their personal lives and their clinical work.[6] Ironically, while the status quo assumptions of traditional psychology continue to ignore spirituality, the psychologists themselves are apparently finding it important and relevant to their work.

Second: As noted earlier, in *Megatrends 2000* John Naisbitt named increased interest in spirituality as one of the ten megatrends in contemporary American society.[7] Therefore, it seems that both the field of psychology and the culture at large may be ready for more emphasis on the spiritual dimension.

Third: The American consumer knows that psychotherapy is a way to deal with the existential and spiritual issues of life. In *Habits of the Heart*, a landmark sociological study of American life, Robert Bellah pointed out that it was in the 1960s that psychology, which had previously been viewed as a treatment for mental disorders, came to be seen as a vehicle for personal growth.[8] Many Americans went into therapy, participated in encounter groups, or became involved in other growth-oriented experiences. We became a psychological nation. Psychology became the number one major in colleges and universities, and an entire generation discovered that psychology could help them not only with mental illness but also with nonmedical matters. Therapists helped clients clarify their values, become more assertive, increase their sexual joy, release their creativity, increase their athletic performance, enhance their work satisfaction, reduce their stress, find more meaning in their lives, resolve relationship problems, and deepen their spirituality.

The clock can never be turned back. Millions of baby boomers have learned that psychotherapy is not simply for the mentally ill, but is for all those who are struggling with problems in living or who simply wish to deepen and enrich their lives. For the past thirty years the vast majority of those utilizing psychological services have been normal people dealing with normal problems. Practically every American family has a family member, relative, or close friend who has been in therapy. Thus, many American consumers know the value and multiple uses of therapy far better, it seems, than the health care bureaucracy, which continues to insist on defining therapy in narrow medical and mechanistic terms.

Maureen O'Hara is executive vice president and Dean of Faculty of Saybrook Graduate School and also a member of Meridian Institute, a futures think tank in the Bay area. O'Hara believes that American consumers constitute a huge and largely untapped market for therapists who are willing to abandon the medical model and "reinvent themselves as practitioners of what Abraham Maslow called 'a psychology of being.'"[9] Citing a Rand Corporation study, she points out that many Americans still avoid psychotherapy because of its connection to the medical model which tends to pathologize patients, seeing them as mentally sick. Thus, O'Hara feels the future of the field may belong to those therapists who see their work as "something akin to a sacred calling" and who wish to minister to "troubled souls." She urges psychotherapists to take this historical opportunity to dissociate themselves from doctors, medicine, and the entire managed care system.

Fourth: The medical and mechanistic models that now dominate psychology can never bring the spiritual dimension back into psychology. The basic assumption of the medical model is that our patients are sick and must be diagnosed and given treatment in order to get well. Psychiatry has gone so far as to literalize the medical metaphor, using drugs and invasive procedures to cure the mentally ill. But whether interpreted literally or metaphorically, the medical model leaves little room for the soul.

Likewise, mechanistic models view the client as a complex machine, highly responsive to environmental stimuli and conditioning, and subject to malfunction, and the job of the therapist is to fix the machine. Historically, classical behaviorism, based on a mechanistic model, acknowledged neither the mind nor the soul. Today, the mind has been accepted into the model, thanks to the influence of cognitive therapy, but there is still no place for the soul.

Certainly medical and mechanistic models have made useful contributions that should be integrated into any comprehensive theory of psychotherapy. But when these models serve as the *foundation* of counseling and psychotherapy, they produce a psychology that is barren of soul; they unintentionally participate in the further desacralization of our society and the de-souling of individual lives. Make no mistake: soul-less therapies produce soul-less results. And when psychotherapies, which are designed to help clients, become permeated by the same desacralizing assumptions which operate in our society and which often are the causes of clients' problems in the first place, perhaps it is time to seek approaches that support rather than destroy the soul.

These are revolutionary times for psychology. Thousands of therapists are disillusioned with the medical and mechanistic approaches of managed care, and millions of American consumers are hungry for a therapeutic experience that addresses the existential and spiritual issues of their lives. If these two forces ever catch sight of each other, a revolution in psychology will take place. However, two things could abort this revolution. First: psychologists may be unable to dissociate from medicine and managed care. If so, they will miss this historical opportunity to redefine themselves and the profession. Second: American consumers, tired of a psychology that pathologizes them, treats them with quick-fix techniques, and ignores their deeper concerns, may turn to alternative approaches which honor their spiritual quest. In fact, this is already happening; and if this trend continues, a revolution will occur, but psychology will not be involved. It will be left behind to become a narrow specialty in medicine. It would be a shame for psychology, with all of its knowledge and historical promise, to be consigned to some small room in the medical establishment when it has the potential to be a clearinghouse for the soul, a huge edifice dedicated to all areas of human endeavor.

A NEW VISION OF PSYCHOTHERAPY

We desperately need a new vision of counseling and psychotherapy, one that honors the soul and the spiritual nature of the human being. Creating such a vision may be the most important task facing psychology. Working out such a vision will require time and the efforts of many creative therapists. I would like to present a few ideas that might be a beginning for such work.

James Hillman defines psychotherapy as soul-making and views the therapist as an attendant to the soul-making process.[10] I personally define psychotherapy as the art of nurturing and healing the soul. I take seriously the idea that psychopathology is the suffering of the soul and that the primary task of the therapist is *cura animarum*, the cure and care of the soul. Thus psychotherapy from the perspective of soul proceeds from two basic assumptions: the first is that the client is suffering at the soul level, and the second is that psychotherapy is the process by which the client's soul is nurtured and healed.

Psychopathology: The Suffering of the Soul

Throughout the history of therapeutic psychology, many practitioners have recognized that psychopathology is often the result of conflicts and deprivations at the spiritual level. Erich Fromm emphasized the importance of the soul and believed psychotherapy must address the spiritual dimension.[11] Viktor Frankl believed meaninglessness is the major existential issue of our times and that the failure to find purpose in our lives often results in psychological problems.[12] Abraham Maslow believed that we have certain higher needs—the need for love, beauty, truth, goodness, and other Being-values, as he called them. If these needs are not met, we fall into a type of metapathology, which is the direct result of deprivation at the spiritual level.[13] Irvin Yalom, an existential psychiatrist at Stanford University, has written a comprehensive textbook showing the relationship of existential themes to psychopathology.[14]

This list could go on, but the point is clear: many of our most renowned psychologists and psychiatrists have recognized that psychopathology is not simply the result of problems in the mental and emotional dimension, but that some forms of psychopathology are rooted in the spiritual dimension. And whether we describe this dimension in philosophical, existential, religious, spiritual, or psychological terms, it is profoundly involved in the etiology of psychological problems as well as in the healing that comes through psychotherapy. When viewed in this way, the idea that psychopathology is the suffering of the soul is not new to psychology at all. It is simply describing in the language of the soul what many others have said throughout the history of psychology.

Psychopathology is the cry of the soul, and psychological symptoms are messages of pain from the deepest part of our being. The soul suffers when it is deprived of love, goodness, truth, beauty, and passion. It experiences agony when it confronts death, meaninglessness, isolation, and loneliness. The soul is ontologically thirsty, and if this thirst is not quenched, life becomes barren and dry, and the soul begins to die. There are also some violations and betrayals in life that cut so deeply that they can only be called wounds to the soul. When the soul is deprived, neglected, hungry, thirsty, wounded, or abused, it suffers. This suffering of the soul is what we label as pathology and then try to fit into the categories of our diagnostic manual.

Psychotherapy: The Art of Nurturing and Healing the Soul

Psychotherapy is the process by which we try to assuage this pain by nurturing and healing the client's soul. When Freud posited the unconscious as the source of neurotic conflicts, he then had to discover the paths to the unconscious, ways to access that dimension of his patients. If we posit the soul as the source of our clients' suffering, we must then find paths to the soul in order to nurture and heal at that level. Fortunately, human beings have been nurturing and healing the soul for thousands of years, and this makes our task easier. I would like to suggest some paths to the soul that can be used in therapy.

First: the therapist's relationship with the client is a primary route to the soul. We have known for many years that the quality of the relationship is a crucial factor in therapeutic healing. Yalom pointed out that there are hundreds of research studies showing that the quality of the therapeutic relationship is significantly related to therapeutic outcome. He said that the most important lesson the psychotherapist must learn is that "it is the relationship that heals."[15]

But what does it mean that the relationship heals? I believe this is another way of saying that the therapist nurtures the client's soul and that through this nurturing the client is healed. Love is the most powerful healer of the wounded soul. In the therapeutic relationship, love manifests as empathy, caring, warmth, respect, honesty, and acceptance of the client. The presence of these factors turns therapy into a container for soul-making. They make soul-to-soul contact possible, and they heal because they soothe and nurture the client's soul.

This has implications for the therapist. I can only be a healer of the soul when I am in contact with my own soul. We can touch the other only as deeply as the place from which we come within ourselves. If I reach out to my client from a shallow place within myself, I will not be able to make contact with the soul of my client. But if I am familiar with the regions of my soul and can readily access this dimension of my being, I will be able to make contact with my client at a more profound level and foster a relationship in which healing of the soul becomes possible. As Paul Tillich said, "Depth speaks to depth."

Second: The therapeutic relationship is important; but it is also important that the client sees therapy not simply as a situation where people come to have their souls nurtured by someone else. Psychotherapy is an apprenticeship in which clients learn how to care for their own souls. The client should be shown that there are countless activities and experiences that feed the soul. In fact, almost anything that touches, stirs, or speaks to our depths has this capacity. Literature, poetry, music, paintings, sculptures, movies, plays, dance, religion, nature, and the creative process are all potential sources of soul-nurturing.

Like a shaman carefully choosing roots and herbs for a ritual healing, the therapist must help each client find those things in life that nurture and heal his or her soul. It is extremely important that the therapist realizes that what nurtures the soul differs dramatically from person to person and avoids falling into the elitist assumption that only classical music, art, literature, and so forth can nurture the soul. While some clients may find Mozart, Beethoven, Van Gogh, or Rilke wonderful sources of soul food, for others a country song by Willie Nelson or Garth Brooks may go straight to the soul. A hike in the mountains or a camping trip to the desert may nurture the soul of another client who would find art galleries and operas a bore. So if we wish to help our clients nurture and heal their souls, we must first help them discover the activities and experiences that truly meet the needs of their own unique soul.

It is also important for the client to begin a regular, consistent program of engaging in these soul-nurturing activities and experiences. For one person this may mean taking regular walks on the beach or along the river; for another it may mean collecting poems or making a tape of all the songs which touch him or her most deeply; for still another it may mean going to the theater more regularly. A few years ago I had a client who went to see *Phantom of the Opera* and then wept in my office as she told me how profoundly the story and the music had touched her soul. A few years ago when I was going through a difficult time in my own life, I happened to see the movie *Dead Poets Society*. The film's existential themes touched my soul and gave me a new perspective. I know a woman who loves Beethoven's music and once got through a painful depression by playing his works over and over. She says the music is what sustained her. I know an older colleague who holds two doctorates, one in psychology and one in literature. For years he has helped clients in mental hospitals nurture and heal their souls by encouraging them to write and share poems with one another in therapy groups. A few years ago I had a client who was in great pain and was feeling somewhat suicidal. When I asked her what she felt would help, she said, to get away by herself to the seashore. Somewhat cautiously I agreed, on the condition that she promised me that she would not harm herself and that she would stay in contact. She agreed, and her time at the beach was deeply healing.

Thus, psychotherapy from the perspective of soul means that the soul is placed at the very center of the therapeutic endeavor. Psychotherapy then becomes an arena in which the therapist nurtures the client's soul, and a training ground for the client to learn how to nurture his or her own soul. This does not mean that other techniques based on other theories are not used; but it does mean that everything is placed in the service of soul and is evaluated from that perspective.

NEW METAPHORS FOR PSYCHOTHERAPY

To replace the medical and mechanistic models that dominate counseling and psychotherapy today, I would like to suggest some alternative metaphors that honor the soul and the spiritual dimension of the human being.

Psychotherapy as an Artistic Process

The best description of psychotherapy I know comes from a writer, not a psychologist, and her topic in fact was creative writing, not psychotherapy. Isabel Allende, who wrote *The House of the Spirits* and other novels that have received international acclaim, was asked to describe how she writes. She replied:

> I write in a very organic way. Books don't happen in my mind; they happen somewhere in my belly. It's like a long elephant pregnancy

that can last two years. And then, when I'm ready to give birth, I sit down. I wait for January 8th, which is my special date, and then, that day, I begin the book that has been growing inside me.

Often when I sit that day and turn on my computer or my type-writer and write the first sentence, I don't know what I'm going to write about because it has not yet made the trip from the belly to the mind. It is somewhere hidden in a very somber and secret place where I don't have any access yet. It is something that I've been feel-ing but which has no shape, no name, no tone, no voice. So I write the first sentence—which usually is the first sentence of the book. That is the only thing that really stays. Then the story starts unfold-ing itself, slowly, in a long process. By the time I've finished the first draft I know what the book is about. But not before.

Somehow inside me—I can say this after having written five books—I know that I know where I am going. I know that I know the end of the book even though I don't know it. It's so difficult to explain. It is as if I have this terrible confidence that something that is beyond myself knows why I'm writing this book. And what the end of the book will be. And how the book will develop. But if you ask me what the book is about or where I am going I can't tell you. I can't tell anybody. I can't even tell myself. But I have a cer-tainty that I would not have started the book without knowing why I'm writing it.[16]

Allende has put into words a process that stands at the center of all creative art and that also characterizes the best psychotherapy. Psy-chotherapy has far more in common with such artistic processes than it does with medical and mechanistic models. I believe the best way to understand therapy is to approach it as an artistic endeavor and to use the creative process as its central metaphor.

Most clinicians do recognize that, in the best psychotherapy, there is a creative process that takes on a life of its own and carries the client toward some unknown yet deeply sensed destination. That is to say, in the best therapy the client sooner or later begins to experience the subtle flow of her own creative becoming. Like Allende, the client knows that she knows where she is going. But also like Allende, if you ask her where she is going, she can't tell you. She can't tell anybody. She can't even tell herself. But she has a certainty that she would not have started the journey without knowing why she was making it.

Therapy is the facilitation of this natural, creative process of be-coming; it is an intensive endeavor in which both client and therapist focus on that which is trying to emerge or be born in the client. There is a lot of waiting. There is not much knowing. Yet there is a strong sense that this becoming is important, perhaps even a matter of life and death. The client knows that destruction will be associated with this creative process. Old ways of being, old patterns and outdated structures will have to be relinquished. She knows that, before the process is over, she may experience more anxiety, depression, and pain. Yet there is an underlying belief in the creative process, an unshakable sense of being carried by forces greater than self toward a new and ultimately more fulfilling way of being in the world.

In his book *Existence*, Rollo May said that the word existence comes from the root *ex-sistere* and means to "stand out" or "emerge." He said that existential psychologists see "the human being not as a collection of static substances or mechanisms or patterns but rather as emerging and becoming, that it to say, as existing."[17] May saw psychotherapy as a creative process in which the therapist facilitates that which is emerging or becoming in the client. I take seriously the idea that human beings go through periods of growth in which they leave old patterns behind and are carried forward toward the deeply sensed but unarticulated new. I also take seriously the idea that anxiety, depression, and other clinical problems more often than not are signals telling us that we have ceased to grow, that we are dying inside, suffocating in the old, untenable structures that no longer serve us. Just as the artist works with what is trying to become manifest in the painting, sculpture, or poem, so the creative therapist works with what is trying to emerge in the actualizing process of the client. The client and therapist meet and give birth to that which is struggling to be born in the client's soul.

Psychotherapy as an artistic endeavor stands at the opposite end of the continuum of therapeutic practices from the shallow, mechanistic approaches that now dominate the field. It is a deeper, more mature form of therapy because it relies on a more complex understanding of the human condition. It honors and draws upon the vast cache of wisdom found in the world's literature, poetry, arts, philosophies, religions, and ancient healing methods. Yet, there is nothing in this approach that contradicts or closes its door to either science or to new knowledge about the healing process.

By contrast, the technician-driven model of psychotherapy generally ignores the human context. It pays little attention, if any, to the existential and spiritual questions that are often at the root of the client's problems. Like the well-trained mechanic who can tune our car but has nothing to offer if we ask how to develop a better life, so the technican-therapist can change behavior or remove symptoms but seems to know little about nurturing the soul or helping the client create a deeper, more passionate existence.

For twenty years I have worked in hospital, community mental health, and private practice settings. I have found that while clients often initiate therapy because of a painful symptom, they quickly begin to discuss their lives—the complex fabric of who they are, where they are going, and what is present and what is missing in their lives. Once clients enter this deeper process, it is almost impossible to convince them to do what they consider to be "gimmicky" techniques or homework assignments directed only at symptom alleviation. They sense that they have embarked on a journey that will not only alleviate their symptoms but will also lead them to a deeper, more meaningful life.

In a bureaucratically driven profession that demands, after only one or two sessions, linear treatment plans with clearly defined goals, specific methods to reach those goals, and a list of criteria for determining when therapy will be finished, the therapist who wishes to honor the deeper, creative process in the client is at a woeful disadvantage. Just as our technological society allows little room for art and artists, so in psychology the artistic therapist goes unhonored. Rather, the model therapist is quickly becoming a left-brained, scientistic, hyper-rational technician who knows little or nothing about the soul. The health care industry, driven by economics and a quick-fix mentality, supports this kind of therapist. The faster a therapist can get the job done and return the suffering individual to the assembly line or the corporate ladder, the more money the managed care company makes. Sadly, in America money is more important than clients' souls and therapy is becoming a quick-fix center owned by Wall Street.

Rollo May once told a friend of mine who was immersed in study of the hard sciences at the time, "You need to read less science and more poetry." That says it for me. In therapist training programs and the therapy profession generally, we need to read less science and more poetry. Therapy is more than linear science, medical procedures, and mechanistic methods. It is also poetry and art. And it is the artistic, creative, spiritual, poetic dimensions of therapy that are central, because they reflect and facilitate the process of growing, becoming, and birthing one's soul.

Psychotherapy As Working with Being

Psychotherapy is an ontological process. The raw material of soul-making is *ontos*, "being," and in therapy I have often had the sense that I am working with ontological clay, that the client's being is emerging and that the client and I, like two sculptors, are gently molding, shaping, and working it until it begins to take form.

As noted earlier, Rollo May believed that the natural state of the human being is emerging, becoming. Emotional problems develop when this natural process is hampered or blocked. Therapy, then, addresses that which is trying to emerge or become in the client, as well as those things that are blocking the process. In this same vein, Eugene Gendlin has developed a therapeutic approach called focusing, which is specifically designed to help clients connect with their preverbal flow of experience, with that which they know but cannot yet put into words.[18] In this sense, one might say that focusing is a way to help clients access that which is trying to become.

This language may sound a bit mysterious to those who think of therapy in linear and mechanistic terms. But to the creative artist, this language is not strange at all. In making art, one must access dimensions of inner experience and rely on processes that cannot be described in linear ways. How does a painter, for example, know how much of which color to put where in order to move toward his intuitive vision of what the painting is to become? How does the writer know when to throw a page away and when to keep one, especially when the intuitive vision is not yet completely clear? In creating art there are mysterious processes, almost impossible to describe in words, which guide the artist. There is an internal sense—a dynamic, intuitive reference point—to which the artist returns again and again to make sure the work of art is developing in the proper direction. Psychotherapy relies on some of these same mysterious processes; only the client and therapist are working with *ontos*, with the being of the client that is trying to emerge or become. And just as the creative artist must follow his intuitive sense to produce the work of art, the creative therapist must follow the authentic nature and emergence of the client's being in order to help it become what it is trying to become. These creative processes simply cannot be described in linear terms;

and that is exactly why mechanistic models of therapy are limited and inadequate when it comes to understanding and describing the complex processes involved in the therapeutic encounter and in psychological growth.

Paul Tillich contributed another piece to this perspective. Tillich spent much of his life translating religious concepts into ontological language in order that people in the modern age for whom religious words have lost their meaning could see the great underlying truths that these concepts represent.[19] Tillich viewed our basic human condition as one of separation from God, which he called the Ground of Being. He recast the concept of sin to refer not to moral missteps, but to the condition of being separated from the Ground of Being. Reconciliation, another Biblical concept, he interpreted as the process by which we are reunited with the Ground of Being.

Different symbol systems provide different ways of communicating the same basic truths. Using religious language, one could say that human beings are separated from God and need to be reconciled to God. In psychological language, one could say that human beings are out of contact with their deeper self and need to reconnect with it. Using Tillich's ontological language, one would say that we are separated from the Ground of Being and need to be reunited with it. Thus, psychotherapy means helping clients to come home to their essential self, to be reconciled to the ground and source of their being, to reconnect with who they really are.

Similarly, Carl Rogers said that clients come to therapy in a state of incongruence; that is, they are cut off from their inner experience. There is a lack of alignment between their self concept and the truth of the organism. To put it another way, the client is not anchored in her own being, and this produces anxiety and disequilibrium.[20]

To assist the client, the therapist must create a relationship characterized by what Rogers called empathy, unconditional positive regard, and congruence. Rogers originally discovered these three variables by analyzing transcriptions of his own therapy sessions. He found that when he was empathic, caring, and congruent with clients, they tended to improve. Rogers came to believe that these variables were the necessary and sufficient conditions of therapy, and he and his colleagues backed up this claim with hundreds of studies which showed a positive correlation between these conditions and successful therapeutic outcome.

I believe these three variables are ontological, that they have to do with being. In uncovering these variables, Rogers discovered something a bit more profound than his psychological language could indicate. For example, at one level, empathy is simply an effort to enter the phenomenological world of the client and to reflect back to the client what one sees there. But at a deeper level, empathy can be seen as an ontological tool for uncovering the authentic being of the client. From an ontological perspective, empathy is not simply mirroring the client's thoughts, feelings, and inner experiences; it is also becoming attuned to the client's authentic being. Accurate empathy uncovers the client's unique essence. As Heidegger might say, it is *aleitheia*, the truth of being, in action. Thus therapy is not simply psychological work; it is ontological endeavor.

Rogers's concept of unconditional positive regard is a nonjudgmental caring that accepts the client as he is. Rogers found that when clients are accepted as they are, they are then free to evolve and change. I suspect that this paradox is actually an ontological dynamic. If judgment or rejection inhibits the process of becoming, perhaps acceptance is the ontological condition that allows the client to begin evolving again. Thus, ontological healing means being seen for who we truly are through empathy, and then being accepted as we are through unconditional positive regard.

In his sermon "You Are Accepted" in *The Shaking of the Foundations*, Tillich described the powerful effects of being accepted.

> It happens or it does not happen. And certainly it does not happen if we try to force it upon ourselves, just as it shall not happen so long as we think, in our self-complacency, that we have no need of it. Grace strikes us when we are in great pain and restlessness. It strikes us when we walk through the dark valley of a meaningless and empty life. It strikes us when we feel that our separation is deeper than usual, because we have violated another life, a life which we loved, or from which we were estranged. It strikes us when our disgust for our own being, our indifference, our weakness, our hostility, and our lack of direction and composure have become intolerable to us. It strikes us when, year after year, the longed-for perfection of life does not appear; when the old compulsions reign within us as they have for decades, when despair destroys all joy and courage. Sometimes at that moment a wave of light breaks into our darkness, and it is as though a voice were saying: "You are accepted." You are

accepted, accepted by that which is greater than you, and the name of which you do not know. Do not ask for the name now; perhaps you will find it later. Do not try to do anything now; perhaps later you will do much. Do not seek for anything; do not perform anything; do not intend anything. Simply accept the fact that you are accepted! If that happens to us, we experience grace. After such an experience we may not be better than before, and we may not believe more than before. But everything is transformed. In that moment, grace conquers sin, and reconciliation bridges the gulf of estrangement. And nothing is demanded of this experience, no religious or moral or intellectual presupposition, nothing but acceptance.[21]

Therapist congruence—the alignment of the therapist's outward behavior with her inner experience—is ontological in nature, in that the therapist is in contact with her own being and is thereby bringing authentic being into the therapeutic encounter. In the presence of an authentic therapist, the client's being, no matter how repressed, will resonate and respond. The authentic therapist is a lit candle of being that lights the candle that has gone out in the client's soul.

Psychotherapy as Facilitating Archetypal Processes

The genius of Carl Jung is his recognition of the fact that archetypal processes are at work in the depths of the soul. We are not blank tablets on which experience simply writes its story. Rather, we are born with archetypal predispositions, universal tendencies which can be rather easily activated by our experiences in life. The activating of these predispositions tend to be powerful psychological events. Though they are part of our individuation process and ultimately contribute to our growth, they can also generate strong emotions and be psychologically painful while taking place. Clients may come to psychotherapy because they are caught in an archetypal process, struggling to make sense of the feelings that have been unleashed. In such cases, psychotherapy involves assisting the client through the process.

To illustrate what I mean by an archetypal process, I will use clinical depression as an example. David Rosen, a Jungian psychiatrist and author of *Transforming Depression*, maintains that depression is an archetypal experience that can best be understood as part of the individuation process, and that "at the core of the transformation process is an archetypal death-rebirth experience."[22]

In depression one confronts the dark and monstrous archetype of death and then, as one begins to come out of the depression, the frightening forces of rebirth. These archetypes are powerful, and one could not undergo a more fundamental archetypal experience. As Fritz Perls, the founder of Gestalt therapy, said, "To suffer one's death and to be reborn is not easy."[23]

Depression feels like death. If one has not been through this experience, it is difficult to understand the psychological pain that is involved. In my own life I have, at times, struggled with depression. On my worst days, I would awaken in the morning with anxiety and a sense of dread. It took all the will power I could muster to get out of bed and face the day. I felt lethargic, almost as though I were walking through a river of molasses, forcing myself to take a shower, brush my teeth, get dressed, and go to work. Sometimes I felt sad and cried; but most of the time I felt like an emotionless robot with a depleted battery simply trying to get through the day. I felt no enthusiasm for life, nor for activities that had once given me pleasure. I dreaded giving a lecture or presentation, fearing that my anxiety would interfere with my ability to think, fearing that my students and colleagues would see the embarrassing truth that I, a psychologist, was depressed. I wondered if I would ever get better, or if I would be trapped forever in this dark dungeon. I did not want to see friends; I just wanted to run away, withdraw, hibernate. Life seemed heavy, dark, hopeless. And if I felt a little better at night, still I knew that when I awoke the next morning, the black monster would be back.

Rosen believes that during this phase of depression the old ego-identity is dying. In other words, the old structures of our life are crumbling; the old way of being, with which we may be strongly identified, is no longer working, and we have to let it go. Rosen himself became depressed when his wife left him, an event that forced his old identity to die. He had to go through the death experience of relinquishing his former life and then, eventually, through the birth experience of a new way of life.

People sometimes feel suicidal during the death phase of depress-sion. But of course suicide is not the answer. As Jane Wheelwright says in her article "Old Age and Death," suicidal tendencies indicate that the depressed client has literalized the death feelings and has not yet understood the symbolic, archetypal meaning of what is taking place. Wheelwright writes:

The downward pull and immobilization that accompany deep depressions are mistaken for sensations of physical death rather than of the psychic death which, as a matter of course, precedes psychic rebirth. Suicidal people often fail to recognize that it is nature's demand for a change in attitude or an increase in self-awareness which brings on the depressed state. They do not realize that to bring about a change in their lives, they have to experience despair and to face the black night of their tunneled state of mind in order to come out into the light of change.[24]

Perhaps nowhere is the archetypal process of death and rebirth seen more clearly than in bipolar disorder, which used to be called manic-depressive illness. In its extreme form, clients with this disorder may swing in a matter of hours from one pole to the other. One day they are so depressed that they can think of nothing but suicide and death. The next day, in the manic phase, they are so caught up in the energies of rebirth that they become grandiose, effusive, and cannot be calmed down. While bipolar disorder is an extreme example, with clients sometimes manifesting psychotic symptoms, the disorder provides a dramatic picture of symbolic death and rebirth. In *Touched with Fire: Manic-Depressive Illness and the Artistic Temperament,* Kay Redfield Jamison observed, "The rhythms and cycles of manic-depressive illness, a singularly cyclic disease, are strikingly similar to those of the natural world, as well as to the death and regeneration and dark and light cycles so often captured in poetry, music, and painting."[25]

My own story demonstrates the workings of the death-rebirth process. For years my life was dedicated to ego pursuits connected with my work. At my university I was chair of several committees and sometimes worked sixty hours or more per week to get everything done. But as I reached midlife, I began to realize that I did not enjoy most of the things I was doing. The old ego-identity, which had always given me such a "high," now seemed dry and stale. By the fall of 1988, when I was forty-three, I felt depressed and saw little value in the things I had accomplished. I went into therapy and finally acknowledged that I could not continue to live the way I was living. My old identity, my old way of life, was dying. In therapy I faced its death, mourned its passing, eulogized it where I could, conducted its funeral, and buried it. I found this hard to do because I had become attached to that old way of life, even though it was killing my soul.

Then, much to my surprise, as I let go of the old life, new life began to stir in me. I found myself turning to art, poetry, and creative writing—things which had always attracted me but which I had always put on the back shelf, as it were. I stopped working so many hours and began to do more things that nurtured my soul. I made new friends who knew about living life with passion or who wanted to explore it with me. My marriage took on new life and became better than ever. This book you are reading, with its focus on soul, is a product of my rebirth experience.

I do not like depression. I do not romanticize it. I do not idealize it. I do not wish it on anyone. Depression is a black monster that crushes life and takes away all joy. Nevertheless, I will say this: If someone told me that I could live my life again free of depression provided I was willing to give up the gifts depression has given me—the depth of awareness, the expanded consciousness, the increased sensitivity, the awareness of limitation, the tenderness of love, the meaning of friendship, the appreciation of life, the joy of a passionate heart—I would say, "This is a Faustian bargain! Give me my depressions. Let the darkness descend. But do not take away the gifts that depression, with the help of some unseen hand, has dredged up from the deep ocean of my soul and strewn along the shores of my life. I can endure darkness if I must; but I cannot live without these gifts. I cannot live without my soul."

Seeing depression from an archetypal perspective gives it meaning. Hopelessness is a major problem in depression, mainly because those who give up all hope often commit suicide. Perhaps the best antidote for hopelessness is the sense that there is meaning in one's suffering. There are many kinds of depression, and I am not saying that all depressions are meaningful. Certainly the world is filled with meaningless pain, and I have no desire to paint a Pollyannaish picture of depression. But I have no doubt that some depressions are deeply meaningful; that they are archetypal experiences designed to bring us back to our true selves and show us the road to our destiny.

If we nurtured our souls and took care of our inner lives on an ongoing basis, such extreme reckonings might not be necessary; we might be able to find our way without the sledge-hammer experience of depression. But many of us are made up in such a way that depression seems to be necessary to get our attention. We have strong egoistic tendencies that pull us toward false ego-identities. At the same time, we have a soul that will not let us go, that refuses to let us waste our life in empty pursuits. In spite of the ego's resistance, our soul pulls us toward our destiny, forces us to live out our karma. Since we are unable to learn humility any other way, the soul pulls out its heavy artillery and drops us "bone by bone," to use Emily Dickinson's words. In such cases, depression, while extremely painful, is also our salvation. It is the corrective force that puts us back on the road to our destiny, a destiny we would have missed had it not been for the depression bringing us back into contact with our soul.

I believe there are thousands, maybe even millions, of depressed people who can relate to this. If you are one of these, let me assure you that your depression, as dark and monstrous as it seems, is ultimately your guide. It was sent from beyond to bring you home to your soul, your deepest self. Do not give up or fall into hopeless despair. The phoenix still rises from the ashes, spring still follows winter, resurrection still comes after death, and the joy of rebirth follows the darkness of depression. Find yourself a good, caring therapist who knows that something sacred is taking place, who understands that the forces of death and rebirth are stirring within you, who can walk with you in the darkness and serve as midwife to the new self that is trying to be born. And one fine morning, not too long from now, you will notice that the world looks a little brighter, that the dark clouds are scattering, that the sun is shining on your face, and that hope is finally returning. In the dark smithy of your soul, painful depression may already be forging the contours of the man or woman you are meant to be, hammering out the strength, humility, and wisdom you will need to fulfill your destiny in the world.

Myth is the secret opening through which
the inexhaustible energies of the cosmos pour
into human cultural manifestation.
—Joseph Campbell

PATH FIVE

MYTHOLOGY
The Path of Story, Ritual, and Symbol

Mythology is the oldest path to the sacred. In the course of evolution, when humans first became aware of the spiritual dimension, mythological stories, rituals, and symbols emerged as a way to represent that experience and to help them connect with the sacred domain. Joseph Campbell, one of the major mythologists of this century, said,

> Our first tangible evidences of mythological thinking are from the period of Neanderthal Man, which endured from ca. 250,000 to 50,000 B.C.; and these comprise, first, burials with food supplies, grave gear, tools, sacrificed animals, and the like; and second, a number of chapels in high-mountain caves, where cave-bear skulls, ceremonially disposed in symbolic settings, have been preserved.[1]

From these early beginnings to our present postmodern age, mythological thinking has been part of the human experience. As we will see, mythology is not simply a collection of quaint stories from ancient places and times. Rather, mythology is and has always been a path to the sacred, a mystical bridge that connects us to the spiritual world.

DEFINING MYTHOLOGY

Someone has said that we call our own mythology "religion" and other people's religions "mythologies." I suspect there is some truth

191

to this. Most of us like to think that our religion is special, that it contains the truth, and that all other religions are merely myths that reflect a culture's flawed efforts at understanding God and the universe. But a deeper understanding of mythology reveals the religiocentrism of this view.

Each world religion and each mythology contains its own stories, rituals, and symbols. If one considers these at the surface level, the diversity is almost overwhelming. But if one looks more deeply, it becomes apparent that these highly diverse stories, rituals, and symbols are merely the masks of God, as Campbell called them.[2] For example, on the surface, a funeral in an Episcopal church may look radically different from a simple burial ceremony in an indigenous culture, but both are rituals to help the bereaved through the experience of loss, which is universal. A wedding celebration in a European village may go on for days, while a similar union in a primitive tribe may involve little more than ritually entering the marriage hut; but, again, the two rituals are essentially the same. All mythologies, along with their attendant rituals and symbols, are ways to address the universal events and concerns of human life. While theologians may argue about which religion is right, I suspect that all have something to offer, that each contains insights and spiritual perspectives that must not be lost.

One of the common misconceptions about mythology is that *myth* means "falsehood," something that is not true. On the contrary, a myth often contains the deepest kind of truth. A myth is a metaphorical story, somewhat like an allegory or parable, that contains insights and profound truths about the human condition. The reason we confuse myth with falsehood is that, from a literal point of view, the myth itself is usually not true. For example, there never was a god named Eros who fell in love with a mortal woman named Psyche; this is a myth, an imaginative story that grew out of the culture of ancient Greece. If taken literally, the story is obviously false. But if understood metaphorically, the myth contains important truths about human life. Because our culture is obsessed with propositional truths and hard facts, many people have trouble understanding how something so unscientific and factually untrue as mythology could be of any value. But this attitude reflects more negatively on us than it does on mythology; it suggests how far removed we are from things of the soul and how disconnected we are from the ancient wisdom contained in mythic images. As Rollo May said in *The Cry for Myth*, "There can be no stronger proof of the impoverishment of our contemporary culture than the popular—though profoundly mistaken—definition of myth as falsehood."[3]

Both Western religion and science in their orthodox forms have trouble with mythology. Fundamentalist religion, with its dogmatic need to interpret literally and concretely, is a religious expression of our culture's general lack of understanding of the soul and the imaginal world. Orthodox science, with its rigid commitment to empirical facts, manifests the same inability to appreciate the kind of truth revealed through myth, metaphor, image, symbol, and other intuitive and artistic approaches. This is a scientific form of fundamentalism that has much in common with its religious cousin. Both are obsessed with their own brand of logic and "left-brain thinking," and both have little appreciation for the soul and the value of imaginal truth. So it is no wonder that myth doesn't "play" well in either fundamentalist religion or orthodox science. It challenges their need for a well-ordered universe where everything stays in its place. Myth opens the door to a world that cannot be predicted and controlled, where truth is more amorphous, multifaceted, relative, pluralistic. Myth takes us out of the world where hard-edged facts lie about like stones and leads us into the depths of the imaginal sea which has currents and truths of its own; for while the stories of mythology may not be literally true, this does not mean that they are not metaphorically and existentially true.

Another misconception about mythology is the view, held by some, that mythology is nothing more than a primitive form of science, an attempt by early men and women to understand and control the forces of nature by engaging in various rituals and ceremonies designed to supplicate and appease the gods. There is some truth to this, because mythology did, at times, serve this function. But the origins and purposes of mythology go much deeper than this rather superficial understanding suggests. In fact, this view of myth is a good example of how we impose our modern biases and scientific world-view on ancient cultures, making them little more than crude and imperfect forerunners of our presumably more enlightened age. This is more a sign of our own cultural egocentrism than an accurate analysis of the origin and functions of mythology. When we view mythology as superstition or an inferior form of science, we dismiss it as irrelevant to the modern age. As long as this attitude prevails, we will not be able to see the real value of mythology as a path to the sacred and a way to nurture the soul.

If mythology cannot be dismissed as falsehood or as primitive science, then what is it, and how can it contribute to our lives today?

Mythology is a container for the spiritual and existential wisdom of a culture in the form of stories, rituals, and symbols. It provides a map, as it were, to guide us through the various passages and major events of life. We are all novices when it comes to life; we have never made the journey before, and each section of the road presents questions and dilemmas we have not previously encountered. But millions of others have preceded us. Countless generations have gone through birth, childhood, adulthood, parenthood, midlife, old age, and death. Mythology is the code which contains the record of their journey; it is the depository of the archetypal wisdom they have left behind. So when we are faced with a major life event, we are not alone. These ancient mentors surround us in a great circle, and through the stories, rituals, and symbols of mythology they share their wisdom, helping us understand what is happening and how to deal with it. As Joseph Campbell said, "One of the most wonderful things about these age-old realizations that are constellated in the mythic image is that they let you know what it is you are experiencing."[4]

But mythology is more than a guide map. It contains a mystical power that may reflect its most essential character. Campbell was alluding to this when he said, "Myth is the secret opening through which the inexhaustible energies of the cosmos pour into human cultural manifestation."[5] He was also referring to mythology's mystical function when he said, "Mythology is a rendition of forms through which the formless Form of forms can be known."[6] In the famous interviews with Campbell conducted by Bill Moyers, Campbell said that "the basic theme of all mythology is that there is an invisible plane supporting this visible one."[7] For these two worlds to interact, there must be bridges between them. Or, to use Campbell's metaphor, there must be openings where the sacred can enter our world. Mythology is one of those openings.

While this mystical language may sound strange to modern ears, Campbell was merely reminding us who live in the modern age of what the human species has always known: that mythological stories, rituals, and symbols have sacred power. Like art, music, dance, poetry, literature, and other openings through which the sacred appears, mythology is a channel for spiritual energies that nurture the soul and support our spiritual lives.

How does mythology do this? Do the gods of Mount Olympus zap us with bolts of lightning, igniting our souls and filling us with passion? Well, yes and no. To understand the dynamics of mythology, we must turn once again to Carl Jung's psychological theory. Jung believed that mythology is a projection or externalization of the archetypes of the collective unconscious. Mythology contains stories, rituals, and symbols that reflect images in the depths of our own souls and speak to the universal concerns of the human being. Thus, the gods and goddesses of ancient Greece were creations of the collective unconscious, the externalized symbols of archetypal images and universal energies that reside in the deeper layers of the human psyche. Because myths originate in the images of the collective unconscious, mythological stories, rituals, and symbols have the power to constellate our own archetypal energies and lead us into deeper awareness of our inner world. One might say that mythology serves as an existential spark to ignite the fires in the caverns of the soul, providing us with the light we need to explore this primordial domain and thus deepen our spiritual lives. Or, to use another metaphor, mythology is an existential stimulant which awakens the archetypal forms of the inner life, releasing their energy and wisdom into our lives.

THE BREAKDOWN OF MYTH IN WESTERN CULTURE

In the nineteenth century, Nietzsche recognized the death of Western mythology and knew the abyss of despair this would open up for modern men and women. In *The Birth of Tragedy*, he wrote, "Man today, stripped of myth, stands famished among all his pasts and must dig frantically for roots, be it among the most remote antiquities."[8]

Carl Jung saw this same beast that "slouches toward Bethlehem," to use Yeats's image. In *Man and His Symbols* he wrote:

> Modern man does not understand how much his "rationalism" (which has destroyed his capacity to respond to numinous symbols and ideas) has put him at the mercy of the psychic "underworld." He has freed himself from "superstition" (or so he believes), but in the process he has lost his spiritual values to a positively dangerous degree. His moral and spiritual tradition has disintegrated, and he is now paying the price for this break-up in worldwide disorientation and dissociation. . . . We have stripped all things of their mystery and numinosity; nothing is holy any longer."[9]

Joseph Campbell agreed. He said that mythology supports civilization and when a culture loses its myths, deterioration is the result. He wrote:

> We have seen what has happened, for example, to primitive communities unsettled by the white man's civilization. With their old taboos discredited, they immediately go to pieces, disintegrate, and become resorts of vice and disease. . . . Today the same thing is happening to us. With our old mythologically founded taboos unsettled by our own modern sciences, there is everywhere in the civilized world a rapidly rising incidence of vice and crime, mental disorders, suicides and dope addictions, shattered homes, impudent children, violence, murder, and despair.[10]

As Campbell indicates, the crux of our modern problem is that science has dispelled many of the myths we once believed. Until the modern era, we took our myths literally and viewed them as divine revelations, factual accounts of the universe and the workings of God. When the findings of science undermined the literal truth of these myths, millions of people in Western culture concluded that there was nothing left to believe in, nothing to hold on to. As Nietzsche put it, we lost our mythic home, our mythic womb.[11] Science, with its emphasis on empirical facts, displaced "superstitious" belief systems that could not stand the critique of research and reason. Mythology was viewed as nothing more than another form of superstition, an inaccurate and outdated description of how the universe works. And so in the scientific age we have managed to pull the mythological rug out from under ourselves. By destroying our mythology, we have destroyed the cohesive center of our culture. The result is that our society is disintegrating. "The center cannot hold," as Yeats said, and the centrifugal forces of our times are causing pieces to fly off in all directions.

Now, as the modern age ends and we enter the postmodern period, it appears that we may have placed too much trust in science and reason. Ironically, we made them into the mythological gods of the modern era, but it now appears our scientific gods have feet of clay. We placed so much trust in reason, objectivity, and the scientific method providing the route to absolute truth, that we completely ignored other epistemological approaches and disparaged entire realms of human experience that would not fit neatly into that paradigm, including such things as mythology and the soul. As a result, our society has lost contact with the sacred dimension and is now falling apart. As Rollo May said:

> When we in the twentieth century are so concerned about proving that our technical reason is right and we wipe away in one fell swoop the "silliness" of myths, we also rob our own souls and we threaten to destroy our society as part of the same deterioration."[12]

When mythology dies, life loses its sustenance. Man does not live by bread alone, and so also the soul cannot live off science, reason, logic, and linear thought. She requires story, ritual, symbol, and other expressions of the mythic imagination. Without a life-giving river of mythology, existence becomes a desert, passion dies, creativity evaporates, and meaning turns to dust. As Joseph Campbell said, "Hell is life drying up."[13]

To see what happens when a culture loses its mythology, one only has to look at the Native Americans. One of the great tragedies of American history is the way the white man systematically destroyed the Native American mythology and traditions. As the American nation established itself on the East Coast and pressed westward across the continent, the government felt perfectly justified in taking Native American lands, confining the people to reservations, placing their children in schools, and destroying the people if they fought back. We stole their lands and undermined their traditions. To see the result, one only has to look at the desolation evident on many reservations—the poor living conditions, the high levels of alcoholism, the loss of pride, the absence of traditional rituals, and the general destruction of the cultures that once flourished across this country.

STORY

Story is an essential dimension of mythology. Before humans learned to write, stories were memorized and passed orally from generation to generation and were the primary vehicles for transmitting the history, values, and traditions of a culture. For thousands of years, human beings sat around campfires listening to storytellers weave their magical tales. In ancient Greece, some of the world's first playwrights transformed story into its more complex form, the play. Actors strode across the stage and invited audiences into a make-believe world where the ancient story was taking place now instead of in the past. In our own time, this ancient art form has found new expression through radio, television, and movies. In the early days of radio, families and neighbors would sit around this new invention listening to the stream of stories created by the writers for this new medium, just as their ancestors once sat around campfires. And when television came along, story-telling was again transformed. No longer limited to sound alone, television writers now became modern playwrights, turning out episode after episode of stories, programs that viewers could both see and hear. Movies, which began as silent stories told in visual images, have become one of the most sophisticated and complex art forms of our day.

With the invention of writing, early historians and poets were able to record facts, stories, and poems that, once written down, required no storyteller. Those who could decipher those strange markings on the clay tablets or the papyrus or the vellum were able to enter the world of the storyteller and through their imaginations, ignited by the written word, could entertain themselves, experience deep emotions, and add to their understanding of the world. In those early days, it must have seemed strange indeed to those who could not read or write to see someone sitting alone, poring over such marks, and periodically stopping to laugh, cry, or gaze off into the distance with a look that said he was in another world. But such is the magical power of the word and the human imagination. In the beginning was the Word and the Word was with God and the Word was God. Today, in the modern literate world, story and the word remain staples of our imaginative worlds. Thousands of novels are published each year, and millions of people around the world read them sitting on park benches, curled up before fireplaces, relaxing on beaches—even during lunch breaks at work.

Story is a powerful medium. Research experiments on neural activity have shown that when one is reading a story, both hemispheres of the brain are active; whereas, when a subject is given technical material to read, there is relatively little neural activity and it is concentrated in the left hemisphere. Thus, it seems our brains are evolutionarily "hard-wired" to process stories. This, no doubt, is the reason we remember the stories a speaker tells long after we forget the more abstract points she made. This may also explain why children are enchanted by stories, especially when told by someone with dramatic storytelling abilities. It also helps to explain why the media spend billions of dollars every year turning out stories for our entertainment and education. Both neurologically and archetypally, we seem to be predisposed to the impact of story.

Personification—the ascribing to an abstract idea or image the attributes of a person—is part of what makes stories so powerful. For example, we speak of "Father Time" or "Mother Earth" or "Baby New Year." Gods and goddesses, also, are personifications of principles; while theologians and philosophers often remind us that the word God points to a mystery so deep that it can never be captured in human form, most of us continue to personify God. While the mind can certainly handle abstract symbols, personification seems to be a more powerful and primordial form of human thinking and speaks to the soul in ways that abstractions cannot. Mythology and the stories which comprise it are replete with personifications. This is, no doubt, one reason why mythology touches us at such profound levels and why we are so fascinated by these ancient stories. Personification is one of the dialects of the soul; it is congruent with the imaginal and poetic nature of the deeper levels of the psyche.

RITUAL

Campbell said, "A ritual can be defined as an enactment of a myth. By participating in a ritual, you are actually experiencing a mythological life, and it's out of that participation that one can learn to live spiritually."[14]

All societies have rituals. There are rituals connected with birth, puberty, marriage, death, and other major life events. There are rituals associated with education, religion, medicine, the military, the courts, and with practically every other cultural institution and arena. Ritual serves many social functions: it provides structure, promotes social cohesion, and marks important events.

A primary function of ritual is to mark transition. Puberty rites move the adolescent out of childhood into adulthood. The wedding ceremony changes one's status from single to married. Most religions have formal ceremonies that mark the transition from one's old life into a new life as a believer. Transition rituals have two major elements—death to the old reality and passage into the new. For example, in Western culture the wedding ceremony usually begins with the bride coming down the aisle on the arm of her father, signifying the old reality of her status as a daughter, a member of her father and mother's family. But as the ceremony begins, severance with the old reality takes place. The father gives away the bride, takes his seat, and his daughter takes her place at the side of her husband-to-be. The ceremony continues, culminating as the new reality begins with the words "I now pronounce you husband and wife." The reception is a way of celebrating and further solidifying the new reality from a social perspective; the honeymoon is an opportunity for the couple to establish their new reality in a private context. "Old things have passed away; behold all things are become new" is the maxim that describes the work of transition rituals.

I believe we miss the deeper meaning of ritual if we view it only in terms of its social functions. In its purest form, a ritual is a mystical act that connects us with the sacred. Like mythology, ritual is based on the assumption that there is an invisible world that lies beyond the one in which we live our lives. And whether we call this world the sacred, the spiritual, or the unseen dimension, ritual is a primary route to that world, a way of making direct contact with the eternal verities pointed to by the stories and symbols of mythology.

But more than this, many rituals are designed to affect or influence the unseen world. For example, the ritual of Catholic confession is designed to take away the penitent's sins so that they exist no more in the eternal record of God. And the rituals associated with Yom Kippur, the Jewish Day of Atonement, are likewise designed to erase the sins of the people and reestablish their "at-one-ment" with the Lord. When one stops to ponder this, one realizes that the mystical and psychological power of ritual is quite incredible. All of us know that there is a sense in which moral mistakes cannot be undone. If we have done an unworthy thing, simply confessing it and seeking forgiveness does not change that fact. Yet ritual takes us into a timeless place where reality is malleable, where the mistakes or shameful realities of our lives can be wiped away as though they never occurred. As Campbell said, "Ritual belongs to the nonhistorical dimension of existence."[15] Ritual has the power to bring grace into our lives and restore hope, giving us a chance to rewrite the story of our lives. To put this in nontheological language, one could say that rituals are mystical events designed to affect the ontological reality of our lives, a way to reconnect with the Ground of Being and to find the forgiveness and acceptance we need in order to try again. So to understand the meaning of ritual, one must attend to its mystical power as a path to the sacred.

SYMBOL

One of the early meanings of the word *symbol* is quite striking. In ancient Greece the word referred to a token of identity verified by comparing it with its other half. In those days, before driver's licenses, passports, or social security numbers for identification, when it was important to ensure the identity of someone, one way to do this was to break an object in two, give the person half and send the other half on ahead to the party that would be meeting him. Once he arrived, the receiving party could compare the stranger's half of the object with their own, thus verifying that he was indeed who he claimed to be. While we don't use this method of identification now, the idea is still around. For example, lovers sometimes share a heart-shaped piece of jewelry which symbolizes their relationship. The heart is in two pieces, and each partner keeps a piece.

Another meaning of *symbol* comes from the etymology of the word and was pointed out by Rollo May: it comes from two Greek words, *syn* and *ballein*, and means "to draw together."[16]

As both of the above definitions imply, a symbol is something that points beyond itself, just as one half of the heart-shaped piece of jewelry implies that someone holds the other half. This is the basic difference between a religious symbol and an idol. An idol does not point beyond itself; the believer is asked to worship it, rather than to look through it to the transcendent. The reason idolatry is condemned in the Old Testament is because the worshipper's consciousness is focused on the graven image rather than on God. A religious symbol, on the other hand, points to the sacred; it calls for the believer to look through it to the transcendent which it represents.

Another characteristic of a symbol is that it participates in that which it symbolizes, as Tillich said.[17] That is, the symbol is not only a sign pointing to something beyond; it also partakes of the nature of what it points to, like the sacred objects in indigenous tribes which are imbued with mana. To the Christian believer, the cross is not simply two juxtaposed pieces of wood, nor even a sign reminding one of Jesus. Because the cross participates in that which it symbolizes, it has sacred power, or numinosity, for the believer; it has the power to touch, stir, and move the soul. Just as an ordinary piece of iron can be magnetized by placing it in contact with a powerful magnet, a symbol, which is usually an ordinary object, is "magnetized" by the power and being of that which it represents. Carrying this metaphor a step further, one could say that the believer's soul, in the presence of the symbol, feels this magnetic power and is drawn toward God. Thus the symbol draws together the soul and the transcendent.

Another characteristic of a symbol is that it doesn't stand for one idea or a single truth, but always holds a multiplicity of meanings. As May said, "Symbols speak on several levels at once" and encompass a "multitude of dimensions."[18]

While I had no words to describe my understanding at the time, even as a child I intuitively sensed that linear truths and singular ideas were too narrow and confining. I was always drawn to symbols and found them more congruent with my own intuitive perception of the world precisely because I sensed the diversity of meanings they represent. While some people seem to be born with a linear, analytic, "one truth" approach to life, perhaps others are born with an intuitive sense that the world is pluralistic and that a singular truth, as convincing as it appears, is only one of many possibilities that lie deep in the psyche, only waiting for someone to name them and bring them into actualization. Each of us "contains multitudes," but we tend to construct only certain singular truths by drawing out from the primordial region of the soul only that which fits with the assumptions of our culture or our own epistemological methodology. Just as someone fishing in the ocean might pull up one particular fish and insist that it is the only kind of fish in the sea, so we may pull up one truth and forget that the psyche is a deep ocean filled with a multiplicity of potential truths. Because they engage the multiplicity of the human psyche, symbols enlarge the soul's possibilities and remind us of a pluralistic perspective that Western culture seems to have forgotten.

Finally, symbols unlock levels of reality and regions of the soul that would not be available to us otherwise. Tillich said:

> All arts create symbols for a level of reality which cannot be reached in any other way. A picture and a poem reveal elements of reality which cannot be approached scientifically. In the creative work of art we encounter reality in a dimension which is closed for us without such works. [The symbol] also unlocks dimensions and elements of our soul which correspond to the dimensions and elements of reality. A great play gives us not only a new vision of the human scene, but it opens up hidden depths of our own being.[19]

Here is the power of symbol as a tool for soul-making. Symbols give us access to dimensions of the soul that cannot be reached in any other way. They awaken psychic potentialities that lie in the unconscious depths of the soul and help us incorporate these new regions of experience into our conscious life. Thus symbols illumine our inner life and enlarge our souls.

MYTHOLOGY AS A PATH TO THE SACRED

Because it reflects the archetypal patterns of the human psyche, mythology has the power to stimulate, awaken, and nurture the soul. If understood properly and used wisely, mythology can help us with soul-making and serve as a path to the sacred.

Inner Gods and Goddesses

In recent years we have seen the publication of various books which approach mythology from an archetypal perspective and encourage readers to develop the deeper potentials of their psyche by conscious attention to the various gods and goddesses of ancient mythology.[20] Interpreted from a Jungian perspective, these divinities represent archetypal potentials within our own souls, and by attending to them we can awaken these energies and actualize the potentials represented by these divine images. In an age when we have forgotten the soul-making power of myth, such books are helpful.

However, those using mythology in this way must understand that archetypal images cannot be stimulated simply by reading about an ancient god or goddess and trying to emulate his or her character in one's life. This is not soul work; it is outward behavioral change unsupported by the life-changing power of an underlying archetypal constellation. Accessing the real soul-making power of an archetype requires the fire inherent in numinosity. Without this, one runs the risk of developing a persona which is not sustained from within. An example would be the popularity in recent years of the "wild woman" archetype, thanks to the book *Women Who Run with the Wolves*.[21] For women who were truly seized by this image, incorporating the powerful energies of the "wild woman" archetype into their lives became their soul work. But for other women whose response to the image was at the persona level, real numinosity and real passion were not generated. So even if these women changed their hairstyles or wore clothing that seemed to reflect a wilder nature, they were not really doing soul work. The image was affecting them only at the surface level; it was not reaching into the depths of their collective unconscious and generating archetypal power and heat. Archetypal change occurs when an archetype "grabs" us, when it glows with numinosity in us, when we can feel its power as it moves in the depths of our soul.

It is important, however, to expose ourselves to a wide range of archetypal symbols through mythology, literature, art, music, poetry, and other cultural manifestations of the inner life. Such exposure ensures that if archetypal energies are stirring within our souls below the level of awareness, they will have the opportunity to attach themselves to the outward symbol and, through this numinous union, begin to emerge.

Personal Mythology

In recent years there has been increasing interest in creating one's own personal mythology. Numerous books and workshops have been dedicated to this theme. In an age when cultural myths are dying, it makes sense that people would try to fill this vacuum by searching for ways to create personal mythological structures to undergird and give meaning to their lives. As May said, today each individual "is forced to do deliberately for himself what in previous ages had been done for him by family, custom, church, and state."[22]

The overarching myths of a culture have major impact on how individuals construct their personal myths; but today, because our cultural myths are in disarray, many people are experimenting with different identities and lifestyles, trying to find a personal mythology and way of being that gives them a sense of existential grounding. May pointed out that clients often use psychotherapy as a way to create new myths for their lives. For such clients, "myths may be a reaching out, a way of trying out new structures of life, or a desperate venture at rebuilding his or her broken way of life."[23]

While we may be able to create some personal myths which help orient our lives, this does not make up for the fact that our overarching myths have broken down and that we live in a time of cultural disorientation. Regardless of how hard we work on our personal mythology, I suspect we will not be able to escape the anxiety and groundlessness of our times.

Mythology in an Age of Doubt

Until recently, human beings took their myths literally, believing them to be factual accounts of the gods and the forces that shape human life. Undoubtedly, this belief helped unlock the power of myth by exalting it to the status of divine revelation and infusing it with sacred and mystical significance. But today we live in an age when rationality undermines the literal understanding of myth. So for those who would use myth as a path to the sacred, the crucial question is whether or not mythology will yield up its soul-nurturing power to those who no longer believe in its literal truth. Or to put it another way, is the consciousness of a "true believer" the only key that can unlock the power of myth, or are there other ways to access myth's energy when one no longer accepts myth literally?

Campbell addressed this question head-on. He acknowledged that life seems to require the "life-supporting illusions" of mythology and pointed out that symbols interpreted literally support civilization. He said that "where these have been dispelled, there is nothing secure to hold on to, no moral law, nothing firm."[24] At the same time, Campbell was an ardent supporter of modern science and believed one must not ignore its findings and retreat into "patterns of archaic feeling and thought inappropriate to contemporary life." Campbell framed the issues and set forth our modern dilemma in a nutshell: we need the cultural cohesion that comes from a mythology believed literally, but we can no longer believe in mythology's literal truth because science has shown it to be false. Do we give our loyalty to the myths that sustain our civilization, or to the findings of science? Hinting at a possible way out of this dilemma, Campbell asked, "Are the two, on level, at odds? Or is there not some point of wisdom beyond the conflicts of illusion and truth by which lives can be put back together again?"

Campbell believed the solution to this dilemma is to be found in psychology. He said, "It is my considered belief that the best answer to this critical problem will come from the findings of psychology, and specifically those findings having to do with the source and nature of myth." He suggested that psychologists and comparative mythologists should work together to understand the nature and functions of mythic symbols. Referring to the psychology of Jung, who believed mythology's value lay in its power to illumine the inner life, Campbell wrote:

Our outward-oriented consciousness, addressed to the demands of
the day, may lose touch with these inward forces; and the myths,
states Jung, when correctly read, are the means to bring us back
in touch. They are telling us in picture language of powers of the
psyche to be recognized and integrated in our lives, powers that have
been common to the human spirit forever, and which represent that
wisdom of the species by which man has weathered the millenniums.
Thus they have not been, and can never be, displaced by the findings of science, which relate rather to the outside world than to the
depths that we enter in sleep. Through a dialogue conducted with
these inward forces through our dreams and through a study of
myths, we can learn to know and come to terms with the greater
horizon of our own deeper and wiser, inward self. And analogously,
the society that cherishes and keeps its myths alive will be nourished
from the soundest, richest strata of the human spirit.[25]

So both Campbell and Jung believed that we can accept both science and mythology. While science has undermined the literal truth of
our myths, it has not touched the existential wisdom they contained,
nor has it taken away mythology's power to constellate and illumine
our inner life.

In fact, mythology has always been about the inner life, for it is
a projection into the world of our deepest archetypal patterns. But
it is only in the modern age that we have become aware of this
psychic trick that our collective unconscious played on us. Until the
modern era, we believed that our mythological projections were flesh
and blood realities. It was the findings of modern science, coupled
with the explanations of depth psychology, that finally pulled the
wool from our eyes and made us aware of what humankind has
been doing for thousands of years. So now we can return to mythology with a fuller consciousness of its origins and functions and use
it for what it is, a map of our inner world and a tool for exploring the
deeper dimensions of the soul. One does not have to believe in the
literal truth of the myth, which means believing in its projected form,
in order to benefit from its soul-illumining and soul-making power.
Since mythic images point to dimensions of our own inner life, we can
use these images in soul work. This use of mythology does not depend
on true-believer consciousness; one does not have to believe in the
literal truth of the mythological symbol in order to benefit from its
numinosity.

Just as one can attend a play, knowing it is not "real," yet can still enter a state of receptive consciousness which allows the play to touch and move the soul, so one can approach mythology with an open heart and allow oneself to be drawn into its magical power to enchant and illumine the inner life. Mythology, its secret finally revealed and its literal truth stripped away by modern science, has the last laugh. For the stripping away has only served to reveal its authentic origin and function, which have to do with the inner life of the soul. And while something may be forfeited in the loss of belief in the literal truth of mythology, perhaps, in balance, it is not so bad to learn that the treasures we once thought lay in some far away place are actually within the immediate depths of our own souls.

Can mythology nurture the soul of one who no longer believes its literal truth? The answer is a resounding "Yes!" In fact, I believe this perspective represents a higher level of spiritual maturity, because it forces us to stop seeking the source of our spirituality in gods outside of us and makes us realize that those gods are really planes of experience that exist in the recesses of our own souls. Mythology opens us to the unfathomable depths of our own spiritual nature; and this, it seems to me, is what authentic spirituality is all about.

Quite apart from our religion
There are plum blossoms
There are cherry blossoms.
—Nanpoku

PATH SIX

NATURE
The Path of the Earth and Heavens

Henry David Thoreau first saw Walden Pond when he was five years old on a trip with his family from Boston. This small lake of about sixty acres in size, located in the woods outside Concord, Massachusetts, had a profound impact on the young Thoreau. Later, he would write in his journal, "That woodland vision for a long time made the drapery of my dreams."[1] In 1845, twenty-three years after his first visit, Thoreau built a hut near the pond and lived there for two years by himself. During this period of solitude, he communed with nature and recorded his thoughts and observations. *Walden* has become an American classic. It continues to awaken and express, in a most powerful way, our love and longing for the earth.

In one of *Walden*'s best-known passages, Thoreau explained why he dropped out of society to live at Walden Pond. He wrote, "I went to the woods because I wished to live deliberately, to front only the essential facts of life, and see if I could not learn what it had to teach, and not, when I came to die, discover that I had not lived."[2]

For Thoreau, nature was the temple of God. While others went to church, Thoreau would take walks through the woods and fields around Concord. He viewed nature as the perennial source of life, and he wanted to be near it "as the willow stands near the water and sends out its roots in that direction."[3] Thoreau's love affair with nature lasted throughout his lifetime. In the final years of his life, he wrote little that was of public significance, but he kept a private journal filled with observations and descriptions of nature. Thoreau knew from direct experience that nature is a path to the sacred, a way to nourish the soul.

OUR LONGING FOR NATURE

Like Thoreau, we all have a longing for the natural world. Each spring, millions of Americans take out their garden tools, fall to their knees, and work the soil in suburban yards, flower beds, and "postage-stamp" vegetable gardens. Every weekend the highways near urban areas are jammed as people who have been cooped up in a world of concrete and asphalt all week pour out of the cities toward lakes, rivers, mountains, beaches, and deserts. In the summer months many of our national parks and campgrounds are filled to capacity.

At some level we all know that nature is the perennial source of life, the nourisher of both body and soul. We are all *pagans* in the original sense of the word, meaning "country dwellers" or "people of the earth." We all come from the earth, depend on it while we are here, and return to it when we die. Narritjin Maynuru Yirrkala, an Australian aborigine, said, "We belong to the ground. It is our power. And we must stay close to it or maybe we will get lost."[4]

OUR ORIGINAL CONNECTION WITH THE EARTH

For thousands of years as our species evolved, we lived close to the earth and in consonance with the rhythms of nature. We knew in our blood the movement of the moon and stars, the rising and setting of the sun, the changing of the seasons. We slept when it was dark, arose when the sun came up, ate directly from the earth, drank from her streams, and ordered our lives by the seasons of the year. We were nomadic, lived in tribes, and ate berries, nuts, fruits, and roots on our journeys. We were hunters and gatherers, and, eventually, herders and farmers. But always, from our earliest beginnings to recent times, we lived in direct contact with the earth and under the sacred canopy of the heavens.

In ancient times, humans not only lived close to nature but actually worshipped her as the source of all. In early agrarian societies, nature was regarded as the Great Mother whose fertile womb produced the grains, vegetables, and fruits that sustained human life. Storms, earthquakes, and volcanoes were signs of her wrath or fury. Certain rivers, mountains, natural formations, and groves of trees were regarded as sacred, and ancient people went to these places to commune with the earth and absorb her divine energies. In these early societies, one's religion was synonymous with one's relationship with nature, because nature and the Goddess were one.

Estrangement from Nature

But with the coming of the modern age, we began to lose our connection with nature. In our own country, as the Industrial Revolution gained momentum, people left the farms and rural areas to work in the factories. They moved away from a life close to nature to become cogs in an industrial machine that produced other machines and products for human consumption. Some of those in the cities remembered their roots, the childhoods spent roaming the open fields, walking through the woods, and swimming in the creeks and rivers. On vacations they took their children back to grandparents' farms, to national parks, or to other places in nature, hoping to show their children the wonders of their own childhood experiences. But as generations passed, the majority of Americans have gradually lost contact with their rural past and become increasingly estranged from nature. They are unfamiliar with the music of crickets, the croaking of frogs, and the cry of whippoorwills in the dark. No longer can they name the constellations or describe the phases of the moon. No longer can they draw comfort from the sounds of the night, but are startled if an owl hoots outside their bedroom window. Sleep is conditioned to the sounds of traffic, horns, and sirens, not to the relative silence and gentle sounds of the country. After living with nature for thousands of years, human beings were cut off from the earth in a split second of evolutionary time, wrenched from the arms of the mother that had given them birth.

According to some scholars, our estrangement from nature began when patriarchal religions, with their masculine, warrior-like gods, replaced the Goddess religions, which had regarded the earth as the Great Mother. In *The Chalice and the Blade* Riane Eisler says that patriarchal invaders overran the peaceful agrarian communities and set up their own masculine gods.[5] Eisler identifies Yahweh, the God of the

Hebrews, as one of those gods and traces the patriarchal attitudes of Judaism and Christianity to these early beginnings. Experts in ancient religions such as Marija Gimbutas, who worked at both Harvard and UCLA, and Joseph Campbell, widely regarded as the most knowledgeable mythologist of this century, share Eisler's basic view that Goddess religions eventually gave way to patriarchal religions.[6] The ancient Hebrews, it seems, were especially intent on eliminating the Goddess and all signs of nature worship. Yahweh was a jealous and wrathful god who insisted that he was the only true God and sanctioned the destruction of those who disagreed. Yahweh had no wife or female counterpart. Among his followers there seems to have been little respect for women or for the feminine principle. Men were accorded superior status and women were regarded as inferior, existing primarily to serve men.

This patriarchal outlook had a major impact on the way nature was regarded. While the agrarian communities worshipped nature as the embodiment of the Goddess, the patriarchal nomads regarded nature in a more secular and functional way. They were herders of animals, and their nomadic lifestyle brought them into conflict with others. Thus they became adept at fighting and developed weapons of war. Unlike the Goddess, Yahweh was not considered to be immanent in the creation; he was *supernatural*—literally, "above nature." Yahweh created the world, it belonged to him, and he therefore had the right to do with it as he pleased—including giving it to his people. They, in turn, had the right to own and use the land. Thus, under Yahweh's religion, nature was objectified and was no longer regarded as the sacred body of the Goddess.

By the time the Book of Genesis was written, this estrangement from nature had become the new order. After creating Adam and Eve, God told them, "Be fruitful and multiply and replenish the earth, and subdue it: and have dominion over the fish of the sea, and over the fowl of the air, and over every living thing that moves upon the earth." This is the language of patriarchy—the language of war, domination, and territorial kingship. These are not the words of the Goddess religions; they do not reflect an attitude of reverence for nature, a desire to live in sacred harmony with the Mother and Source of all.

Some of the stories in the early chapters of Genesis may have been specifically designed to discredit attitudes common in the Goddess religions. For example, the story of the Garden of Eden tells how the serpent tempted Eve to eat of the forbidden tree and how Eve, in turn, tempted Adam. The serpent, an important symbol in Goddess religions, is blamed, along with the first woman, for the fall of man.

The story of Cain and Abel, the sons of Adam and Eve, can be read as a story of conflict between the nomadic herders who worshipped Yahweh and the agrarian people, generally associated with the Goddess. Abel was a "keeper of the flock," and Cain was a "tiller of the ground." Each of them brought an offering to God, Abel bringing the "firstlings of his flock" and Cain bringing the "fruit of the ground." The Bible says, "The Lord had respect for Abel and his offering, but for Cain and his offering he had not respect."

Of course, these interpretations are speculative. It is difficult, if not impossible, to reconstruct ancient history in such detail that we can know the motives behind these old stories. But it does seem clear that the Goddess religions, with their reverence for the earth, were replaced by patriarchal religions, which emphasized the domination and subduing of the earth.

DOMINION OVER THE EARTH

I am convinced that the Biblical injunction to dominate and subdue the earth has helped create and maintain one of the most damaging attitudes possible in regard to our relationship with nature. It has allowed us to regard nature as existing simply for our sake, a "store of resources to be used up," as Sam Keene put it.[7] In the name of science, progress, and technology we have subjugated nature, forcing her to yield up her virgin timberlands, rich soil, clean rivers, sparkling lakes, verdant rain forests, clear atmosphere, pure water, and countless species of animal and plant life. We in the First World, consumed with consumerism, continue to exploit Third World countries so that we can feed our voracious appetites. We euphemistically rename these countries "developing nations" as we bring them our science, technology, and corporate attitudes of rape and plunder. Yet in doing so, we change and even destroy traditional cultures which have lived without our brand of progress for thousands of years. Today there is hardly a place on earth that has not been scratched, mauled, or gutted. As we look at the great, bleeding wounds of the planet, it seems we have finally fulfilled the Biblical injunction to dominate the earth. Perhaps in the Christian year of A.D. 2000 we should raise a great marker, draped in black, on some international piece of ground, with an inscription that reads: "Matricide: nature, at last, has been subdued."

Certainly modern science and technology have made wonderful contributions to our culture, and most of us have no desire to return to primeval times. But we must look at the assumptions underlying science and the way we use it. Grounded in the principles of objectivity and the subject-object dichotomy, Western science contains many of the same attitudes toward nature found in the Western religions' disposition to subdue the earth. Lorraine Anderson wrote, "Francis Bacon, the principal founder of modern science, described nature as a woman and defined science as a quest to capture her, subdue her, and wrest her secrets from her."[8] By viewing nature as an object to be studied, measured, dominated, and controlled, science and technology have contributed to our estrangement from the earth.

Men with picks and shovels, axes and crosscut saws, guns and fishing nets were limited in the violence they could do to the earth. But the Industrial Revolution gave us the machine, the ultimate weapon for dominating and subduing the earth. The machine can destroy entire rain forests, plow millions of acres to dust, change the course of rivers, and bite into the earth with drag lines the size of football fields. They also provide a sense of anonymity and separation from the violent deed. When a man uses an ax or crosscut saw to cut into a redwood that has stood for two thousand years, he sees the wound he makes; it is "up close and personal," like hand-to-hand combat in war. But with the machine, an entire rain forest can fall at the command of a corporate bureaucracy thousands of miles away and no one seems to be responsible. The corporate bureaucracy, insulated by its protective circle of lawyers, is almost impenetrable; and the machine operators and on-site crew—those who inflict the damage—insist that they are just ordinary folks doing what they are told.

THE OBJECTIFICATION OF NATURE

Forty years ago, Alan Watts warned that objectification is the major problem in Western culture's relationship with nature. Objectification allows us to distance ourselves from nature, to see her as a collection of objects "to be conquered and reordered, to be made subject to the technology of the rational intellect."[9] Watts said we must realize that "nature is ordered organically rather than politically, that it is a field of relationships rather than a collection of things." The objectification of nature is based on the delusion that human beings are not in the loop, that we have somehow managed to transcend nature and can therefore sit godlike and removed as we observe, manipulate, and exploit her. But Watts reminds us that "man is a loop in the endless knot, and as he pulls in one direction he finds that he is pulled from another and cannot find the origin of the impulse."

Because everything is connected to everything else and because we know so little about this relational complexity, we are taking enormous risks when we exploit any resource. As Watts said, we have only "the most fragmentary knowledge of the complex relationships so disturbed." Rachel Carson, author of *Silent Spring,* was known as the grandmother of the environmental movement and was awarded the Presidential Medal of Freedom posthumously in 1980. She warned us of the unforeseeable dangers of disturbing nature's delicate balance.[10] Today, ecological textbooks contain countless examples of how seemingly benign acts have had disastrous consequences for the ecological balance in various regions of the world. To think that we can control nature and direct her course may be the most dangerous delusion in the history of the world.

While we may think that we are separate from nature, the truth is that we, too, are embedded in her complex relational network. We are only one species among million of others which nature has produced. Perhaps this is the most important lesson of Darwin's thesis: we are nothing more and nothing less than one of earth's countless offspring. The fact that we learned to walk upright and developed what we consider a rather complex brain may be nothing more than an evolutionary experiment. If we are foolish enough to turn this small, calculating brain against nature, I suspect she will find a way to diminish us. We must realize that nature is the parent here and we are the children. She has been around for billions of years, and we are only a blip on the evolutionary screen. Therefore, the proper attitude toward nature is humility, along with a certain gratitude that she has allowed us to rise out of the primordial darkness to see the light of day.

I am connected to everything else. Who I am does not stop at my skin, but extends outward through a complex matrix of interconnectedness to encompass the entire universe. I interact with and interpenetrate my environment as I inhale and exhale, drink water, and eat food. Carbon, a major building block of life and one of the oldest elements, was created in the incredible blast of the Big Bang. The stars are made of carbon, and so am I. The same God that hurled the stars into the vast darkness of space also bent over my body and sprinkled "star stuff" into my bones and flesh. Thus, I am a sibling of the stars, the sun, and the galaxies. We have the same parent, share the same origins, come from the same womb.

So perhaps St. Francis, the nature-loving mystic of Assisi, knew something we have forgotten when he called the celestial bodies of our sky "Brother Sun" and "Sister Moon." And maybe Thoreau, too, was right when he asked how we can possibly be lonely as long as we can look up into the night sky and see the dancing lights of the Milky Way.[11] Compassion for nature grows out of awareness of our interconnectedness with everything that exists. As a friend of mine put it, "If you objectify something, you can imagine that it's separate from you, so it's easier to use, hurt, or abuse it. But if you are intimately connected with something, it becomes part of you, and to hurt it hurts yourself."

In 1997, thirty-nine people committed mass suicide near San Diego, only forty minutes' drive from where I live. As I watched the videos some of them had made before their deaths, I was struck by their sense of estrangement from this planet. They did not feel part of this earth; they felt it was not their home. So they fell for a scheme that told them they could escape this world by killing themselves and being whisked away on the tail of a comet. This is one of the problems with belief systems which emphasize how much better things will be somewhere else; they tend to alienate us from the earth, making us believe this world is not our home. While I would not deny the possibility of life after death, all I can know for sure is that right now, in this moment, I am alive. And this blue planet, endlessly circling the sun, with its oceans, mountains, prairies, and deserts, is both my mother and my home. In 1945 she gave me birth, has now sustained me for more than fifty years, and someday, not too many years from now, I will be buried in her crust. For comrades she has surrounded me with a collage of flowers, trees, woods, streams, animals, birds, fish, and human companions, including a wife and two sons whom I love more than life itself.

I have no desire to catch a comet, go to Mars, or take up residence in some other distant place. I love this earth and want to live these short years with gratitude and appreciation. I truly want to leave this planet in good shape—not only because she is my mother, but also because I have three grandchildren who will drink the water, breathe the air, and eat the food of this earth. I don't want to take the risks of participating in a scheme that might poison, pollute, or destroy this human habitat. I want future generations to have a good place to live.

A CHANGE IN SPIRITUAL CONSCIOUSNESS

So what is to be done? How can we re-sacralize our attitudes toward nature and begin to see her as a path to the sacred? In his book *Earth Memory*, Paul Devereux says that for this change to occur, a radical shift in spiritual consciousness is required.[12] He is well aware of those who denounce spiritual approaches, insisting that "modern science and technology will triumph over the problems we face; that there will be a technological fix." He points out, on the other hand, that "this attitude is rapidly losing its appeal for many people who are seeing with increasing clarity the environmental mess our technology, our applied science, is creating under the present worldview." Devereux does not believe that science or other mainstream institutions of society will save the earth. Rather, he believes that what is required is nothing less than a fundamental change in consciousness, a major reorientation in the way we view nature. He said, "It is our mentality, literally our worldview, which needs healing in the first instance. The environmental healing will then be a natural consequence."

Devereux believes there are hopeful signs that this change in consciousness has already begun. He points, for example, to the increased ecological awareness that has led to the various "green" movements, to the widespread interest in the wisdom of traditional cultures, and to the New Age movement's interest in healing the earth—although he fears that New Agers sometimes forget that it is we, rather than the earth, who need to be healed. Devereux also views the various pagan and goddess movements in a positive light, seeing them as "a manifestation of a profoundly deep memory within humanity: the essentially universal Earth religion."

COMMUNION WITH NATURE

If what is called for is a radical change in consciousness, how do we bring about such a change in ourselves? How does one who was raised to objectify nature, who has always felt separated and estranged from her, go about changing those basic attitudes?

It will not happen by simply reading books on ecology. Today there are thousands of books and articles on ecology and hundreds of scientists who have dedicated themselves to the study of environmental issues. This work is crucial, and I admire those who are doing the research and amassing the data that can direct us to saner policies in our treatment of the earth. But more than information is required if we are to change our basic attitude toward nature. We must lay down our textbooks and enter into a personal, communal relationship with her. This is what has been lost, and this is what must be restored. Nature has secrets she only reveals in the context of an intimate relationship with her. It is only there that we discover her sacred character.

Communion with nature involves letting go of our objectifying attitudes and opening our souls to her depth, beauty, darkness, and power. It requires a more poetic, mystical, feminine, intuitive, meditative, and intimate way of relating. Walt Whitman understood these matters. He wrote:

> When I heard the learn'd astronomer,
> When the proofs, the figures, were ranged in columns
>   before me,
> When I was shown the charts and diagrams, to add, divide,
>   and measure them,
> When I sitting heard the astronomer where he lectured
>   with much applause in the lecture-room,
> How soon unaccountable I became tired and sick,
> Till rising and gliding out I wander'd off by myself,
> In the mystical moist night-air, and from time to time,
> Look'd up in perfect silence at the stars.[13]

This poem, properly understood and applied, contains all the wisdom we need to change our consciousness and make nature a path to the sacred. But like the "learn'd astronomer," too many of us approach nature with charts and diagrams instead of opening our souls to the perfect silence of the stars. While objective approaches have their place, communion means leaving the lecture hall and going out into the mystical, moist night air, where nature reveals herself directly to the soul that is open to wonder and awe. Communion means approaching nature with a soul-based reflectiveness that is willing to wait, listen, and allow nature to reveal herself in her own way, in her own time. Communion involves an attitude of not imposing, a lack of predetermined categories, and even a sort of "philosophical vagueness," as Alan Watts called it. Of course, to the tough-minded, aggressive Western realist, this makes no sense; surely research, measurement, precision, and hard-edged clarity are always preferable to vagueness. But in some arenas of life the hard-nosed approach simply does not work. Intimate human relationships, for example, require a completely different approach, and so does our relationship with nature. To know her deepest secrets, we must be willing to enter a communal relationship with her, reaching out with what Watts called "a warm, melting, vaguely defined, and caressing touch."[14]

In other words, communion involves a tender-minded way of perceiving, a comfortableness with what is misty, vague, obscure, mystical, and indistinct. Watts suggested that Eastern cultures are more at home with the subtle dimension of life, more attuned to the beauty of mist-covered mountains or the flight of wild geese half-hidden in the clouds, while Western culture produces a "brash kind of personality" which is "ever ready to rush in and clean up the mystery, to find out just precisely where the wild geese have gone." He also said, "It is just this attitude which every traditional culture finds utterly insufferable in Western man, not just because it is tactless and unrefined, but because it is blind. It cannot tell the difference between the surface and the depth."[15]

What we are talking about here is an alternative way of knowing. Communion is an effort to overcome the subject-object split and to open ourselves to the oneness and interconnectedness of all things. Frankly, most Westerners do not know how to do this. We have been shaped by a culture that idealizes objectivity and denigrates subjectivity. Consequently, we are estranged from our own inner experience and cannot rely on it as a way of knowing the world. Instead, we have learned to rely on the ego—the rational-logical-analytic mind—which allows us to operate in the world without really "being there" in body or soul. The glorification of objectivity, an attitude so dominant in all areas of Western life, can only occur in a culture in which individuals are estranged from themselves, cut off from their own subjectivity. No wonder other cultures think us strange. The idea that life can be lived in the head, without any real need for body, soul, and emotions, is indeed strange.

Martin Buber was well aware of these two fundamentally different approaches when he said we can have both I-It and I-Thou relationships with nature. In the I-It mode, nature is an object, a thing, and we retain an objective distance. In the I-Thou mode, we enter into a deeper type of relationship; the scaffolding of I-It falls away and we merge into unity with nature. As Buber put it:

> I contemplate a tree. . . . I can assign it to a species and observe it as an instance. . . . I can dissolve it into a number, into a pure relation between numbers, and externalize it. Throughout all this the tree remains my object and has its place and its time span, its kind and condition. But it can also happen, if will and grace are joined, that as I contemplate the tree I am drawn into a relation, and the tree ceases to be an It. The power of exclusiveness has seized me. This does not require me to forego any of the modes of contemplation. There is nothing that I must not see in order to see, and there is no knowledge that I must forget. Rather is everything, picture and movement, species and instance, law and number included and inseparably fused."[16]

Thoreau also understood the I-Thou relationship with nature. Some passages in *Walden* are pure communion. On one occasion, after he had been at the pond for a few weeks, Thoreau began to feel lonely and wondered if he could survive without others. But then something happened. He described the event:

> In the midst of a gentle rain while these thoughts prevailed, I was suddenly sensible of such sweet and beneficent society in Nature, in the very pattering of the drops, and in every sound and sight around my house, an infinite and unaccountable friendliness all at once like an atmosphere sustaining me, as made the fancied advantages of human neighborhood insignificant, and I have never thought of them since. Every little pine needle expanded and swelled with sympathy and befriended me. I was so distinctly made aware of the presence of something kindred to me, even in scenes which we are accustomed to call wild and dreary, and also that the nearest of blood to me and humanest was not a person nor a villager, that I thought no place could ever be strange to me again.[17]

Even if he had known the term, Thoreau might have been too modest to call this a peak experience. Yet clearly, he felt a nourishing communion with nature and was aware of a presence of something kindred to himself. From that time on, throughout his stay at Walden Pond, he never felt lonely again. To those who raised the topic, he replied, "Why should I feel lonely? Is not our planet in the Milky Way?"

Thoreau knew that poetic sensitivity was required to relate to nature. The scientist approaches nature with charts and measurements, the lumberjack with ax and saw; even farmers may view their farms as little more than means of production. But the poetic soul simply contemplates nature, communes with her, and receives her gifts. Thoreau wrote:

> I have frequently seen a poet withdraw, having enjoyed the most valuable part of a farm, while the crusty farmer supposed that he had got a few wild apples only. Why, the owner does not know it for many years when a poet has put his farm in rhyme, the most admirable kind of invisible fence, has fairly impounded it, milked it, skimmed it, and got all the cream, and left the farmer only the skimmed milk."[18]

STORIES OF COMMUNION

On the other hand, there are farmers and ranchers who have a poetic relationship with the land. I have a good friend who owns a ranch in northern Wyoming that was homesteaded by his grandparents in the early 1900s. The old adobe house, built by his grandfather, still stands only a few yards from the new house in which my friend, along with his wife and daughter, now lives. That ranch is in John's blood; he knows every hill, meadow, and clump of trees. He knows where the white-tail deer sleep, the fields where the sage grouse hatch their young, the varieties of grass and wildflowers that spread over the ranch. Sometimes he gets in his truck or rides his horse over the ranch just to see the beauty and richness of the land. If I told John that he had a poetic sensitivity and that he communed with the land, he would laugh at me for my "highfalutin" words; but he would know exactly what I meant and his eyes would twinkle with a knowing smile. John is a rancher-poet, a hard-working man with a heart attuned to a Wyoming ranch.

My family and I moved to Wyoming in 1979. Although we lived there for only three years, I fell in love with that wild, wonderful state. Our house was at the base of the Big Horn Mountains near the town of Sheridan. That region is teeming with wildlife; nature seems to be almost bursting at the seams. One rainy afternoon Sara and I counted ninety-four deer as we drove along the back roads near Sheridan. Antelope are so numerous that one can see them in herds along the interstate highway. Wyoming has one of the largest elk populations in the world. There are also moose, bear, fox, wolves, bobcats, mountain lions, geese, pheasants, ducks, grouse, owls, eagles, squirrels, rabbits, chipmunks, porcupines, beavers, and countless other animals. The mountains of Wyoming are covered with pine, cedar, aspen, and other breath-taking varieties of trees. Its crystal-clear streams and blue mountain lakes are teeming with trout, bass, brim, perch, and other fish.

When Sara and I return to Wyoming to visit, we like to drive out to our friends' ranch at the end of the day. When twilight descends over the rolling hills and pastures, the only sounds that can be heard are the croaking of frogs at the pond, the hooting of an owl in the distance, and the chirping of crickets. We watch deer make their way down from the hills to the rich alfalfa fields. Once we saw a porcupine waddle across an open field. Rabbits come out in the twilight to play in the dirt road. These things nourish my soul.

I also love to drive up into the Big Horn Mountains. Once at the top, a narrow dirt road runs along the ridge of these blue mountains. There are no tourists here snapping pictures, no commercialization of any kind. One can go for miles and never see another human being. The mountain road leads through dark pine forests, across cold mountain streams, and through large, open meadows. In the distance, at higher altitudes still, one can see jagged blue peaks covered with snow, thrusting upward into the clear blue skies. Frequently, one sees deer, moose, and sometimes even an elk or two. In springtime, wildflowers are in abundance and the mountain streams, filled with melting snow, flash and sparkle as they rush down the mountain. Needless to say, I feel true communion with Wyoming. On one of my visits, I wrote the following poem, which I titled "Here the Animal is Sustained in Me: A Poem for Wyoming":

Here the animal is sustained in me.

Leaving veneered civilization,
I step naked into the wilderness
of raw, primitive life.

Here plastic things do not matter:
brand name clothes,
money in the bank,
degrees on the wall.

Shedding all that is not real,
I fall back into the pool
of instinctual existence,
put the apple back on the tree,
and know the beauty of original things.

Here I drink from natural springs,
sleep nestled against mountains,
eat food cooked on open fire,
run with deer, elk, wolves, and bear,
fly with eagles, hawks, grouse, and owls.

Here my body slowly sinks into the sacred
and knows the rhythm of ancient ways.
I "chop wood, carry water,"
fish, sleep, eat, make love,
and know in my whole body
that this is home.

Here the animal is sustained in me.[19]

When I first saw the giant redwoods of California, I was over-whelmed not by their size, for I had expected that, but by their sense of solid, eternal presence and, for lack of a better word, their *indifference* to the affairs of humankind. Some of those trees were standing there when Jesus walked the streets of Jerusalem, when the Roman Empire flourished, when the Dark Ages descended, when the Renaissance broke out, when Columbus sailed to America. Those trees felt like ancient elders to me. I simply could not objectify them; they were "personages." They reached out to me with a huge warmth and wrapped me in their sacred silence and darkness. By their gentle presence, they put my small life in perspective. At some point I began to cry, and I did something I had never done before: I talked to trees, particularly to one old fellow standing right in front of me. I don't remember all I said, but I can tell you it was pure worship. For the first time, I understood why people once worshipped trees. For the first time, I understood why ancient women in the time of the Goddess religions built their altars in the groves. I also understood what a female client had meant when she told me that a huge tree in the woods behind her house had given her love and protection as a child—kindnesses often missing in her young life. Before I left that grove of redwoods, I wrote in my journal, "I shall not soon forget this first meeting." Later, I wrote a poem about this experience which I titled "To the Redwoods":

> Now I know why my foremothers
> worshipped trees
> and danced their moonlight rituals
> in darkened groves.
>
> Here amid your pachyderm trunks
> there is power and some huge warmth
> inviting midnight fires and rituals wild
> to hold back centuries of darkness
> that hover close by.
>
> And you alone survived to tell
> of those pagan days
> and the patience it takes
> to make a life.[20]

The psalmist said, "The heavens declare the glory of God and the firmament shows his handiwork." Nature speaks of the sacred and points to the Great Mystery. For those who wish to restore their souls and regain their sense of what is truly important, communing with nature is one answer. She will open your soul, fill your heart, and whisper ancient secrets in your ears.

*Even though Western society has created separation and
alienation by stressing rugged individualism and material
wealth, we are, essentially, tribal people meant to live
together, share the load, and care for one another as
we pass through the many phases of life.*
—C. S. Kasl

RELATIONSHIPS

The Path of Friendship, Family, and Community

I have a friend who moved here a few years ago from Argentina.
Recently, I asked him about the differences between his country and
the United States. He replied that one of the major differences is that
in Argentina family and friends are primary and one's work is secondary. He said, "When I first came to California, I would go to lunch
with my associates, but all they wanted to talk about was work. In
Argentina, we would never talk about work at lunch. We would talk
about our families, our friends, or what we were doing in our lives." He
said, "Also, I have noticed that here everybody waits for the weekend
to get together with friends; in Argentina we would do this almost
every night of the week. We would go to a park after work or have
people over for dinner." Then he smiled and said, "I think in Argentina we work to live, but in America you live to work."

THE BREAKDOWN OF COMMUNITY

My friend's observation goes to the heart of one of our problems
in America. Relationships are important, but they tend to take a back
seat to work and career. When Americans lived on farms and in rural

communities, relationships were more central. Farming was hard and required many hours, but there was always time for family, friends, and community, especially in the autumn and winter when the crops were in and things slowed down. In those days work itself often had a social dimension. Fathers and sons worked together in the fields while mothers and daughters took care of household chores. And major tasks such as harvesting, canning, quilting, butchering, cutting hay, and barn-raising were often done with community help.

Urbanization and Community

As Americans moved to the cities, much was lost in terms of community. The web of extended family, so common in rural areas, was unraveled as people left parents, grandparents, uncles, aunts, cousins, and other relatives to go to the big cities and get factory jobs. The nuclear family came into being. Many of the new urbanites liked the anonymity the city provided and the freedom it gave them to create their own lives. But this freedom often came at the price of gradually losing contact with family, relatives, and friends back home. Many people had to work twelve to fourteen hours a day and found that they had little time for friendships and community. Certainly, there were exceptions. In many ethnic neighborhoods, for example, a sense of community prevailed. But in general, urbanization not only left large holes in the social fabric of rural life; those who moved to the city were unable to reestablish the close sense of community that had characterized life in rural and small town America.

Eventually, with the help of labor unions, working conditions in the factories improved and the forty-hour work week was invented, with the idea that this would give the workers more free time— shorter workdays and the weekends off. But today, with commutes on crowded freeways, long commuter train rides, and the overtime hours that companies often require, it is not unusual for employees, both blue- and white-collar, to spend fifty to sixty hours per week in work or work-related activities. In "traditional" families, where dad goes to work and mom stays home, fathers often leave before their children get up in the morning and come home after they are in bed. Sadly, it reminds one of the old joke about a young man who complains that his father ruined his life. His father replies, "That's impossible. I wasn't even there!"

It seems strange that we have so readily accepted such an insane style of life. Through thousands of years of evolutionary development, human beings did not sit behind desks for fifty hours a week or punch factory time clocks. For our primitive ancestors survival was difficult, but they also had a lot of "downtime," and they lived in tune with the seasons and rhythms of nature. We are not evolutionarily "wired" to sit in an office or to stand on an assembly line doing the same boring tasks year after year. Yet this is the life most Americans live. Our culture is dedicated to material things, and we have bought Madison Avenue's vision of the good life: we all want to have good jobs and make lots of money so that we can have nice things. Despite our nostalgia for a simpler life, most of us could not imagine living in a hut by Walden Pond. We would want a waterfront mansion, a speed boat for the pond, an aviary for the birds, and gardeners to care for the surrounding woods!

Our demanding schedules and obsessions with material things are taking a staggering toll on our relationships. In most families both partners have to work in order to make ends meet, and some see their children for only two or three hours a day. On the weekends, if mom and dad don't have to work at second jobs or put in overtime, the family may be able to spend a few hours together in between grocery shopping, doing the laundry, cleaning the house, and tending the lawn. And for single parents the stress is even greater. I know single mothers who juggle dozens of responsibilities and keep a long line of plates spinning as they rush frantically through an impossible day, only to find that the next day is just like the one before.

Western industrialized society has sold us a stress-filled, body-damaging, soul-killing, and relationship-destroying existence; and we have bought it lock, stock, and barrel. And because these forces operate at the societal level and shape the world we live in, most of us feel we have little choice but to jump on the treadmill as soon as we get out of high school or college and continue working for the rest of our lives.

From the woods of New England we can sometimes hear Thoreau's warning: "Simplify, simplify, simplify. Don't come to the end of your life and realize you never lived." But it is hard to hear Thoreau amidst the clanking of the factories, the sirens of the city, and the whirr of the treadmill. And so we continue our exhausting lifestyle, only half conscious of how, like a cancer, it is eating away at our family relation-

ships, our friendships, our sense of community, and the other things
that really matter.

Individualism and Community

A less obvious but perhaps more insidious factor contributing to the
loss of community is the extreme individualism that has increasingly
characterized America. In *Habits of the Heart* Robert Bellah said that
the overemphasis on individualism has undermined community values
and commitments.[1] Bellah reminded us that individualism and community are reciprocally related and that individualism only makes
sense against the background of community. In other words, to stand
out as an individual, one needs a community to stand out against.
Without community, individualism degenerates into little more than
random and anarchical expressions of loneliness and alienation.

In America we are so committed to "being ourselves" that we sometimes cut off family, friends, and community involvements if they seem
to infringe on our personal freedom. Unfortunately, psychotherapists
sometimes contribute to this by encouraging clients to make personal
growth the dominating theme of life and eliminate relationships that
interfere with self-actualization. But this intention ignores the fact
that authentic actualization occurs in the context of community and
compassionate commitments in the world. To insist that one's own life
is all that really matters is narcissism, not actualization. Relationships
and compassionate involvement, not self-centered navel-gazing, are
the arena for personal growth and becoming. And while it is true that
some relationships are damaging and should be terminated, it is also
true that every relationship has its problems and that the very nature
of relationship requires a willingness to accommodate, rather than
insisting that the relationship must not, in any way, infringe on one's
freedom.

Viktor Frankl often pointed out to his graduate students that self-
actualization cannot be attained if sought directly. Rather, self-actualization is a by-product of commitment to a meaning or purpose larger
than oneself. Frankl said that those who set out with the specific goal
of becoming actualized are doomed to failure. On the other hand,
those who, in self-forgetfulness, commit their lives to a cause greater
than themselves will discover in time that they have also grown in
maturity and depth. Frankl's view echoes that of many spiritual traditions, including Christianity, which emphasize that in losing ourselves

we find ourselves. The historical figures whom we admire as having truly become self-actualized are invariably those who committed themselves to a humane and just cause. One only has to think of such individuals as Albert Schweitzer, Abraham Lincoln, Eleanor Roosevelt, Mother Theresa, or Martin Luther King, Jr. to see that authentic self-actualization involves commitments to others, not a focus on one's own development.

In the field of psychology in recent years there has been a great deal of talk about codependency. Numerous books and countless workshops have been dedicated to this theme, all heralding its dangers. It is true, of course, that relationships can be pathological and that individuals can lose their own sense of self through enmeshment with another. In this sense, no doubt the codependency movement has been helpful to those caught in such relationships. But unfortunately, for many Americans *codependency* became a catchword for almost any form of caring or act of self-sacrifice. In my opinion, the popularity of this movement was due in part to the fact that its message could so easily be twisted to support our preexisting tendency toward extreme individualism. It provided us with an excuse to disconnect from others and to place ourselves, once again, at center stage.

Something is desperately wrong in a culture when people begin to pathologize attachment, connection, compassion, and self-sacrifice. Such extreme individualism, as Robert Bellah warns, destroys the fabric of community. Many Americans who see a narrowly defined personal fulfillment as the goal of existence cannot imagine "wasting their lives" caring for an elderly parent, a retarded child, or a paraplegic mate, and certainly cannot understand how someone might actually find such a life fulfilling. The fact that we cannot understand this tells us something about the real pathology in America—how far we have drifted from the values of commitment and compassion. Thus, the individualism that has always characterized Americans and is one of our greatest assets can, in its extreme and narcissistic form, become a monster that destroys connection and community.

LONELINESS AND ISOLATION

When community breaks down, loneliness and isolation prevail. As a therapist, I have heard hundreds of clients speak of the pain of disconnection from others—women whose husbands neither hear nor see them; men who have not one friend with whom to share their lives; young children desperate for parental attention; teenagers so isolated and alone that suicide, in their minds, becomes a viable option; older people, their spouses and friends all dead, starving for any kind of contact. Some say that this is the age of anxiety, and so it is. But it is also the age of loneliness and isolation.

When I was a minister, I once delivered a sermon on loneliness. After the service, an older woman who was known in the congregation for her aloof and bitter personality came up to me and, fighting back tears, said, "I just want to tell you that I have spent many nights crying myself to sleep out of loneliness." With that, she quickly turned and walked away. I was touched by her confession, and from then on I saw her in a different light; I knew that behind those crusty defenses was a deeply isolated and lonely soul.

After my mother died, my dad would tell me, "I'm doing okay except I'm so lonely I feel like I'm going to die." They had been together sixty years. Some might say my dad was too dependent on my mother, and from some outside psychological perspective, they would probably be right. But when my mother died, it broke my dad's heart, and somehow that seems deeply human, not pathological at all.

We all long for connection, and this longing comes from the very center of our souls. A few years ago I had a client, a man in his forties, who loved women and wanted a relationship so badly that each time he spoke of it he would begin to cry. I often felt that this strong but gentle man was expressing the universal longing for connection, the desire to have someone share our life.

Some existentialists say that loneliness and isolation are simply part of the human condition: We come into the world alone and we die alone. Regardless of how much two people love each other, how close they become, they are still separate, isolated individuals. Thus, isolation and loneliness are ontological, simply part of being human. While there is a certain truth in this, there is also something ontological about love and human relationship. In fact, the deeper ontological truth may be that we are all connected. In that light, loneliness would be the longing of the soul for the realization of that ontological truth in the lived reality of one's life. Or to put it more simply, perhaps love is not illusion; perhaps, in fact, it is the only truth that can salve the painful loneliness of the heart. Erich Fromm believed this. He wrote, "Love is the only . . . answer to the problem of human existence."[2]

FRIENDSHIP

A few years ago one of my doctoral students wrote her dissertation on soul-to-soul friendships.[3] A soul-to-soul friendship is one which goes to the deepest levels of intimacy, each friend inviting the other into the inner chambers of the soul. Two hearts touch, listen, resonate, intertwine. Soul-to-soul friends become part of each other, so that it's hard to tell where one stops and the other begins. They commune with each other, even when they are silent in each other's presence. When they are apart, each holds the other in his heart and is nourished and sustained. And when they meet again, it is as though they were never apart. This is not a romanticized description. As those in such relationships know, these are the hard-edged, empirical facts of soul-to-soul friendship.

The Lebanese poet Kahlil Gibran understood this kind of friendship. In *The Prophet* he wrote:

> And let there be no purpose in friendship save the deepening
> of the spirit.
> For love that seeks aught but the disclosure of its own
> mystery is not love but a net cast forth: and only the
> unprofitable is caught.
> And let your best be for your friend.
> If he must know the ebb of your tide, let him know its flood
> also.
> For what is your friend that you should seek him with hours
> to kill?
> Seek him always with hours to live.[4]

I am struck by Gibran's statement, "Let there be no purpose in friendship save the deepening of the spirit." This is exactly what happens in soul-to-soul friendships. Unlike friendships which are built on doing things together, these friendships are more about being together in a certain way. Soul-to-soul friendships focus on speaking from the heart, on listening, caring, and truly being present for each other. Thus, these friendships are not so much about playing golf or going shopping together, although the friends may do these things too; they are about nurturing the soul and deepening the spirit. In this sense they are paths to the sacred.

Soul-to-soul friendships, when they occur, often fall into our lives like gifts from God. Sometimes they begin in childhood, sometimes in high school or college; but they can happen at any time. One day we go to lunch with an associate at work, but instead of the usual social chatter he says, "I'm sorry, but I've just got to talk to somebody about what I'm going through." Before lunch is finished two hearts will have touched, and it may be that a soul-to-soul friendship will have been born.

However they happen, these are sacred moments—these openings of two souls, and the trusting, risking, vulnerable way they give themselves to each other. There are no words to describe such friendships. They are anchors in our lives, and they nourish and sustain our souls.

My Views on Friendship

Through the years, from my work as a therapist and from my own personal relationships, I have learned a few things about soul-to-soul friendships.

First: It takes two people to have a soul-to-soul friendship. While this may seem obvious, I have been amazed at how many people work for years trying to create a soul-to-soul relationship with someone who has no interest in this kind of intimacy. If one person in a friendship, marriage, or any other relationship has no desire to move into the deeper regions of the soul, then that relationship is slated to remain on the surface.

Second: One of the best ways to nourish a friendship is to talk about the relationship itself. Friends often talk about topics of mutual interest—their marriages, their children, their parents, their job, their hopes and dreams. Such conversations can certainly draw friends closer together. But for the friendship to become a soul-to-soul relationship, the two friends must find the courage to talk about the friendship itself. To talk honestly about how one experiences the friendship and how one sees the other person, both positively and negatively, involves a level of risk that is not present when other topics are discussed. Nevertheless, this kind of sharing is one of the most effective ways to deepen a relationship. It allows the friends to work the soil of the friendship—pull the weeds, affirm their caring, clear up misperceptions, and re-attune their souls. It creates an arena for nourishing the relationship directly and doing the relationship maintenance all intimate friendships need.

However, this does not mean that friends should do nothing but process their relationship; friendship is meant to be lived, not analyzed and discussed. But, as one part of their relationship, friends should set aside time to talk about the friendship itself. In my experience, this is the most effective way to nourish the relationship and deepen its intimacy.

Third: The essence of a soul-to-soul friendship is the ability to see and affirm each other's authentic being and growing edge. Heinz Kohut, a psychoanalyst, developed a therapeutic approach called self psychology, which has important implications for friendship.[5] In his analytic work, Kohut found that some clients had a damaged sense of self, an inadequately developed self structure. He came to believe this damage occurred in the earliest years of life due to a failure of empathy on the part of the mother. To develop a healthy self structure, the infant needs a mother who is "there"—who is empathically attuned to her baby and mirrors back the child's experiences and feelings. Kohut felt that clients with a damaged self structure could be healed by the empathy and care of the therapist. In other words, by providing the conditions that were missing when the client was a child, the therapist can heal and restore the self that was damaged or that failed to develop.

Kohut's theory illumines friendship. He said that we need people who mirror our inner feelings and growing sense of self back to us not only in childhood, but throughout our lives. In other words, we need friends who truly see us in our authentic being, and who accept us as we are. We need friends who can see our growing edge, the person we are becoming. Unfortunately, our families often cannot do this for us; they are often too invested in seeing us the way we were or in imposing their own values on us. But soul-to-soul friendships provide an arena for unconditional acceptance and empathic care—exactly what we need to be and become the person we truly are. True friends affirm each other's authentic being and help each other on the road to becoming.

Fourth: Erotic energy is present in most, if not all, intimate friendships. Because sexuality is our deepest form of communication, it should be no surprise that erotic feelings often arise in soul-to-soul friendships. Friends sometimes feel uncomfortable with the erotic dimension of their relationship, viewing it as a problem. Yet this energy, if properly handled, can be a wonderful, enriching part of friendship. Erotic energy is an expression of life force; it is a source of creativity, passion, and vitality. It enlivens friendship and can be a source of spir-

itual nourishment. If we were more accepting of sexuality in this culture, I suspect that we would celebrate this dimension of friendship,
knowing that we could make intelligent decisions about how and
when to express our erotic energy. Because eros is such a vital, beneficial part of life, I think friends should acknowledge and discuss its
presence in the relationship, instead of trying to pretend it isn't there.

Further Reflections on Friendship

Friendships can be extremely intimate. One may feel closer to a
friend than to one's own family. One may tell a friend things that could
never be told to anyone else. Some friends would even be willing to die
for each other. Yet, as important as friendship is, it is the only relationship of such depth that is not ritualized in our society. We have
wedding ceremonies to symbolize the union of a husband and wife;
we do not have a similar ceremony to ritualize friendship, even though
the friendship may last longer than the marriage. Perhaps it is this very
lack of structure, the realization that the friendship exists not out of
social pressure or public commitments but in and for itself, that makes
it so special.

A friend is someone who abides. *Abide* is an old word which means
"wait" or "remain." A friend is one who is simply there, waiting or
standing by as we go through the various stages of life. He may offer his
thoughts, but he does not judge, criticize, or insist that we do it his way.
He is just there, loving us and giving us freedom to be ourselves, even
to make our mistakes. If you have friends like this, you should take
Shakespeare's advice and "grapple them to thy soul with hoops of
steel."[6]

Another truth is that friendships sometimes end. Regardless of how
intimate a friendship may be, sometimes things happen that make it
impossible for it to continue. Sometimes we outgrow a friend, or the
other person outgrows us, or we simply grow in different directions.
Sometimes we hurt each other, and the hurt goes to a place where
apology and forgiveness cannot reach. When a soul-to-soul friendship
ends, the experience can be excruciatingly painful. A woman who lost
her best friend told me that the end of that friendship was far more
painful than her divorce. Soul-to-soul friendships are rooted in our
very being. If they end, it is like tearing our soul out by the roots; we
are shaken at the very foundations of our being. We may find that we
are no longer sure about the world—whether it is a safe place or not.

We think, "If this could end, this which I thought was so sure, then how can I trust anyone or rely on anything?" After such an experience, it may take a long time before we finally open our heart to life again.

If friendships do not end in life, they will certainly end in death. When I was younger, I did not think about these things. But I have watched my father, who is now eighty-nine, lose one friend after another. He recently told my sister, "I have no one left. All my friends are gone." When my doctoral student interviewed one woman about her soul-to-soul friendship, the woman said, "We have been friends all our lives, and someday one of us will attend the other's funeral." Such reflections remind us that we should be filled with gratitude for the friendships we have.

FAMILY

Perhaps no bond between people is as strong as that of common blood. Family relationships can be the source of our highest joys and, sometimes, of our deepest despair. No matter how hard we try, we cannot escape family relationships. They are imprinted on our souls, and our common blood binds us together from birth to death.

To discuss all family relationships would be a book in itself. Therefore, I have chosen to focus on parents, children, and marriage.

Parents

Raising a child is a tremendous responsibility, yet most parents have no training for this important task other than the often flawed lessons they received from their own parents. Even the best parents often make mistakes, saying and doing things that are harmful to the child. As a result, most of us grow up with at least a few parental scars, and some grow up with serious psychological damage.

For the first thirty years of our lives, many of us use our parents as Rorschach cards, projecting onto them all our frustrations and unhappiness. In youth it is always easier to blame our parents than to take responsibility for our own lives. But by the time we reach our thirties, and especially if we have children of our own, many of us begin to see that this business of being a parent is not quite as easy as we had imagined. For the first time, we may have some empathy for our own parents and for what they went through with us. We may begin to feel that our parents, within the limits of their abilities and their own scars, did the best they could. And for the first time, forgiveness may enter our hearts.

As one of my clients, a man in his late forties, told me:

> In adolescence and through my early twenties, I was angry at my parents for their inadequacies and the ways they had hurt me as a kid. I thought I had gotten over it, but then, a few years ago, some of these old issues flared up again, especially in regard to my dad. When I was a kid, we seldom did father-son things like going fishing or playing catch. I had always felt that he just wasn't there for me. So, even though he was in his seventies, I decided to talk to him about my feelings. After I told him all the things that had hurt me, he was quiet for awhile and then said, "It sounds like you're pretty mad at me. I know I made mistakes, but I was under a lot of pressure in those days. I was working two jobs just to provide for the family. I got up at 4:30 each morning and worked until 8:00 at night. On the weekends I had to do things around the farm to catch up. I was doing my best to put a roof over your head and food on the table. I know I should have done some things differently, but I did the best I could."
>
> When he finished, I had tears in my eyes. I had forgotten all that. As kids, we see our own disappointments and usually have no idea what our parents are going through. After listening to dad, I felt compassion for him—and gratitude. I realized that while he had his faults, failure to love me was not one of them. My bitterness went away that day, and I have never felt angry about my childhood since.

And so it goes, generation after generation. In childhood we set our parents on pedestals, believing they can do no wrong. Then in adolescence and young adulthood we see their faults and blame them for not being perfect. But, if we are fortunate, there comes a time when we forgive them, see them for the human beings they are, and reestablish a relationship on a more mature and compassionate basis.

But this is not an easy process. Before we can forgive our parents, many of us must go through various stages of anger, hurt, blame, and sometimes even rage. Slowly we realize that we cannot change the past, but that by reestablishing a relationship with our parents, we may be able to get a taste of the intimacy and care we so desperately wanted as children. We also may discover that as adults we are able to give our parents what they always needed and perhaps never had. Of course, some parents were physically and sexually abusive and their children later want nothing to do with them. This is understandable; such parents have betrayed their children and the sacred responsibilities of parenthood. But most of us did not endure such pain, and we need to forgive our parents and get on with our lives. Even if they are set in their ways and unwilling to discuss the past, we can still forgive our parents in our own hearts. Fortunately, forgiveness is something we can do by ourselves. It is a solitary act which comes from a courageous heart and has the power to release us, and sometimes them, from the prison of bitterness, loneliness, and hurt.

Children

Harvard psychiatrist Robert Coles is one of the leading scholars in the field of children's spirituality. In his book *The Spiritual Life of Children*, he makes it clear that children are intensely interested in spiritual matters and often have profound insights into life's deeper questions. Cole believes that children need to feel connected to something larger than themselves and that nourishing our children's spirituality is extremely important.[7]

Deepak Chopra agrees. In *The Seven Spiritual Laws for Parents* he says that every child already has a spiritual life and emphasizes that it is our responsibility as parents to nurture this natural capacity and "place our children firmly on the journey of spirit."[8]

Stephen Covey, in *The 7 Habits of Highly Effective Families*, compares our children to the Chinese bamboo. For four years after planting, one sees nothing but a small shoot. All the growth is underground as the tree develops a powerful root structure. Then, in the fifth year, it suddenly shoots up to as much as eighty feet! Our children are like that. Throughout childhood we provide them with love, instill in them important values, nurture their spirituality, and guide them in their day-to-day decisions. We help them develop a strong root structure so that in time they will be able to grow to great heights.[9]

The Christian mystic Meister Eckhart said that we are born with a God seed, an inherent tendency toward spiritual growth, within us. He wrote:

> The seed of God is in us. Given an intelligent and hard-working farmer and a diligent field hand, it will thrive and grow up to God, whose seed it is; and accordingly its fruits will be God-nature. Pear seeds grow into pear trees, nut seeds into nut trees, and God seed into God.[10]

How do we as parents help our children to grow spiritually? How do we nourish this natural inclination and ensure that the God seed within them germinates and grows?

Perhaps the place to begin is with ourselves. We live in a world where success is often judged by money and possessions. In such a world it is easy to neglect our children's spiritual development and to focus on their material success. So the first step is to examine our own attitudes and priorities. As Deepak Chopra said:

> Many people assume without question that success is essentially material, that it can be measured in money, prestige, or an abundance of possessions. These can certainly play a role, but having such things is no guarantee of success. The success we want our children to achieve has to be defined in many nonmaterial ways as well. It should include the ability to love and have compassion, the capacity to feel joy and spread it to others, the security of knowing that one's life serves a purpose, and finally, a sense of connection to the creative power of the universe. All of these constitute the spiritual dimension of success, the dimension that brings inner fulfillment.[11]

Many parents would agree with Chopra's comments. They know that spirituality is extremely important, and they want to give their children a solid spiritual foundation for life. But for those who are no longer affiliated with religion, for those who think of themselves as spiritual but not religious, it is not easy to know what to do. Once children come into the picture, some parents feel that creating a spiritual life outside the walls of institutional religion is fine for adults, but that their children need the foundations that traditional religion provides. In fact, many baby boomers who once rejected religion have now returned to church because they want their children to have the spiritual and moral grounding they believe religion provides.

For those of you who are thinking about taking your children to church, I would encourage you to consider the following:

Why do you believe that traditional religion is the best way to give your children the spiritual foundations they need? Most of us automatically assume that taking our children to Sunday school and church is a good thing; after all, who could question something so worthy? Nevertheless, I would encourage you to question it.

Have you considered, for example, the possibility that exposing your child to traditional religion might actually be *damaging* to your child's spirituality? While this may sound preposterous, ask yourself how many people you know who feel that their early religious training damaged them. As a psychotherapist, I have heard client after client describe how the teachings of their church warped their growth as human beings and seriously undermined their interest in spiritual matters. I believe it is naive for parents to assume that taking their children to Sunday school will provide them with healthy spiritual values. Religion can be for better or worse; it can nourish your child's soul or damage it, depending on the religion and what it teaches.

Churches differ widely in the values they teach, and some hold values that are highly questionable if not reprehensible. Do you want your little girl to be told that when she grows up she is to be in submission to her husband? Do you want her to be taught that the ideal wife and mother is one who stays home rather than one who pursues a career? Do you want your children to be taught that sex is only for procreation and that birth control in marriage is wrong? Do you want your children to be taught that their erotic feelings are bad and that lust will cause them to go to hell? Do you want your children to be told that homosexuality is a sin and that all gays and lesbians must either give up sex or spend eternity in hell? Do you want your children to be taught that abortion is a sin? Do you want your children to be told that Christianity is the only true religion and that all other religions are false and opposed to God? Do you want them to be told that the theory of evolution was invented by godless men and that the Biblical account of creation is to be accepted literally? Do you want your children to be told that if they do not believe and obey the church's laws, they will go to hell and burn forever? Many churches, especially those at the fundamentalist end of the continuum, hold such views. Ironically, the teachings of traditional religion are not always as moral and righteous as we like to think. In the name of God, some churches promote bigotry, sexism, hate, fear, and other objectionable values. And you can be sure that if your children attend such a church, they will, in one way or another, be exposed to these values.

In his book *Raising Spiritual Children in a Material World,* Phil Catalfo raises serious concerns about parents who expose their children to such churches. He asks, "What attracts people—decent, sincere, hard-working people who love their children and want a better life—to fundamentalist creeds?"[12] Catalfo suggests that in today's world many parents are so stressed that they find it easier to say,

"Just tell me what to do," which, of course, fundamentalist religion is always ready to do. But Catalfo believes this sort of choice on the part of parents sends the wrong message to their children; instead of teaching them self-reliance in spiritual matters, it teaches them to be dependent, to let others tell them how to live their lives.

Catalfo points out how some Christian families insulate themselves from life; they watch Christian television, read Christian books, go to Christian theme parks, and send their children to Christian schools. Catalfo says:

> Of course, there's nothing "wrong" with that, and people should remain free to do so. However, I believe that monoculture is inimical to life. That's certainly true in ecosystems, and it's no less true in society, let alone in the world of the spirit.[13]

Catalfo believes that, instead of raising children in a Christian monoculture, it is far better to teach them how to bring spirituality into their lives. We need to "discover how we can infuse our role as parents with an enlivened spirituality, and therefore be able to raise 'spiritual' children while remaining in the material world where our journey will be carried out."

While some churches are dangerous to children's spiritual welfare, there are also churches that are tolerant, loving, and engaged in compassionate action in the world. The clergy of these churches are openminded, well-trained, and hold none of the narrow attitudes described above. So if you plan to take your child to church, it might be wise to meet with the pastor or priest and ask him (or her) what the church believes on various issues. If the reason you are taking your children to church is to give them a solid moral and spiritual foundation, then it makes sense to know beforehand the kinds of values the church holds.

While some parents will take care of their children's spiritual instruction by sending them to church, others have no interest in taking this route. Some feel that, just as archaic educational systems cannot adequately prepare children for today's world, traditional religion is equally incapable of providing the kind of spiritual grounding children need to live in a complex postmodern world. Parents who are nourishing their own spirituality outside of traditional religion must think creatively about how to nourish their children's spirituality. I can imagine that if concerned parents got together and creatively addressed their children's spiritual welfare, they could come up with fascinating possibilities. There are wonderful children's books on such themes as love, compassion, friendship, divorce, death, sexuality, equality, and respect for differences. There are also movies, stories, songs, creative games, and other materials which focus on spiritual themes. Much information is also available on the beliefs, rituals, and customs of the world's religions. Creative parents could put together a highly stimulating set of activities and learning experiences for their children's spiritual nourishment; and I believe this could be done, if the parents wished, outside the walls of traditional religion. This is an area that is wide open to anyone interested in developing new, alternative ways to nurture their children's souls.

Certainly the most important thing parents can do for their children's spiritual development is embody and practice spiritual values in their own lives. As Chopra said, "As a parent, you will teach more effectively by who you are, not what you say."[14] If parents place spiritual values above material ones; if they are kind to each other, love their children, value their friends, and treat others with fairness; if they seek to rid their own hearts of racism, sexism, and other forms of intolerance; if they speak up for the dispossessed and engage in compassionate action in the world; if they love God and treat their neighbor with respect—their children will observe and absorb these values. Ultimately, parents' personal spirituality is the most potent influence on the spiritual development of their children.

One of the great rewards of parenthood is to see one's children eventually grow into men and women of both stature and depth. Sometimes my graduate students, many of whom are parents, ask my advice about child-rearing. After making it clear that I'm no expert, I then tell them something like the following:

> Love your children. They will be gone before you know it. Be gentle with yourself as a parent. You don't have to be perfect; you only have to love them. Do the best you can. But don't make your children your life. Martyrs set horrible examples for their children.
>
> Have a life of your own, and give your children a parent who is strong, vibrant, passionate, and alive. If you have a good marriage, make it a priority. Love your mate and make sure your children know it. Nothing makes a child feel more secure. It is true that the best gift you can give your children is to love their father or mother.
>
> Most importantly, listen to your children and see them for who they truly are. Don't impose your own dreams on them or make them

live the life you missed. They have one life, and it belongs to them and God—not to you.

Finally, listen to their anger with you, but don't take it too seriously, especially in the teenage years. Hold your ground; don't acquiesce to every demand; but continue to show them in countless ways how much you love them.

And one other thing: Be sure to keep yourself healthy so you can live long enough to see them grow up and have children themselves. Watching them deal with children of their own who are giving them hell is one of the sweetest experiences of déjà vu you will ever know!

My favorite poem about children is from *The Prophet* by Kahlil Gibran.

Your children are not your children.
They are the sons and daughters of life's longing for itself.
They come through you but not from you.
And though they are with you, yet they belong not to you.

You may give them your love but not your thoughts,
For they have their own thoughts.
You may house their bodies but not their souls,
For their souls dwell in the house of tomorrow, which you
    cannot visit, not even in your dreams.

You may strive to be like them, but seek not to make them
    like you.
For life goes not backward nor tarries with yesterday.

You are the bows from which your children as living arrows
    are sent forth.
The archer sees the mark upon the path of the infinite,
    and He bends you with His might that his arrows may
    go swift and far.

Let your bending in the archer's hand be for gladness;
For even as He loves the arrows that flies, so He loves also
    the bow that is stable.[15]

Marriage

Despite affairs, divorce rates, and other problems that plague modern marriage, I believe a soul-to-soul relationship with someone whom we deeply love offers the greatest opportunity for personal and spiritual growth available.

Marriage is not sacred because the church says so or because a clergyman performs the ceremony. Marriage is sacred because it involves the joining of two hearts and souls for life—an awe-inspiring commitment that has "sacred" written all over it. As Stephen and Ondrea Levine say in their book *Embracing the Beloved*, "When true hearts truly join there is mystical union."[16]

As the years unfold, this mystical union takes on increasing depth until it becomes itself a third presence. This is not easy to describe, but it is similar to what Martin Buber called "the between" and what some have called the "us" of relationship. A few years ago, I had a graduate student whose husband had recently died. One day she told me, "I miss him so much." Then she added, "But I also miss 'us.' When I go to places we once went to together, I am now alone. There's no more 'us,' and I miss both him and 'us' terribly." In the Levines' book, the Beloved is not one's spouse, but rather, that sacred "third" in which both partners meet and find sustenance. Hugh and Gayle Prather, who wrote *I Will Never Leave You*, say that the relationship "is like a candle they hold between them, lighting their way through the world."[17] This sacred third is ontologically viable; it has a being and reality of its own. In fact, the Levines say that when we experience this presence at its core, we may tend to call it God.[18] In wedding ceremonies, the minister or priest sometimes tells the couple, "It takes three to make a good marriage—the two of you and God." This is a religious way of acknowledging that a marriage is not so much a two-way street as it is a triangle in which the sacred sits at the apex. Whether one calls it God, the presence, the between, the third, the "us," or the candle that lights the way, it is the mystical power that brings sacred energy into the heart of the marriage.

Marriage is a spiritual training ground, a place where we slowly give up self-centeredness and learn the meaning of patience, forgiveness, compassion, and love. Most of us fling ourselves into marriage on the wings of infatuation and the dream of living happily ever after. But we soon discover that marriage is not so much about living happily ever after as it is about loving each other regardless of what comes. In the context of this kind of commitment, the passion of infatuation fades away and is replaced by a passion forged in the pain and joy of real life. The rough edges of our personality are rounded and polished, and gratitude rises in the heart for this person who loves us so deeply. Immersed in love, we learn to love; and in learning to love one, we learn to love the world.

COMMUNITY

One of the greatest difficulties in building a spiritual life outside the walls of traditional religion is that there seems to be no established community for this enterprise. Those following alternative spiritual paths often walk alone. Unlike those in traditional religion, they have no ready-made community for encouragement and support.

Community is extremely important. While there are many things one can do alone to nurture the soul, few things are as important for spiritual life as having companions who understand and support one's journey. My sense is that those who are following alternative paths do find informal ways to find community, through friendships, workshops, organizations, and by simply sharing books, articles, movies, and other materials with one another. But I sometimes wonder if a more formal community might be useful.

Typically, those who are spiritual but not religious have no interest in creating a formal community. One of the most attractive features of many alternative paths is that they are free of the heavy institutional obligations that characterize traditional religion. But I wonder if it might be possible and desirable to create new structures and forms of community that would provide a setting for spiritual sharing and development without the rigid structures and demands that often accompany organizations. For example, those interested might want to meet in a small, flexible, informal community, perhaps as a small group in someone's home, to discuss alternative approaches to spirituality and give each other mutual support. I have personally engaged in such gatherings and found them to be extremely stimulating and supportive.

One of the questions that arises is whether or not a spiritual community can exist in the absence of a common belief system. In other words, is it possible to have a spiritual community based on difference as well as similarity? It seems that this is what such a community would call for, given the diversity and pluralism of alternative spirituality. Yet most of us find this difficult; we feel more comfortable with those who are like us, and it is much easier to create a community based on commonality than to create one flexible enough to incorporate a wide range of spiritual perspectives.

A more mature spirituality, one that honors the spiritual views of others, calls for a more mature form of community. Maurice Friedman, reflecting the views of Martin Buber, has emphasized that true community must be based on " confirmation of otherness" as well as on similarity.[19] Perhaps it is time for us to transcend old tribal models based on divisions of "us" and "them" and construct communities that support diversity. No doubt, if we form spiritual communities which incorporate differences, we will experience friction at times. But I suspect such communities will also be exciting, creative, and growth-promoting.

Rather than calling for conformity to a common belief system, my vision of spiritual community is one which supports each person in his or her own spiritual journey. This would not mean that people could not question or raise concerns about the path of another; but such discussion should be done with respect for that path. The overarching structure of the community would be a respectful tolerance for diverse perspectives.

A few years ago the Levi Strauss company launched an experiment that might serve as a metaphor for this new kind of community. The famous blue jeans company built a computerized factory which could quickly make a pair of jeans to the exact measurements of the customer, rather than requiring individuals to fit themselves into the standard sizes. In the same way, spiritual communities could be created which would support individual journeys rather than requiring everyone to fit into standard belief systems. I am convinced that traditional religion often kills the soul by forcing it into a small, suffocating box. A community which promotes freedom for the soul and creative searching for answers to life's spiritual questions would indeed be a godsend to spiritual seekers disillusioned by traditional religion. Such a community, it seems to me, would be a path to the sacred.

Relationships are essential to the life of the soul. As the epigraph at the beginning of this chapter says, we are a tribal people and we need one another, not only for physical survival but also for spiritual sustenance as we journey together on the road to the sacred. As Jung said, "The unrelated human being lacks wholeness, for he can achieve wholeness only through the soul, and the soul cannot exist without its other side, which is always found in a "you.'"[20]

Man is never helped in his suffering by what he thinks for himself, but only by revelations of a wisdom greater than his own. It is this which lifts him out of his distress.
—Carl Jung

DARK NIGHTS OF THE SOUL
The Path of Existential Crises

Most of the time, nurturing the soul is a positive, uplifting experience. But there is also a dark side to soul-making. Buddha's enlightenment came after he saw the pain, suffering, and death of humankind. Jesus, whose spiritual depth has brought solace to millions, was described as a man of sorrows and acquainted with grief. David, that spiritual giant of the Old Testament, described as a man after God's own heart, knew the depths of human despair. He lost his beloved son Absalom and was, at times, overwhelmed with depression and grief. The *Book of Psalms*, so filled with spiritual wisdom, stands as a monument not only to his spirituality but also to his many dark nights of the soul.

Spirituality is connected with the painful as well as the joyous aspects of human existence. The soul grows wiser and stronger through adversity. This chapter will explore dark nights of the soul as a path to spiritual growth.

THE INEVITABILITY OF SUFFERING

"Life is difficult," Scott Peck says in the opening sentence of his book *The Road Less Traveled*.[1] And if we live long enough, we will know great pain and sorrow. We will see our grandparents and our own mother and father die. We may even stand at the grave of our son or daughter, or our best friend, or a grandchild taken by accident or disease. From the time we are small, we learn that life is limited and that pain, suffering, and death are part of the human condition. As time goes on, these existential truths come down from their abstract heights and take up residence among those we love. A friend at school is killed in an accident. A distant aunt dies of breast cancer. Grandpa had a stroke and is not expected to live. The darkness creeps closer and closer, and we see, reluctantly and with our own eyes, that death will eventually take everything we love.

How does the heart endure such pain and where do we ever find the strength to go on? As Rainer Maria Rilke said, "Murderers are easy to understand. But this: that one can contain death, the whole of death, even before life has begun, can hold it to one's heart gently, and not refuse to go on living, is inexpressible."[2]

In a sense, there are no answers to such existential realities. Pain, suffering, and death are simply part of life. Intellectual and philosophical answers provide little comfort; ultimately, they are only attempts to defend ourselves against awareness of our own mortality and the vulnerability of life. But there is a way of approaching these realities that can make all the difference in the world. This way has to do with the soul and the discovery that these experiences, painful as they are, can be paths to the sacred.

DARK NIGHTS OF THE SOUL AND SPIRITUAL GROWTH

The expression, "dark night of the soul," comes from the writings of the Christian mystic St. John of the Cross and refers to those tragic times in life when, because of some pain, suffering, or loss, we are overwhelmed and beyond consolation.[3] All joy departs and we think the sun will never shine again. Each day becomes a burden, a heavy weight that crushes our spirit, and we wonder if we can ever go on. Dark nights of the soul are different from normal struggles. They are existential crises; they have to do with our ultimate concerns, our very existence itself. When we confront these dark realities, they shake the foundations of our very being.

How do such tragic experiences help us to grow spiritually? How can they possibly serve as a path to the sacred? The answer lies in the realization that existential crises open us to the life of the soul. The soul is the only part of our being which is capable of dealing with such crises. As she struggles with these heavy burdens, she grows strong in grace and wisdom. Thus, dark nights of the soul, difficult as they are, nourish the roots of our spiritual life.

Normally, our egos are in control. The ego is there to insure our survival in a shallow, Darwinian sense. The ego never faces the deeper questions of existence; it is dedicated to helping us build the kingdom of self. We are easily fooled by the ego; it seems to be on our side. It is always planning strategies for our self-aggrandizement, always helping us build, brick by brick, the edifice of our own power, prestige, wealth, career, or whatever we have decided is most important.

But then, in the midst of this project, from out of nowhere, an existential crisis descends. Our mate is diagnosed with a life-threatening illness, our child is hurt in a horrible accident, or some other unspeakable tragedy strikes like a tornado at the center of our well-ordered life. And in that moment everything shifts. Priorities rearrange themselves with lightning obviousness, and the house that ego built collapses in a second, revealing it to be the house of cards it always was. Suddenly, we find ourselves sliding helter-skelter down a long, winding chute, dropping into hell and the darkest regions of the soul. Somewhere the sun may shine, but it shines no longer for us. Night closes in, the darkness thickens, and our long, dark night of the soul has begun.

The ego cannot handle these situations. It can only stand by, wringing its hands and repeating its mantra, "Why me? Why me?" But the soul, familiar with the tragedies of life, rises up, pushes the ego aside, and begins to do her work. Drawing from a source beyond ourselves, she channels mercy into our lives and gives us courage, like daily manna, to get us through the day. As she nurses our wounds and binds up our brokenness, she also helps us lay rugged foundations for a new, more solid way of life—a life characterized less by ego and more by humility, compassion, gratitude, and love. Not everyone who goes through a dark night of the soul learns these lessons; but they are always there, waiting to be learned by anyone who has the eyes to see and the heart to receive.

We should never romanticize dark nights of the soul. They are harsh, rugged paths to the sacred, full of jagged rocks that scar the heart forever. We don't ask for these experiences, we don't want them; and when they come, they are so devastating that it feels as though the candle has gone out forever. Nevertheless, out of this unspeakable pain, the soul spins strands of gold and weaves a cloak of wisdom and depth. These ravaging experiences, these trials by fire, purify us and set our lives on firmer foundations. "Extremity is God's opportunity" says the old proverb, and it is true. Dark nights of the soul break our spirits and open our hearts to God. But they are a painful path to the sacred, a trail of tears, an unsolicited opportunity for spiritual growth.

FOUR DARK NIGHTS OF THE SOUL

Dark nights of the soul take many forms. Any tragic experience that shakes the foundations of our lives qualifies. But there are some crises which are especially common, and most of us will have to face these in one way or another.

Meaninglessness

One of the most common existential crises in this postmodern age is the struggle with meaninglessness. Sometimes the belief structures that have given reason and purpose to our lives come crashing down at our feet. Suddenly, we are exposed to the naked questions of existence: Who am I? Where did I come from? Where am I going? What is the meaning of my life? These are not academic questions; they are existential queries that rise from the depths of our soul.

Over 300 years ago, Blaise Pascal wrote:

> When I consider the short duration of my life, swallowed up in the eternity before and after, the little space which I fill, and even can see, engulfed in the immensity of spaces of which I am ignorant and which know me not, I am frightened, and I am astonished at being here rather than there; for there is no reason why here rather than there, why now rather than then. Who has put me here? By whose order and direction have this place and this time been allotted to me? The eternal silence of those infinite spaces frightens me.[4]

It is agonizing to confront such questions. Most of the time we go skipping through life, never thinking about such "morbid" things. But when an existential crisis occurs, we are forced to ponder these matters. There is an old saying: "One clock stopped and knew the meaning of time." Crises make us stop and reflect on the meaning of life.

Viktor Frankl believed that meaning is the foundation of human existence and the key to psychological health.[5] When Frankl was a prisoner in the concentration camps of Hitler, he observed that those prisoners who lost their sense of meaning tended to die shortly thereafter, but those who held on to meaning, who had a purpose to live for, often survived against the odds. Frankl was fond of quoting Nietzsche's statement, "He who has a *why* to live for can bear almost any *how*."

In his book *Existential Psychotherapy*, Irvin Yalom said that there are two types of meaning, cosmic and terrestrial.[6] Cosmic meaning refers to overarching systems of meaning, systems which attempt to explain the overall purpose of life and the universe. For example, Christianity, along with most other world religions, is a cosmic meaning system. Christianity tells us that God created the universe, sent his Son to redeem us, and that the purpose of our lives is to serve Him. Other religions—Buddhism, Islam, Hinduism, Judaism, and Taoism, along with the many indigenous religions—are also based on cosmic systems of meaning. While the systems differ in their contents and explanations, they all attempt to provide a meta-perspective on life. Most people adhere to some cosmic system of meaning; they hold an overarching theological or philosophical perspective which tells them the purpose of existence and gives meaning to their lives.

Terrestrial meaning, on the other hand, refers to the specific, concrete meanings that are found "on earth." Anything in our daily lives which gives meaning to our existence would be an expression of terrestrial meaning. For example, we may find meaning in our family and friends, or in the beauty of a sunset, or in a piece of music, or in playing with our child.

Today, many people are questioning the cosmic meaning systems in which they were raised and which once gave them comfort. When one's existential security has always depended on a particular belief system, it can be devastating to realize that one no longer believes in that system. People going through this experience often feel cut off from their roots and sometimes cut off from the people they love as well. When meaninglessness invades the heart, it is often followed by anxiety, depression, and a deep sense of ennui.

Yet for many, this crisis also marks the beginning of a new life. The spiritual quest often begins when the old system breaks down and we are forced, for the first time, to confront the ultimate questions of human existence. It is frightening to stand naked before the universe, unprotected by hand-me-down answers, and to ask, "Who am I?" "Why am I here?" "Where did I come from?" "Where am I going?" "How ought I to live?" Yet I am convinced that those who ask these eternal questions are in a process of waking up. Many people live their entire lives simply accepting what others have told them; they never know the risk or excitement of embarking on an authentic journey where everything is at stake, even one's own existence. By asking the eternal questions, we embark on a seaward journey of no return, joining all those who have pondered such questions from the beginning of time. Even if we do not find all the answers, we discover that the journey itself is rewarding because it opens us to the mysteries of life and slowly shapes us into men and women of depth.

Suffering

At every moment, somewhere in the world, people are suffering. A parent is watching her child die of incurable disease; a husband is mourning the death of his wife; a teenage girl has just learned that her mother, the center of her life, has a terminal illness. Others live in chronic, unremitting physical pain, unable to find relief. And still others are lost in anxiety, depression, psychosis, or some other form of emotional distress. When we are healthy and feeling well, we seldom think of these painful realities. If the sun is shining in our lives, it is easy to forget that thousands of others are suffering, lost in dark nights of the soul.

In the concentration camps of Hitler, Frankl and thousands of others suffered every day. Constantly under threat of execution, Frankl and his fellow prisoners worked long hours in freezing temperatures without adequate clothing and sometimes without shoes. Fed nothing but a piece of bread and a pint of watery soup each day, their bodies deteriorated until almost nothing was left but skin and bones. Six million people, including Frankl's twenty-four-year-old wife and others of his family, were murdered in the death camps. Yet, Frankl was able to transcend these horrible tragedies, and, instead of becoming bitter, he spent his life helping others.

Elie Wiesel, also a death camp survivor who witnessed unbearable atrocities, fashioned from this darkness a life of spiritual depth and compassion. In 1986, Wiesel was given the Nobel Peace Prize for his lifelong efforts to reach others with a message of healing and peace. Those who have read Wiesel's books cannot help but be moved by his spiritual depth and his rich understanding of the human condition. In his acceptance speech for the Nobel Peace Prize, he said:

> No one is as capable of gratitude as one who has emerged from the kingdom of night. We know that every moment is a moment of grace, every hour an offering; not to share them would mean to betray them. Our lives no longer belong to us alone; they belong to all those who need us desperately. . . . And that is why I swore never to be silent whenever and wherever human beings endure suffering and humiliation. We must always take sides. Neutrality helps the oppressor, never the victim. Silence encourages the tormentor, never the tormented.[7]

Frankl and Wiesel, along with thousands of others who have suffered and thereby grown large, remind us that spirituality grows not only in the light of day but also in the darkest nights of the soul.

Death

Perhaps the harshest reality of human existence is death. Intellectually, we all know that some day we will die, but we tend to ignore this reality as long as possible. Sogyal Rinpoche, the Buddhist monk who wrote *The Tibetan Book of Living and Dying*, said that when he first came to the West, he was shocked by Western culture's denial and lack of understanding of death. He saw how devoted we are to materialism, youth, and power; how we put our old people into homes where they often die abandoned and alone; how we build our lives on false foundations, not taking into account the fact of death. By contrast, in Tibetan culture people focus on the spiritual quest. They are trained to meditate on death, to arrange their life priorities in light of this reality, and to assist others in the dying process.

Rinpoche believes that "one of the chief reasons we have so much anguish and difficulty facing death is that we ignore the truth of impermanence." He writes:

> We so desperately want everything to continue as it is that we have to believe that things will always stay the same. But this is only make-believe. And as we so often discover, belief has little or nothing to do with reality. This make-believe, with its misinformation, ideas, and assumptions, is the rickety foundation on which we construct our lives. No matter how much the truth keeps interrupting, we prefer to go on trying, with hopeless bravado, to keep up our pretense.[8]

But despite our pretensions, sooner or later we must all face the reality of impermanence, the fact that all things pass away. Rinpoche told an old Tibetan story about a very poor man who finally manages to save a sack of grain. He takes the heavy bag of seeds home and hangs it from a rafter with a rope to protect it from rats and thieves. To protect it further, he decides to sleep under the bag. Lying there, he begins to make great plans as to how he will divide and sell the seed in small quantities, make a good profit, and then reinvest the money in even more seeds. In this way he will eventually become wealthy, be respected in the community, and all the women will want him as their husband. He will marry a beautiful woman and with her he will have a son. Meanwhile, as the man is fantasizing, a rat has been gnawing on the rope, and suddenly the heavy bag of seed falls, killing the man instantly.[9]

The point of the story, of course, is that no matter how carefully we plan our lives and no matter how wonderful our dreams, death can come at any moment and end everything. Impermanence is an indisputable fact of human existence.

When I was a minister, there was an old man in my congregation who seemed very sad. One day his grown daughter told me why. Throughout his life, the man had made an excellent salary, but he had insisted on saving every penny so that when he retired, he and his wife could travel the world. His wife supported his dream and was extremely frugal, often denying herself things that other women enjoyed. Then, only a few months before her husband's retirement, she was diagnosed with cancer and soon died. They had lived their entire lives for retirement, for the "golden years," but for her those years never came. And the man was left with nothing but his money and the memory of how his wife had sacrificed all her life, ultimately for nothing.

Because death can come at any moment, Rinpoche believes it is important to meditate on the impermanence of things and arrange our lives accordingly. Instead of trying desperately to grasp and hold on to things, Rinpoche says that we must learn detachment, or letting go. Detachment is not indifference; rather, it is coming to terms with the fact that everything passes away. This is a difficult lesson to learn; it is only natural to want to hold on to that which we love or care about. But because impermanence is the truth of life, we must make peace with this existential fact. To do otherwise is to build our lives on false foundations. Coming to terms with death and impermanence releases us to live in the now, to appreciate things in the moment, knowing that we cannot control or hold on to them forever. Rinpoche quotes William Blake, who had understood this same lesson:

> He who binds to himself a joy
> Does the winged life destroy
> But he who kisses the joy as it flies
> Lives in eternity's sun rise.[10]

But how can meditating on impermanence help? Won't it simply plunge us into the demoralizing realization that death invades everything, that ultimately nothing has any meaning? Rinpoche does not think so. He says that "the purpose of reflection on death is to make a real change in the depths of your heart" and that through deep contemplation we may "truly open our eyes to what we are doing with our lives."[11] Rinpoche believes that through meditation we can discover a deeper mind, a solid place to stand as we face the impermanence of life. This deeper mind is our true nature, the essence of who we really are. Rinpoche believes this part of us is eternal, that it does not participate in the impermanence of all things. Therefore, it is the place from which we can live in this changing world, and it is the place from which we can die. While Rinpoche uses the word *mind* to refer to this deeper dimension of our being, I believe he is referring to that same region of the psyche that I am calling *soul*.

For many of us, it is not only our own mortality that troubles us, but the realization as well that at any moment our loved ones could be taken away. In fact, this possibility can be more frightening than thinking about our own death. And for many, this nightmare becomes reality.

Rabbi Harold Kushner, who wrote *When Bad Things Happen to Good People*, lost his son to a rare disease called progeria, or "rapid aging." The child was diagnosed at an early age, and Kushner and his wife had to watch as their happy little boy slowly turned into an old man before their eyes and then died in his early teens. Going through this excruciating experience, Kushner grew into a man of depth. His book, so human and wise, has helped thousands to face their own tragedies. Near the end of the book, Kushner expresses with disarming honesty how his son Aaron's life and death changed him:

> I am a more sensitive person, a more effective pastor, a more sympathetic counselor because of Aaron's life and death than I would

ever have been without it. And I would give up all of those gains in a second if I could have my son back. If I could choose, I would forego all the spiritual growth and depth which has come my way because of our experiences, and be what I was fifteen years ago, an average rabbi, an indifferent counselor, helping some people and unable to help others, and the father of a bright, happy boy. But I cannot choose.[12]

Kushner's touching statement captures the truth of those whose souls have grown wise from painful loss: he would give it all up in a second if he could have his son back. This is how it is with dark nights of the soul. Our souls grow strong, and we develop an authentic capacity to console others; but we cannot celebrate this growth like an egoistic victory, because the price we paid was far too high.

Growing Old

It is not easy to watch ourselves grow old, to feel the aches and pains, to see our once youthful bodies deteriorate, to look in the mirror and see an old man or woman where just yesterday there was a boy with a crew cut or a girl in pigtails. But this, too, is part of the human condition, and those of us who escape disease or accident will face old age.

My father is now eighty-nine and still lives in the same Arkansas county where he grew up. My mother passed away in 1990. All three of my dad's brothers are dead, and nearly all his friends are gone. His heart is giving him trouble, sometimes he can't get his breath, and he knows that he will not be around much longer. Because of the pain in his legs, he can only take a few steps, so he sits in his easy chair all day, staring out the window or trying to watch baseball on television. He loves to read, but he can't see well enough now, so this pleasure has been taken away. Yet despite his circumstances, he maintains a wonderful outlook on life. He jokes with visitors, tells stories to anyone who will listen, and tells anyone who inquires about his health, "Why, I'm just doing a hundred percent!" He is a remarkable man who has mastered, better than anyone else I know, the difficult process of growing old. A few years ago, in one of our more intimate conversations, I told him, "When I was a boy, you taught me how to live. Now, by your example, you are teaching me how to grow old."

For many people, the older years are filled with loneliness, loss, failing health, and emotional depression. How can we face old age with dignity and grace? Is there a way to look these realities in the face and still maintain our composure, perhaps even find a way to celebrate this final phase of our lives? The answers are not easy, but there are people who can give us some clues.

Frankl believed we cannot wait until we are old to address this issue. He believed the answer to old age is to live life so fully each day that one has no regrets at the end. He wrote:

> At any moment, man must decide, for better or for worse, what will be the monument of his existence. . . . The pessimist resembles a man who observes with fear and sadness that his wall calendar, from which he daily tears a sheet, grows thinner with each passing day. On the other hand, the person who attacks the problems of life actively is like a man who removes each successive leaf from his calendar and files it neatly and carefully away with its predecessors, after first having jotted down a few diary notes on the back. He can reflect with pride and joy on all the richness set down in these notes, on all the life he has already lived to the full. What will it matter to him if he notices that he is growing old? Has he any reason to envy the young people whom he sees, or wax nostalgic over his own lost youth? What reasons has he to envy a young person? For the possibilities that a young person has, the future that is in store for him? "No, thank you," he will think. "Instead of possibilities, I have realities in my past, not only the reality of work done and of love loved, but of suffering suffered. These are the things of which I am most proud, though these are things which cannot inspire envy." [13]

Poet Mary Oliver also gives us a clue in the following lines from her poem "In Blackwater Woods":

> To live in this world
>
> you must be able
> to do three things:
> to love what is mortal;
> to hold it
>
> against your bones knowing
> your own life depends on it;
> and, when the time comes to let it go,
> to let it go. [14]

Rumi believed we must learn to dance even in the midst of our pain. He wrote:

> Dance, when you're broken open.
> Dance, if you've torn the bandage off.
> Dance in the middle of the fighting.
> Dance in your blood.
> Dance, when you're perfectly free.[15]

If we live our lives with passion and learn the lessons life has to teach, there is a gentle wisdom that comes with age, a capacity to embrace life, even its pain and sorrow, and to be grateful for the dance. As W. B. Yeats said,

> An aged man is but a paltry thing
> A tattered coat upon a stick
> Unless soul begin to clap its hands
> And louder clap for every tatter
> in its mortal dress[16]

COMES THE DAWN

Fortunately, most dark nights come to an end, and we finally see the dawn. When Frankl was freed from Auschwitz at the end of World War II, he had no place to go. His family had been killed, the city that had formerly been his home lay in ruins, Europe itself was decimated. The despair of the war still hung in the air and filled Frankl's heart. His long, dark night had done irreparable damage that would stay with him all his life. Nevertheless, there came a time when dawn lit the eastern sky and new life put forth its first green branches in his heart. Frankl described this experience:

> One day, a few days after the liberation, I walked through the country past flowering meadows, for miles and miles, toward the market town near the camp. Larks rose to the sky and I could hear their joyous song. There was no one to be seen for miles around; there was nothing but the wide earth and sky and the larks' jubilation and the freedom of space. I stopped, looked around, and up to the sky—and then I went down on my knees. At that moment there was very little I knew of myself or of the world—I had but one sentence in mind— always the same: "I called to the Lord from my narrow prison and He answered me in the freedom of space."
>
> How long I knelt there and repeated this sentence memory can no longer recall. But I know that on that day, in that hour, my new

life started. Step for step I progressed, until again I became a human being.[17]

Life is filled with tragedy and pain, yet, as Frankl and thousands of others have discovered, help is available. When all seems lost and we have let go of our last hope, something greater than ourselves reaches out with a gentle hand, surprisingly strong, and gives us a strength that is clearly not our own. Sometimes through jubilant larks in a meadow, sometimes through friends, sometimes when we are all alone in the middle of the night, our salvation quietly arrives. The soul glows with numinosity, the sacred surrounds us, and we feel connected to the Source of all. In those moments, dawn lights the eastern sky, and we fall to our knees in gratitude that the dark night has ended and that we have been given new strength to carry on.

Carl Jung said, "Man is never helped in his suffering by what he thinks for himself, but only by revelations of a wisdom greater than his own. It is this which lifts him out of his distress."[18]

The soul is our connection to the sacred, to that which is greater than ourselves. The soul knows pain, suffering, and death. She contains the eternal archetypes of life's dark realities. She has lived with them for thousands of years; and she alone has the wisdom to give us what we need. No long explanations. No false words of comfort. The soul simply says "Yes, that's the way life is." But in that "yes," we hear the eternal "Yes" that bids us welcome to the human race and to a drama as old as life itself. And sometimes, in that moment, we hear a drum from some distant shore playing the song of life. We rise from our ashes, still broken and bleeding, and catching the rhythm of the loudening drum, we dance in our blood, bandages flying in the wind. We dance with the sacred. We dance with our souls. We dance, dance, dance until we're finally free.

Our task is not to endure the pain and difficulties of life but to give ourselves over to the soul and to that which is greater than ourselves. The ego cannot handle suffering and death. It cannot believe that what happens to all will also happen to it. In youth the ego always dominates, except perhaps in those who have "old souls" or in those who have already been purified by suffering and death. But as we mature, we begin to see that we will not get through life unscathed after all. The deterioration of our once robust parents and the aging of our own bodies wipe away any lingering delusions that we will somehow escape. And as the ego bows to the argument of age, the soul finally has a chance to rise up and show us the way. With the soul as our guide, we begin to see that life is a potent mix of joy and sorrow, light and darkness, mountain and valley, life and death.

And the soul, which knows all these realities and has weighed them for centuries, whispers her judgment in our ears: "Life is worth it," she says, as she begins to clap her hands. "Life is worth it. So get up and dance!"

*Truth exists for the particular individual only
as he himself produces it in action.*
—Sören Kierkegaard

WALKING THE PATHS
A Personal Program for Spiritual Growth

As we have seen, spiritual growth is the by-product of the nurturing of a soul through ongoing contact with the sacred dimension of life. Therefore, the key to spiritual development is to identify those experiences which constitute your own path to the sacred and engage in these activities on a regular basis.

In this chapter I will show you how to design a three-month pilot program for spiritual growth. To ensure that the program meets your specific needs, I will first lead you through a series of exercises to help you pinpoint the kinds of activities and experiences that nourish your soul. Then I will show you how to use this information to set up your own personal program for the care of the soul. The program itself consists of engaging in several soul-nourishing activities over a three-month period and of keeping a daily record of your spiritual journey in a Soul Journal.

This program puts you in charge of your own spirituality. Because of this, I believe you will find it to be exciting, relevant, and growth-inducing. Essentially, the program provides you with the framework and tools you need to build a spiritual life outside the walls of traditional religion.

RATIONALE FOR A SPIRITUAL PROGRAM

I realize it may seem strange to speak of a program for nurturing the soul. The soul is that dimension of our being which cannot be regulated or contained, and thus transcends all techniques and programs.

Yet I am convinced that a regular, structured approach to caring for the soul is crucial to spiritual development. Programs are only destructive when, instead of supporting the soul, they force it in directions alien to its nature. But a personalized program designed by oneself and based on one's true needs is very different from a program imposed from without.

Nurturing the soul is an art and, like any art, it can only be learned by disciplined practice. Therefore, think of this program as an introductory course in the care of the soul. If you practice these rudiments faithfully, you will grow spiritually. In time, you will become an artist of the soul, skilled in the care of your own soul and capable of assisting others on their spiritual journeys as well.

ORIENTATION TO THE PROGRAM

As you begin this program, there are several important points to keep in mind.

First: You are unique, and your spiritual needs are different from those of everyone else. So as you work on identifying the experiences which nourish your soul, do not be overly influenced by what others tell you. There are countless books, articles, cults, religions, gurus, and sometimes family members and friends ready to tell you how to be spiritual. Certainly you can read the books and listen to what others say, but maintain your own freedom and individuality. This is your spiritual journey, and you can be sure that it will be radically unique. So trust your soul and follow wherever it leads.

Second: Realize that your spiritual needs will change over time. For example, this book has presented you with eight different paths to the sacred. If you are like most people, some of the paths appeal to you and others are of little interest. This is because right now you have certain needs; perhaps due to your age, stage of life, or the problems with which you are struggling, some of the paths speak to your soul and others do not. If you read this book again in the future, you may find that the paths that seem relevant now will have faded in significance and other paths will have become crucially important. This is how it is with the spiritual journey. While the soul always needs to be fed, the food it prefers changes over time.

Third: As you begin this venture, I would encourage you to adopt an open, adventurous attitude. Realize that you may discover food for your soul in strange and unlikely places. Life is a smorgasbord with hundreds of soul-nourishing possibilities. So don't limit yourself to the familiar or restrict your search to conventional places.

Fourth: Be willing to redefine spirituality based on your experience and on the truths you discover for yourself. Most people hold very conventional ideas about spirituality; I would suggest, instead, that you disregard traditional definitions and see what your own experience teaches you. I cannot predict where your journey will take you and what spiritual insights you will achieve, but I can assure you that an authentic spiritual journey will always take you into new and unexpected places of the soul.

Fifth: Remember that soul work cannot be rushed. The soul has its own timing and rhythms. You may need to spend several hours or even a few days on one exercise before it is finished. Let your soul be your guide. Soul work is somewhat like making bread. It takes a lot of kneading and working of the dough. Then it has to be set aside so the yeast can do its work before the bread is placed in the oven. So with each exercise, "knead the dough." Work the material thoroughly and then set it aside for awhile and come back later. Only when you feel the exercise has done its work should you move on to the next exercise.

Sixth: Be open to the sacred. The purpose of this program is to help you connect with the sacred and allow its life-giving energies to nourish your soul. Simply going through the steps of the program will not accomplish this. It requires, in addition, that you open your heart and engage in each activity with a genuine desire to touch the sacred dimension of life. If you approach the program with this attitude, it is likely that you will have many poignant moments and perhaps even a peak experience or two in which you feel the power of the sacred.

CREATING A SACRED PLACE

While it is not an absolute requirement of the program, I would strongly recommend that you create a sacred place in which to do this work and reflect on your spiritual life. Joseph Campbell pointed out the importance of this when he said:

> This is an absolute necessity for anybody today. You must have
> a room, or a certain hour or so in a day, where you don't know

what was in the newspapers that morning, you don't know who your friends are, you don't know what you owe anybody. . . . This is a place where you can simply experience and bring forth what you are and what you might be. This is the place of creative incubation. At first you may find that nothing happens there. But if you have a sacred place and use it, something eventually will happen.[1]

Ideally, this would be a room or a part of your home that you can set apart specifically for this purpose. You might even consider decorating this space with items that reflect your soul—symbols, souvenirs, keepsakes, pictures, quotations, poems, and other items that are meaningful to you. You might choose to include candles, incense, or other such items. For some people, nature sounds such as rainfall, desert winds, ocean waves, night sounds, and even the lonely howling of wolves can be relaxing and centering. These are only suggestions. Choose and arrange your sacred place intuitively, letting your own soul be your guide. But make the area rich with things of your soul, and add additional items as your spiritual journey unfolds. Creating a sacred place can be a spiritual adventure; the process itself can nourish your soul.

Once you have created your sacred place, try to set aside time each day to ritualistically leave the secular world and enter there. Use this time to reflect on your life, write in your journal, or think about your spiritual quest.

THE SOUL JOURNAL: THE HEART OF THE PROGRAM

The Soul Journal is the heart of this program. You are asked to write two pages about your spirituality in the Journal every day, without exception. The writing should be very personal, describing your thoughts and feelings related to your spiritual life. It does not have to be brilliant, insightful, or well-written; it can be silly, superficial, angry, sad, complaining, or whatever. Don't revise or change it. Just write whatever comes. But do it every day.

> Example: Sherry is a teacher in her thirties. She has been married to Jim for five years, and they have a daughter, Sara, who is almost two. When Sherry first began this program, she had difficulty writing the two pages each day in her Soul Journal. But as she became more involved in the program and more attuned to her own spiritual issues, this became much easier. In fact, she sometimes found that two pages were not enough to record all her thoughts. On the tenth day of her program, Sherry began her entry as follows:

I can't believe I had trouble coming up with something to say in the beginning. This program really makes me think . . . and feel. I've noticed a difference in myself. I look forward to the soul-nurturing experiences and even to writing in this journal. Yesterday, Julia told me I seemed calmer, less harried. It's true. I'm more present to my students. I'm feeling more energy. But I've also noticed something else. This program makes me realize how much I hate my life. I feel I'm on a treadmill, always trying to keep up. The more I get in contact with my soul, the more I hate the hectic, insane life I'm leading. I've got to talk with Jim about this. I don't want to live like this all my life. Maybe we can figure out a way to change things as time goes on.

In addition to writing the two pages each day, you will also be recording your responses to the exercises and activities associated with the program itself in the Journal. So before starting the program, purchase a notebook to use as your Soul Journal.

STEP ONE: DISCOVERING WHAT NURTURES YOUR SOUL

Step 1 will lead you through five exercises designed to help you identify the activities and experiences that nurture your soul. When you have completed these exercises, you should have a much deeper understanding of the kinds of nourishment your soul needs.

Exercise One

The goal of this exercise is to help you identify the kinds of experiences that have nurtured your soul in the past.

Think back over your life and ask yourself the following question: What experiences have touched and moved me most deeply? Think of the most poignant moments you have experienced, events that touched and stirred your soul. You may have felt awe, reverence, wonder, humility, or gratitude. Tears may have come to your eyes. These experiences may have occurred when you were in a natural setting, listening to music, making love, talking with your mate, playing with your child, spending time with a friend, reading a poem or piece of literature, or attending a movie or play. These moments often have occurred in connection with archetypal events such as births, weddings, and funerals. Parents sometimes have experienced such moments when their child started kindergarten, when a son or daughter left for college or got married, or when a grandchild was born.

Poignant moments can occur at any time and in connection with almost any event. So reflect on your life, perhaps beginning with your childhood and progressing to the present, and try to remember as many such experiences as possible. When you recall an experience, write it down in your Soul Journal.

Don't worry if this doesn't come easily. Many people can recall only one or two events at first; but as they live with the question for awhile, other experiences begin to come to mind. So don't rush this exercise. Work on it for awhile and then set it aside. Your mind will continue to work on it as you do other things. Stay with the exercise for several hours or even for two or three days. While some may recall as many as fifteen to twenty such experiences, one should recall at least eight before moving on.

Once you have completed your list, analyze it carefully to see if you can identify certain themes or categories. Did most of your soul-nurturing experiences occur in relationships with others? Did some occur in nature? Did any have to do with romantic experiences? Did any occur in religious settings? Did some have to do with the arts? If so, what kind of art—music, poetry, paintings, drama? Continue analyzing your list until you discover certain themes and gain insights about the types of experiences that have nurtured your soul in the past.

Before ending this exercise, be sure you have recorded all these experiences in your Soul Journal. Then, following your list, write at least one paragraph describing what you learned from this exercise regarding the kinds of things that have nurtured your soul. This information will be used later when you design your program.

> Example: It took Sherry two days to complete this exercise. When she tried to remember things that had touched her most deeply, the first thing she remembered was the birth of her baby, and the second was the day she got married. She couldn't really think of anything else for awhile, but as she continued to consider the question, more memories began to come to mind. She remembered her first kiss, when she was in ninth grade, and how ecstatic she had felt. She remembered Angela, her best friend in junior high school, and the intimate conversations they had shared as friends. She remembered going camping with her family when she was about twelve and how overwhelmingly beautiful the night sky was when they sat around the campfire.
>
> Sherry continued to add to her list until she had fourteen different experiences that had touched her quite deeply. When she analyzed

her list, she found the majority had to do with relationships—with her husband, her child, her parents, and certain friends. However, three of the fourteen had to do with experiences in nature; two had to do with music; and two had to do with romantic and sexual experiences. Sherry listed all these in her Soul Journal and then wrote the following summary about what she had learned from the exercise:

First, I learned (or really just reminded myself) that relationships nurture my soul. I also remembered how important nature is to me. When I was a kid, I loved to go camping or just spend a day playing with my friends in the woods behind our house in Connecticut. Thinking about this made me realize how much I've lost contact with nature. Also, I realized sex is really important to me. After the baby came, we let it slide and now it has become a bit boring and routine. I'm going to talk to Jim about this. This is definitely an area we need to work on.

Exercise Two

This exercise is more structured than the preceding one, but its goal is the same: to help you discover and clarify the kinds of experiences that nurture your soul.

Listed below are categories of various activities which often nurture people's souls. Read each category and then try to recall any soul-nurturing experiences you have had in that particular category. For example, in regard to the first category, "movies," try to recall all the movies that have touched you most deeply. Remember that you are not looking for movies that you merely enjoyed or found exciting; you are looking for experiences that truly touched and moved your soul. Feel free to include the experiences you listed in exercise 1, but try to come up with additional experiences based on the categories in this exercise. Again, take your time with this exercise. Spend a few hours or even a few days on it. Again I want to emphasize that the goal of these exercises is not to do them quickly, but to do them with depth and thoroughness. The categories are as follows:

> Movies
> Music
> Poems
> Nature
> Religious experiences
> Spiritual experiences
> Vacations

Theater
Art
Literature
Places
Food or dining
Family experiences
Romantic experiences
Sexual, erotic, or sensual experiences
Friendships

After jotting down in your Soul Journal all the experiences you can recall in each of the above categories, once again analyze your list carefully. Which categories contain the most experiences? Which categories contain none? In which category did your most intense experience occur? If you were asked to choose the two or three experiences that were the most powerful, which ones would they be and which categories are they in? Continue to analyze your list in various ways to learn all you can about what nurtures your soul.

Before ending this exercise, be sure you have written your list of categories and experiences in your Soul Journal, and then write at least a paragraph describing what you learned from this exercise regarding the kinds of experiences that have nurtured your soul.

Example: Sherry found that this exercise helped her recall four additional experiences that she had not included on her first list. Two had to do with plays, one with movies, and the fourth with literature. She listed these in her Soul Journal and then wrote,

This exercise helped me remember just how important plays are to me. Fiddler on the Roof and Les Miserables both really had an effect. I also recalled how much I liked the movie Steel Magnolias, and how much Gone with the Wind and The Thorn Birds had touched me when I read them as a teenager.

Exercise Three

Exercises 1 and 2 were designed to help you discover what has nurtured your soul in the past. While this information is useful in predicting what will nurture your soul in the future, spiritual needs also change over time. Therefore, exercise 3 is designed to help you identify what your soul needs right now. The goal is to allow your soul to speak for herself.

Sit in a comfortable, quiet place where you will not be disturbed. Close your eyes and take several long, deep breaths, until you feel centered and relaxed. If you meditate on a regular basis, you may wish to use your usual meditation techniques to help you become centered and inwardly focused. However you do it, the goal is to let go of the outside world and focus your attention within.

Once you are relaxed and centered, imagine a setting that would nurture your soul in the deepest possible way. It might be a beautiful place in nature, a cabin in the mountains, a church or temple, a certain beach, or any one of a dozen other possibilities. It can be any setting you desire—one that actually exists or one that you create in your imagination. The only requirement is that it is a beautiful, relaxing setting that would truly nourish your soul.

Now, using your imagination, place yourself in this setting. See yourself standing there, as though you have just arrived, peacefully looking all around you. See the colors; hear the sounds; smell the smells. Make it so real in your mind that it's almost as though you are really there.

Now we come to the heart of this exercise. For about five minutes, allow an imaginary scenario, a creative fantasy, to unfold in this beautiful setting. Don't try to control it or make it happen; just let it unfold, as though you were watching a video. It can be any fantasy you wish. The only requirement is that it is something that is deeply nourishing to your soul, exactly what you need right now at the core of your being. Watch as the scene unfolds and see yourself engaging in activities or experiences that are truly nurturing to your soul. Take your time. Savor the experience. Let the fantasy itself nurture your soul.

At the end of the five minutes, bring the scene to a gentle, positive conclusion. Feel that you have been satiated with the nourishing energies you have experienced and that you are now ready to leave. Take a few deep breaths, slowly open your eyes, and sit quietly for awhile.

Next, in your Soul Journal write down your fantasy in detail, just as it unfolded in your mind. Don't try to analyze or evaluate it. Just write it down as quickly and thoroughly as possible. Write in the present tense. For example: "I am in this beautiful, exotic setting on a tropical island. Nearby is a waterfall, and palm trees are all around. I am lying on the warm sand. . . ."

After you have written down your fantasy, analyze it to see if it contains clues as to what your soul needs at the present time. Does your fantasy suggest that you need to be with other people, perhaps some special person, or does it suggest that you need to be alone? What soul-nurturing activity occurred in the fantasy? What was it about the activity, what was the essential ingredient that was so nurturing? Did anything unusual or unexpected occur in the fantasy? What does this fantasy tell you that you need right now to nourish your soul?

Before ending this exercise, be sure you have written the fantasy in your Soul Journal and that you have spent time analyzing it. Then write at least a paragraph summarizing what you learned from this exercise in regard to what your soul needs at the present time.

> Example: When Sherry did this exercise, she thought of a cabin in the mountains of Northern California. In her fantasy she imagined that she had an entire week to spend there by herself. The cabin was in a beautiful setting, surrounded by tall pines and mountain peaks. Inside was a huge fireplace, with a blazing fire giving off warmth. She lay down on a rug in front of the fireplace and read. When she got sleepy, she took a nap. When she was hungry, she ate. When she felt like it, she took walks in nature. She imagined an entire week of doing exactly what she wanted to do in this beautiful setting. Sherry wrote her fantasy in her Soul Journal and then added the following:
>
> *This fantasy tells me that I need to be alone. (This is so true; I feel overwhelmed with people, people, people!) It also tells me I need to be close to nature. To be in a cabin in the mountains, to lie in front of a big fire, to take walks in nature—this sounds like heaven. If I had a few days to actually do this, I think it would make a real difference for me.*

Exercise Four

The first three exercises were introverted activities, designed to have you look within to gather information about what nurtures your soul. Exercise 4, however, takes you into the interpersonal domain, asking you to discuss what you have learned from these exercises with a trusted friend. Talking with another person will help clarify and consolidate what you have learned.

Choose a friend with whom you feel safe—someone who will understand and be supportive. Try to arrange to meet at a time and place where the two of you will not be disturbed. Give some thought to this and choose a conducive situation.

When you meet, begin by telling your friend why you selected him or her. Tell your friend that you want to describe the exercises and what you have learned about your spiritual needs from them, and that you would like him or her to respond with thoughts, reactions, and suggestions. Remember, however, that you have a right to a private life, so if there are certain things you prefer not to share about these experiences, leave those things out of the conversation.

After your meeting, write at least a paragraph in your Soul Journal describing the conversation with your friend. Did you feel understood? Did your friend provide any feedback or insights that were especially helpful? What was the main value of this meeting in terms of your spiritual growth?

> Example: Sherry decided to call Julia, her best friend. They had lunch on a Saturday, and Sherry told Julia about the program. She read some of her journal entries to Julia, and they had a good discussion about the importance of nurturing the soul. After the meeting, Sherry wrote the following in her journal:
>
> *The meeting with Julia went well, as I knew it would. She's so supportive and was so excited for me. She really didn't give me any new ideas but encouraged me to do some of the things I talked about. When I told her about my fantasy of spending some time in the mountains, she said, "Well, do it!" I told her it wasn't realistic, that Jim couldn't work and also take care of the baby by himself. But Julia asked if Mom could take care of Sara for a few days and even volunteered to help out herself on the weekend. I'll talk to Jim about it tonight, and maybe give Mom a call to see if she can help. So the main thing that came out of the meeting today is: I'm going to do it! I can't go away for a whole week, but I could probably work out something for three or four days. I'm really excited. This is exactly what I need to nurture my soul.*

Exercise Five

This is the concluding exercise of step 1. At this point you should have a rather clear picture of the activities and experiences that nurture your soul. In your Soul Journal write an overall summary of what you have learned from step 1.

> Example: Sherry wrote the following summary:
>
> *What I have learned from these exercises is that relationships nourish my soul; but, paradoxically, I also need to get away from people—even Jim and Sara—at times. I've also realized how important nature is to me, how much I need to get out into the woods and mountains. I also*

remembered how much I like plays, even though I haven't been to one in a long time. There are other things I've learned too, but these are the ones that really stand out.

STEP TWO: DESIGNING THE PROGRAM

Based on the information gained from the exercises in step 1, choose some activities or experiences that would truly nourish your soul at the present time. Specifically, choose two "little" activities and three "big" activities. "Little" activities refer to things you can do on a weekly basis and which are quite easy to incorporate into your schedule. For example, listening to music, taking a walk in nature, or watching the sunset would be quite easy for most people to do, so these would be little activities. "Big" activities, on the other hand, refer to things that take more time and planning. Attending a play, going to a workshop, or spending a weekend in the mountains would be examples of big activities, because most people cannot do these on a weekly basis, and they require time and planning.

So first, choose two little activities that you could do on a weekly basis. These should be relatively easy to do in terms of your schedule and other commitments. This program is not intended to add to your stress but to relieve it. For example, if listening to music nurtures your soul, perhaps this would be one of your little activities, and you could set aside specific times each week to do nothing but listen to your favorite music.

Next, choose three big activities and plan on doing these over the next three months. For example, if spending a weekend in the mountains would nurture your soul, you might make arrangements to do that. If going to a concert or play nourishes your soul, you might call and arrange for tickets. Regardless of what you choose, decide on three big activities and put them on your schedule. Try to spread them out over the three-month period, rather than scheduling them close together.

Thus, your pilot program over the next three months consists of doing five things that nourish your soul—the two little activities on a regular, weekly basis, and the three big activities sometime during the next three months. Be sure to decide on the exact days and times you will do the little activities, and schedule the three big activities immediately. If you fail to set aside precise times, the program will, in all likelihood, fall apart. So plan your times very specifically. Once planned, try not to change your plans. Your time for nourishing the soul should be considered important and inviolable.

Finally, write all of this in your Soul Journal, so that you know exactly what you are going to do and when you will do it.

> Example: Sherry made arrangements to go away by herself and stay at a cabin in the mountains for a long weekend; so this became one of her big activities. The other two big activities were going on an overnight camping trip with her husband and baby, and going to a play. She wrote these in her Soul Journal and made specific plans as to when she would do each activity during the three months of the program. For her two little activities, Sherry planned what she called a "sensual night" once a week for her and Jim to explore their sexual relationship in new ways, and she also decided she would take a walk twice a week on the beach near her house. Outlining her program in her Soul Journal, Sherry wrote:
>
> *My pilot program will consist of the following: My three big activities will be going to the mountains by myself July 19–22, going camping with Jim and Sara the weekend of August 8, and going to see Cats September 4. For my little activities, I will take a walk on the beach two afternoons a week—on Tuesdays by myself and on Saturdays with Jim and Sara.*
>
> *The most exciting thing, however, is my "sensual night." I told Jim I want us to set aside Friday nights just for ourselves. I'm going to plan something sensual and different each Friday night for the first six weeks, and then he will do the same for the last six weeks of the program. I'm looking forward to starting this.*

STEP THREE: WORKING THE PROGRAM

Working the program means keeping to your schedule of soul-nourishing activities and writing in your Soul Journal on a daily basis. Each time you engage in one of your soul-nurturing activities, use your Soul Journal to record what you did, how you felt, and any insights you gained. The Soul Journal is truly the heart of the program. Keeping this diary provides you with an opportunity to reflect on your spiritual life and to record your feelings, reactions, and insights as you go through the program during the next three months.

> Example: Each day Sherry wrote two pages in her Soul Journal about her spiritual life. On days when she engaged in one of her planned

soul-nurturing activities, she added another section describing the experience and how it affected her. The following is part of her entry after one of her big activities—the trip to the cabin in the mountains:

> *I cannot put into words what this weekend meant to me. I had three days to do nothing but relax—to do exactly what I wanted to when I wanted to do it. The cabin was wonderful. It had a small fireplace, and I kept the fire going day and night. Saturday night, I slept in front of the fireplace. Sunday was beautiful; the sun was shining and I could see the snow on the peaks. I love being in nature. I really missed Jim and Sara, but I think it was good for all of us to be apart. I got back in contact with myself. I wasn't a mother or a wife or a teacher; I just was myself. This weekend really nurtured my soul; it helped me spiritually, but I can't really narrow it down to one thing. The entire weekend—the cabin, nature, solitude—all of it together did something for me. I think I'm going to make this an annual event!*

STEP FOUR: EVALUATING THE PROGRAM

At the end of the three-month pilot program, evaluate the program and your experience. A good way to do this is to read through all your Soul Journal entries at one sitting, reflecting on the spiritual growth you have experienced and on the strengths and weaknesses of the program you designed. You may find that your spiritual life has deepened, that you are more centered, more relaxed, and that you have more passion and vitality. You may find that your heart is more open, that your feelings are more accessible, that you feel more creative, that you are more easily touched by music, poetry, and other things of the soul. Taking care of the soul has these kinds of effects. On the other hand, you may be displeased with certain parts of the program. You may find that certain activities did not really nourish your soul. You may discover that you took on too many activities or found it difficult to find the time to do the things you had hoped to do. Regardless, be honest with yourself and do a careful, thoughtful evaluation of your three-month experiment.

If you found the pilot program to be beneficial and if you wish to continue nurturing your soul on a regular basis, you can design another three-month program following the steps in this chapter. I would encourage you to vary your activities and open yourself to a wide range of soul-nurturing experiences.

Example: At the end of her three-month pilot program, Sherry made the following entry in her Soul Journal:

My overall evaluation of the pilot program is that it has been very useful. My soul has truly been nurtured by the things I've done, especially by keeping the Soul Journal. All three big activities—the trip to the mountains, the camping trip with Jim and Sara, and the play—worked out well.

In regard to the little activities, I love walking on the beach and this has now become part of my regular routine. But the sensual nights didn't really work out. The first two or three went okay, but then they began to feel kind of "programmed" to both of us. Also, we were sometimes so tired from the week that neither of us had the energy to get into it. We've decided to change this so that we have a "sensual weekend" as one of our big activities during the next three months. (We are going to San Francisco for a weekend by ourselves). This seems much more realistic than trying to have a special sensual night every week.

So for the next three months, my three big activities will be a sensual weekend in San Francisco with Jim, flying to Arizona to visit Audrey, and taking a weekend trip to the desert by myself. We may also go to another play. My little activities will be listening to music for thirty minutes on Monday and Wednesday evenings, and continuing to take my walks on the beach on Tuesdays and Saturdays. I will also keep writing in my Soul Journal every day. This has become part of my life; it helps me relax and focus on my soul each day.

CHECK LIST

In summary, here is a quick check list for your pilot program:

1. Write at least two pages each day in your Soul Journal, reflecting on your spiritual life.

2. Engage in two little activities each week that nurture your soul, and record your reactions and insights about each activity in your journal.

3. Engage in three big activities during the three-month program and record your reactions and insights about each activity in your journal.

4. At the end of the three-month pilot program, evaluate the program and your growth.

5. If you find the program was beneficial, design another three-month program. Continue to do this for as long as you wish.

Epilogue

As I bring this book to a close, I am acutely aware that the year 2000 is looming and we are about to enter a new millennium, an experience that comes to only a few generations. At the last millennium marker, the year 1000, Europe lay in medieval darkness. The printing press had not been invented, the Renaissance had not occurred, the Protestant Reformation had not yet begun, the New World had not yet been discovered by Europeans, and the modern era lay in the future. Today, the postmodern age is upon us, and the changes humans will see in the next thousand years are beyond our ability to imagine.

In this book I have tried to present a new vision of spirituality, one that is relevant to the postmodern age. The essence of this vision is that spirituality is universal, that the sacred river from which we slake our thirst flows throughout the world. This vision calls for us to let go of our narrow theologies and tribal mentalities and open ourselves to the spirit of life. Surely, this is the only spiritual perspective that can work in a postmodern world.

As a final word, I would like to thank all those who are struggling to create a new world and a new vision of spirituality. You are the gentle revolutionaries who will carry us into the future. Each of you, by contributing your own verse, can help write the spiritual poem of the postmodern age.

Remember that the sacred is all around you. As our greatest spiritual leaders have always told us, the sacred is in the ordinary. God seems to care little for temples made with hands; he is more likely to be found in the cry of a newborn, or at the wedding of two lovers, or in the tears of a woman who has lost her life-long mate. The sacred is everywhere; we need only to open our eyes. The look of wonder on our child's face, the passionate love of a husband and wife, the unspeakable joy of a mother who has just given birth, the gentle touch of an empathic friend, the moon and stars on a winter night, the woods and fields after freshly fallen snow, the glorious sunset of an island sky, the rapture of soul-stirring music, poetry, and art—all of these are hierophanies, manifestations of the sacred in human life. They are examples of the wonderful, life-enhancing moments when we touch the sacred and our souls resonate with the power of that experience. And not one of them has to do with church buildings, priests in religious robes, or the rituals of traditional religion. Rather, they have to do with life, with drinking deeply and freely from the sacred stream. As Kahlil Gibran said:

> And if you would know God be not therefore a solver of
> riddles.
> Rather look about you and you shall see Him playing with
> your children.
> And look into space; you shall see Him walking in the cloud,
> outstretching His arms in the lightning and descending
> in the rain.
> You shall see Him smiling in flowers, then rising and waving
> His hands in the trees.

NOTES

Introduction

1. E. Fromm, *Psychoanalysis and Religion* (New Haven: Yale University Press, 1950), 9.

2. C. G. Jung, *Man and His Symbols* (New York: Dell Publishing Co., 1964), 84.

Chapter 1 – The Spiritual Revolution

1. J. Naisbitt and P. Aburdene, *Megatrends 2000* (New York: William Morrow, 1988), 275.

2. See W. C. Roof, *A Generation of Seekers: The Spiritual Journeys of the Baby Boomers* (San Francisco: Harper San Francisco, 1994).

3. See P. Watzlawick, ed., *The Invented Reality* (New York: W. W. Norton & Company, 1984).

4. A. H. Maslow, *Religions, Values, and Peak Experiences* (New York: Viking Press, Inc., 1970), 33.

5. These Gallup poll figures cited in M. Ferguson, *The Aquarian Conspiracy* (Los Angeles: Jeremy Tarcher, 1980), 364.

6. Naisbitt and Aburdene, 293–94.

7. See T. Moore, *Care of the Soul* (New York: HarperCollins, 1992).

8. These figures are from the U. S. Bureau of the Census.

9. See J. Hillman, *Re-Visioning Psychology* (New York: Harper & Row, 1975).

10. Jung, C. G., *Modern Man in Search of a Soul* (New York: Harcourt, Brace & World, 1933), 229.

11. C. G. Jung, in *The Portable Jung*, ed. J. Campbell (New York: Viking Press, 1971), 59–69.

12. See C. P. Estes, *Women Who Run with the Wolves* (New York: Ballantine Books, 1992).

13. See R. Bly, *Iron John* (New York: Addison-Wesley Publishing Co., 1990).

14. *Joseph Campbell and the Power of Myth*, ed. Bill Moyers, prod. C. Tatge (New York: Mystic Fire Video, Inc., 1988), videocassettes.

15. Jung, *Modern Man in Search of a Soul*, 106–7.

Chapter 2 – Toward a New Spirituality

1. R. Johnson, *Owning Your Own Shadow* (San Francisco: HarperSanFrancisco, 1991), vii–ix.

2. E. Kurtz and K. Ketcham, *The Spirituality of Imperfection* (New York: Bantam Books,1992), 24.

3. See W. James, *The Varieties of Religious Experience* (New York: Longmans, Green, & Company, 1902.) A 1982 edition of this book is available from Penguin Books, New York.

4. See A. H. Maslow, *Religions, Values, and Peak Experiences* (New York: Viking Press, 1970).

5. See G. W. Allport, *The Individual and His Religion* (New York: Macmillan, 1961).

6. See P. Tillich, *Dynamics of Faith* (New York: Harper & Row, 1957).

7. J. Fowler, *Stages of Faith* (San Francisco: HarperSanFrancisco, 1981), 5. All quotations are from pages xiii, 5, and 24.

8. Fowler, xiii.

9. James, 38. All quotations from James in this section are from pages 31–38.

10. E. P. Shafranske, and H. N. Malony, "Religion, Spirituality, and Psychotherapy: A Study of California Psychologists" (paper presented at the meeting of the California Psychological Association, San Francisco, February 1985).

11. E. P. Shafranske and R. L. Gorsuch, "Factors Associated with the Perception of Spirituality in Psychotherapy," *The Journal of Transpersonal Psychology* 16(2) (1984):231–41.

12. For a more detailed description of our research see D. N. Elkins, L. J. Hedstrom, L. L. Hughes, J. A. Leaf, and C. Saunders, "Toward a Humanistic-Phenomenological Spirituality: Definition, Description, and Measurement," *Journal of Humanistic Psychology* 28(4) (1988):5–18.

13. For more information on the *Spiritual Orientation Inventory*, see the article cited in note 12, or write to David Elkins, Pepperdine University, GSEP, 400 Corporate Pointe, Culver City, CA 90230.

14. The Dalai Lama made this statement in an interview reported in "Beyond Religion," by J. C. Carriere. *Shambhala Sun*, November 1995, 18–23, 22.

Chapter 2 also contains material from D. N. Elkins, L. J. Hedstrom, L. L. Hughes, J. A. Leaf, and C. Saunders, "Toward a Humanistic-Phenomenological Spirituality: Definition, Description, and Measurement," *Journal of Humanistic Psychology* 28(4) (1988):5–18. © 1988 Sage Publications, Inc. Reprinted by Permission of Sage Publications, Inc.

Chapter 3 – The Soul

1. J. Joyce, *A Portrait of the Artist As a Young Man* (New York: Viking Press, 1964), 252–53.

2. T. Moore, *Care of the Soul* (New York: Harper Collins, 1992), xi.

3. J. Hillman, *Re-Visioning Psychology* (New York: Harper & Row, 1975), 10.

4. Adi al-Riga, "Praise to Early-Waking Grievers," in *The Essential Rumi*, trans. C. Barks (San Francisco: Harper, 1995), xvi–xvii.

5. Joyce, 252.

6. Cited in F. Andrews, *The Art and Practice of Loving* (Los Angeles: Jeremy Tarcher, 1991), 223.

7. Moore, 5.

8. Hillman, *Re-Visioning Psychology*, xvi.

9. Cited in Hillman, *Re-Visioning Psychology*, xi. This quotation is from a translation of fragment 42 of Heraclitus' works in *Heraclitus*, by P. Wheelwright (Princeton: Princeton University Press, 1959).

10. Hillman, *Re-Visioning Psychology*, xi.

11. See H. Kirschenbaum and V. L. Henderson, eds., *Carl Rogers: Dialogues* (Boston: Houghton Mifflin, 1989), 74.

12. Hillman, *Re-Visioning Psychology*, xvi.

13. C. G. Jung, *Memories, Dreams, and Reflections* (New York: Pantheon), 186.

14. See Hillman, *Re-Visioning Psychology*, x–xi and 23.

15. R. May, *The Courage to Create* (New York: W. W. Norton and Company, 1975), 120–22.

16. C. G. Jung, *Psychological Reflections*, ed. J. Jacobi and R. F. C. Hull (Princeton: Princeton University Press, 1978). These quotations are from pages 199–200.

17. Hillman, *Re-Visioning Psychology*, 23.

18. See C. G. Jung, *The Archetypes and the Collective Unconscious*, vol. 2, part 1 of *The Collected Works*, Bollingen Series XX, trans. R. F. C. Hull (Princeton: Princeton University Press, 1959).

19. See C. G. Jung, *The Portable Jung*, ed. J. Campbell (New York: Penguin Books, 1976).

20. St. John of the Cross, "Although by Night," in *St. John of the Cross*, ed. G. Brenan, trans. Lynda Nicholson (New York: Cambridge University Press, 1973), 165.

21. S. Jackson, "The Lottery," in *The Lottery and Other Stories* (New York: Noonday Press, 1991), 291–302.

22. Elkins, D. N., "Tremble, Tremble." Unpublished poem, copyright 1997, by David N. Elkins.

23. *The Psychotherapy Patient* is a professional journal edited by E. Mark Stern and published by Haworth Press, Inc., New York.

24. W. James, *The Varieties of Religious Experience* (New York: Longmans, Green, & Company, 1902), 508–16. A 1982 edition of this book is available from Penguin Books, New York.

25. J. Rumi, in *Birdsong*, ed. and trans. C. Barks (Athens, GA: Maypop, 1993), 36.

26. Hillman, *Re-Visioning Psychology*, xiv–xv.

27. See J. Fletcher, *Situation Ethics* (Philadelphia: Westerminister Press, 1966).

28. See C. Gilligan, *In a Different Voice* (Cambridge, MA: Harvard University Press, 1982).

29. J. Rumi, in *The Essential Rumi*, ed. and trans. C. Barks (San Francisco: Harper, 1995), 36.

30. Tillich, *The Courage to Be* (New Haven: Yale University Press, 1952), 6.

31. Cited in W. Barrett, *Irrational Man* (New York: Doubleday & Company, 1962), 220–21.

32. S. McNiff, *Art as Medicine* (Boston: Shambhala, 1992), 2.

33. Moore, 121.

34. S. Kierkegaard, *The Sickness unto Death* (Princeton: Princeton University Press, 1941), 29.

35. Cited in W. A. Kaufmann, ed., *Existentialism from Dostoevsky to Sartre* (New York: World Publishing Company, 1956), 99.

36. Cited in W. A. Kaufmann, *Nietzsche: Philosopher, Psychologist, Antichrist* (Princeton: Princeton University Press, 1950), 133–34.

37. Cited in R. May, *The Discovery of Being* (New York: W. W. Norton & Co., 1983), 80.

38. Tillich, 51–52.

39. R. W. Emerson, "Self-Reliance," in *Ralph Waldo Emerson: Selected Essays*, ed. L. Ziff (New York: Penguin Books, 1982), 176.

40. J. Hillman, *The Soul's Code* (New York: Random House, 1996), 8.

41. See K. Horney, *Neurosis and Human Growth* (New York: W. W. Norton & Co., 1950).

42. A. Miller, *For Your Own Good* (New York: Farrar Straus Giroux, 1984), 108.

43. A. Maslow, *Toward a Psychology of Being* (New York: Van Nostrand Reinhold Co., 1962), 3–4.

44. M. Friedman, "Introduction," in *Between Man and Man*, by M. Buber (New York: Macmillan, 1965), xix.

45. Cited in M. Ferguson, *The Aquarian Conspiracy* (Los Angeles: Jeremy Tarcher, 1980), 241.

46. J. Rumi, "Say Yes Quickly," in *Open Secret: Versions of Rumi*, trans. J. Mayne and C. Barks (Putney, VT: Threshold Books, 1984), 69.

47. Joyce, 171.

48. R. M. Rilke, "Sonnets to Orpheus, II, 29" in *The Selected Poetry of Rainer Maria Rilke*, ed. and trans. S. Mitchell (New York: Vintage Books, 1989), 255.

Chapter 3 also contains material from D. N. Elkins, "Psychotherapy and Spirituality: Toward a Theory of the Soul," *Journal of Humanistic Psychology* 35(2) (1995):78–98. © 1995 Sage Publications, Inc. Reprinted by permission of Sage Publications, Inc.

Chapter 4 – The Sacred

1. M. Eliade, *The Sacred and the Profane* (New York: Harper & Row, 1961), 32–34.

2. See R. Otto, *The Idea of the Holy* (New York: Oxford University Press, 1961). All quotations are from pages 5–6 and 23–24.

3. See Eliade. All quotations are from pages 10–14.

4. Eliade, 12–13.

5. P. Tillich, *Dynamics of Faith* (New York: Harper & Row, 1957), 41–43.

6. See W. James, *The Varieties of Religious Experience* (New York: Longmans, Green, & Company, 1902). All quotations are from pages 30, 53, and 503–15. A 1982 edition of this book is available from Penguin Books, New York.

7. James, 53.

8. See M. Buber, *I and Thou*, trans. W. A. Kaufmann (New York: Charles Scribner's Sons, 1970). All quotations are from pages 55–62.

9. W. A. Kaufmann, "Introduction" in *I and Thou*, by M. Buber, 23.

10. Buber, 56.

11. See especially the following works of A. Maslow: *Motivation and Personality* (New York: Harper & Row, 1970); *Toward a Psychology of Being* (New York: Van Nostrand Reinhold, 1968); and *The Farther Reaches of Human Nature* (New York: Viking, 1971).

12. A. Maslow, *Toward a Psychology of Being*, 71.

13. A. Maslow, *Religions, Values, and Peak Experiences* (New York: Penguin Books, 1976), 85.

14. G. Gallup, *Religion in America—50 Years: The Gallup Report.* (Princeton, NJ: Princeton Religious Research Center, 1985). See also L. E. Thomas and P. E. Cooper, "The Measurement and Incidence of Mystical Experiences: An Exploration Story," *Journal for the Scientific Study of Religion* 17(4) (1978):433–37; and L. E. Thomas and P. E. Cooper, "Incidence and Psychological Correlations of Intense Spiritual Experiences," *Journal of Transpersonal Psychology* 12(1) (1980):75–87.

15. L. S. Allman, O. De La Rocha, D. N. Elkins, and R. S. Weathers, "Psychotherapists' Attitudes toward Clients Reporting Mystical Experiences," *Psychotherapy* 29(4) (1992):564–69.

16. James, 66–67.

17. Maslow, *Religions, Values, and Peak Experiences*, 19.

18. Maslow, *Religions, Values, and Peak Experiences*, 33.

19. W. Blake, "The Marriage of Heaven and Hell," in *William Blake: The Complete Poems*, ed. A. Ostriker (New York: Penguin Books, 1977), 188.

20. W. Blake, "Auguries of Innocence," in *William Blake: The Complete Poems*, 506.

21. Cited in Sheikh Ragip Frager, *Love is the Wine: Talks of a Sufi Master in America* (Putney, VT: Threshold Books, 1987), 1.

22. F. G. Goble, *The Third Force* (New York: Pocket Books, 1971), 57.

23. James, 399.

24. J. Rumi, "This We Have Now," in *The Essential Rumi*, trans. C. Barks (San Francisco: HarperSanFrancisco, 1995), 261–62.

25. See C. Tart, ed., *Altered States of Consciousness* (New York: Doubleday, 1972). See also C. Tart, *States of Consciousness* (New York: Dutton, 1975).

26. James, 388.

27. A. Maslow, *The Psychology of Science* (Chicago: Henry Regnery Company, 1966), 139.

28. E. Durkheim, *The Elementary Forms of Religious Life*, trans. J. W. Swain (London: George Allen & Unwin, 1915), 416.

29. Cited in R. Bly, J. Hillman, and M. Meade, eds., *The Rag and Bone Shop of the Heart* (New York: Harper Perennial, 1992), 165.

30. Cited in H. Kirschenbaum and V. L. Henderson, eds., *Carl Rogers: Dialogues* (Boston: Houghton Mifflin, 1989), 74.

31. A. Maslow, *Religions, Values, and Peak Experiences*, 103.

32. See M. S. Cervantes, *Don Quixote: Man of La Mancha* (New York: Grosset Dunlap, 1969).

33. See V. Frankl, *Man's Search For Meaning* (New York: Simon & Schuster, 1963).

34. H. D. Thoreau, *The Portable Thoreau*, ed. Carl Bode (New York: Penguin Books, 1977) 563–64.

35. Durkheim, 427.

36. R. M. Rilke, "Buddha in Glory," in *The Selected Poetry of Rainer Maria Rilke*, trans. S. Mitchell (New York: Vintage Books, 1989), 69.

Path One – The Feminine

1. See C. G. Jung, *The Archetypes and the Collective Unconscious*, vol. 2, part 1 of *The Collected Works*, Bollingen Series XX, trans. R. F. C. Hull (Princeton: Princeton University Press, 1959).

2. For example, see J. Hillman, *Anima: An Anatomy of a Personified Notion* (Dallas: Spring Publications, 1985).

3. See C. Gilligan, *In a Different Voice* (Cambridge: Harvard University Press, 1982).

4. See P. Oberon, "Men with Emotionally Absent Fathers Who Developed into Highly Integrated Men" (Psy.D. diss., Pepperdine University, 1993).

5. See R. Eisler, *The Chalice and the Blade* (San Francisco: Harper and Row, 1987).

6. M. Murdock, *The Heroine's Journey* (Boston: Shambhala, 1990), 1–2.

7. See B. L. Harragan, *Games Mother Never Taught You* (New York: Rawson Associates, 1977) and also P. Heim with S. Golan, *Hardball for Women* (Los Angeles: Lowell House, 1992).

8. M. L'Engle, "Shake the Universe," *Ms. Magazine*, Summer 1987, 182–85.

9. See Eisler.

10. See Gilligan.

11. See J. S. Bolen, *Goddesses in Everywoman* (New York: Harper and Row, 1989).

12. A. Nin, *In Favor of the Sensitive Man and Other Essays* (New York: Harcourt Brace Jovanovich, 1976), 32.

13. Murdock, 8.

14. M. Williamson, *A Woman's Worth* (New York: Random House, 1993), 39.

15. Williamson, 123–24.

Path One also contains material from D. N. Elkins, "Betrayal of the Feminine: A Male Perspective," *The Psychotherapy Patient* 8(3&4) (1992): 127–49. © 1992 The Haworth Press, Inc. Reprinted by permission of The Haworth Press, Inc.

Path Two – The Arts

1. W. Cather, "Eric Hermannson's Soul" in *Willa Cather: 24 Stories*, ed. S. O'Brien (Lincoln, NE: University of Nebraska Press, 1987), 94.

2. M. Fox, *The Coming of the Cosmic Christ* (San Francisco: Harper & Row, 1988), 200.

3. E. Fromm, *The Sane Society* (New York: Fawcett, 1955), 301.

4. See M. Heidegger, *Poetry, Language, and Thought*, trans. A. Hofstadter (New York: Harper & Row, 1975). All quotations are from pages 4–19.

5. Heidegger, 4.

6. J. Joyce, *A Portrait of the Artist As a Young Man* (New York: Viking Press, 1964), 252–53.

7. R. May, *The Courage to Create* (New York: W. W. Norton & Company, 1975).

8. R. Frost, "The Lesson for Today," in *The Poetry of Robert Frost*, ed. E. Connery (New York: Henry Holt & Company, 1979), 355.

9. J. Campbell, *A Joseph Campbell Companion*, ed. D. K. Osbon (New York: HarperCollins, 1991), 19.

10. W. Blake, "Auguries of Innocence," in *William Blake: The Complete Poems*, ed. A. Ostriker (New York: Penguin Books, 1977), 506.

11. J. Giraudoux, cited in *The Meaning of Death*, ed. H. Feifel (New York: McGraw-Hill, 1965), 124.

12. W. Shakespeare, "A Midsummer Night's Dream," in *The Riverside Shakespeare* (Boston: Houghton Mifflin, 1974), 5, 1, 12–17.

13. See S. McNiff, *Art as Medicine* (Boston: Shambhala, 1992). All quotations are from pages 1–21 and page 65.

14. McNiff, 16.

15. McNiff, 14.

16. McNiff, 65.

17. McNiff, 15.

18. See McNiff. All quotations in this paragraph are from pages 17–21.

19. M. Eliade, *Shamanism: Archaic Techniques of Ecstasy* (New York: Pantheon Books, 1964), 182.

20. See D. Rosen, *Transforming Depression* (New York: Penguin Books, 1993), 34.

21. Rosen, 15.

22. Cited in R. May, *My Quest for Beauty* (Dallas: Saybrook Publishing Company), 148.

23. See O. Rank, *Art and Artist* (New York: W. W. Norton & Company), 1989.

Path Three – The Body

1. M. Fox, *The Coming of the Cosmic Christ* (San Francisco: Harper & Row, 1988), 163.

2. C. G. Jung, *Psychological Reflections*, ed. J. Jacobi and R. F. C. Hull (Princeton: Princeton University Press, 1978), 105.

3. G. Feuerstein, *Sacred Sexuality* (New York: Jeremy Tarcher/Perigree, 1992), 29.

4. W. Whitman, *Leaves of Grass*, ed. M. Cowley (New York: Penguin Books, 1959), 122.

5. M. Laski, *Ecstasy in Secular and Religious Experiences* (Los Angeles: Jeremy Tarcher, 1990), 145.

6. Feuerstein, 31–32.

7. Feuerstein, 35–36.

8. Feuerstein, 53–54.

9. See the following by Marija Gimbutas: *The Goddesses and Gods of Old Europe* (Berkeley: University of California Press, 1982); *The Civilization of the Goddess* (San Francisco: Harper San Francisco, 1991); *The Language of the Goddess* (San Francisco: Harper & Row, 1989).

10. M. Stone, *When God Was a Woman* (New York: Harcourt Brace Jovanovich, 1976),154–55.

11. R. Eisler, *The Chalice and the Blade* (San Francisco: Harper & Row, 1987), 25–26.

12. Eisler, 39.

13. See N. Qualls-Corbett, *The Sacred Prostitute* (Toronto: Inner City Books, 1988).

14. W. Blake, "The Garden of Love," in *William Blake: The Complete Poems*, ed. A. Ostriker (New York, Penguin Books,1977), 127.

15. See S. S. Janus and C. L. Janus, *The Janus Report* (New York: John Wiley & Sons, 1993).

16. See N. Friday, *Women on Top* (New York: Pocket Books, 1991), 235–349.

17. See D. Heyn, *The Erotic Silence of the American Wife* (New York: Plume, 1997).

18. See R. Denfeld, *The New Victorians: A Young Woman's Challenge to the Old Feminist Order* (New York: Warner Books, 1995).

19. Denfeld, 31.

20. See P. J. Kleinplatz, "The Erotic Encounter," *Journal of Humanistic Psychology* 36(3) (1996):105–23.

21. Kleinplatz, 107.

22. Feuerstein, 51.

23. Stone, 155.

24. Qualls-Corbett, 13.

25. Qualls-Corbett, 14.

26. Qualls-Corbett, 21–25.

27. Jung, C. G., *Mysterium Coniunctionis,* vol. 14 of *The Collected Works,* Bollingen Series XX, trans. R. F. C. Hull (Princeton: Princeton University Press, 1963), 207.

28. Qualls-Corbett, 25.

29. For a discussion of the Black Madonna, see Qualls-Corbett, 152–55.

30. See W. H. Masters and V. E. Johnson, *Human Sexual Inadequacy* (Boston: Little, Brown, 1970).

31. Kleinplatz, 118.

32. N. Berdyaev, *The Meaning of the Creative Act* (New York: Harper & Brothers, 1955), 224.

33. Fox, 178.

Path Four – Psychology

1. D. G. Benner, "Toward a Psychology of Spirituality: Implications for Personality and Psychotherapy," *Journal of Psychology and Christianity* 8(1) (1989):19–30.

2. See A. Giorgi, *Psychology as a Human Science* (New York: Harper & Row, 1970); and A. Maslow, *The Psychology of Science* (Chicago: Henry Regnery Company, 1966).

3. A. Sutich, "Some Considerations Regarding Transpersonal Psychology," *Journal of Transpersonal Psychology* 1(1) (1969):15–16.

4. For example, see the following by Ken Wilber: *The Spectrum of Consciousness* (Wheaton, IL: Quest Books, 1993); *The Atman Project* (Wheaton, IL: Quest Books, 1980); *Up From Eden* (Wheaton, IL: Quest Books, 1996); *Sex, Ecology, Spirituality* (Boston: Shambhala, 1995); *The Eye of the Spirit* (Boston: Shambhala, 1997).

See the following by Frances Vaughan: *Awakening Intuition* (New York: Anchor Books, 1979); *The Inward Arc* (Boston: Shambhala,1986); *Shadows of the Sacred* (Wheaton, IL: Quest Books, 1995). See also R. Walsh, *The Spirit of Shamanism* (Los Angeles: J. P. Tarcher, 1990); and R. Walsh and F. Vaughan, *Paths Beyond Ego* (Los Angeles: J. P. Tarcher, 1993).

See also the following by Stanley Grof and others: S. Grof, *The Adventure of Self Discovery* (New York: SUNY Press, 1988); S. Grof and C. Grof, eds,

Spiritual Emergency (Los Angeles: J. P. Tarcher, 1989); S. Grof and H. Zina Bennett, *The Holotropic Mind* (San Francisco: HarperSanFrancisco, 1992); and C. Grof, *The Thirst for Wholeness* (San Francisco: HarperSanFrancisco, 1993).

5. J. Hillman, *Re-Visioning Psychology* (New York: Harper & Row, 1975), xii.

6. For example, see E. P. Shafranske, and H. N. Malony, "Religion, Spirituality, and Psychotherapy: A Study of California Psychologists" (paper presented at the meeting of the California Psychological Association, San Francisco, February 1985); and E. P. Shafranske and R. L. Gorsuch, "Factors Associated with the Perception of Spirituality in Psychotherapy," *The Journal of Transpersonal Psychology* 16(2) (1984):231–41.

7. J. Naisbitt and P. Aburdene, *Megatrends 2000* (New York: William Morrow, 1988), 275.

8. See R. N. Bellah, R. Madsen, W. M. Sullivan, A. Swidler, and S. M. Tipton, *Habits of the Heart: Individualism and Commitment in American Life* (Berkeley: University of California Press, 1985), 113–41.

9. See M. O'Hara, "Divided We Stand," *Family Therapy Networker* (Sept–Oct 1996):47–53.

10. See J. Hillman, *Re-Visioning Psychology* (New York: Harper and Row, 1975).

11. See E. Fromm, *Psychoanalysis and Religion* (New Haven: Yale University Press, 1950).

12. See V. Frankl, *Man's Search for Meaning* (New York: Pocket Books, 1963).

13. See A. Maslow, *Motivation and Personality* (New York: Harper & Row, 1970).

14. See I. D. Yalom, *Existential Psychotherapy* (New York: Basic Books, 1980).

15. Yalom, 401.

16. This quotation is from an interview with Allende in *Writers Dreaming,* by N. Epel (New York: Vintage Books, 1993), 8.

17. R. May, "The Origins and Significance of the Existential Movement in Psychology," in *Existence: A New Dimension in Psychiatry and Psychology,* ed. R. May, E. Angel, and H. F. Ellenberger (New York: Basic Books, 1958), 12.

18. See E. Gendlin, *Focusing* (New York: Bantam Books, 1981).

19. See P. Tillich, *Dynamics of Faith* (New York: Harper & Row, 1957); and *The Courage to Be* (New Haven: Yale University Press, 1952).

20. C. R. Rogers, "A Theory of Therapy, Personality and Inter-Personal Relationships as Developed in the Client-Centered Framework," in *Psychology: A Study of a Science*, vol. 3 of *Formulations of the Person in the Social Context*, ed. S. Koch (New York: McGraw-Hill, 1959), 184–256.

21. P. Tillich, *The Shaking of the Foundations* (New York: Charles Scribner's Sons, 1948),153–63.

22. D. Rosen, *Transforming Depression* (New York: Penguin Books, 1993), 88.

23. F. S. Perls, *Gestalt Therapy Verbatim* (New York: Bantam Books, 1971), v.

24. J. H. Wheelwright, "Old Age and Death," *Quadrant* (a publication of the C. G. Jung Foundation for Analytical Psychology, New York), 16(Spring, 1983):24.

25. K. R. Jamison, *Touched With Fire: Manic-Depressive Illness and the Artistic Temperament* (New York: The Free Press, 1993), 6.

Path Four also contains material from D. N. Elkins, "Psychotherapy and Spirituality: Toward a Theory of the Soul," *Journal of Humanistic Psychology* 35(2) (1995):78–98. © Sage Publications, Inc. Reprinted by permission of Sage Publications, Inc.

Path Five – Mythology

1. J. Campbell, *Myths to Live By* (New York: Bantam Books, 1973), 31.

2. See J. Campbell, *The Masks of God* (New York: Penguin Books, 1976), vols. I–IV.

3. R. May, *The Cry for Myth* (New York: W. W. Norton & Co., 1991), 23.

4. J. Campbell, *A Joseph Campbell Companion*, ed. D. K. Osbon (New York: HarperCollins, 1991), 40.

5. See J. Campbell, *The Hero with a Thousand Faces* (Princeton: Princeton University Press, 1976).

6. See J. Campbell, *Primitive Mythology* (New York: Penguin Books, 1976).

7. See J. Campbell with Bill Moyers, *The Power of Myth*, ed. Betty Sue Flowers (New York: Doubleday, 1988).

8. F. Nietzsche, *The Birth of Tragedy* in *The Birth of Tragedy and The Genealogy of Morals* (New York: Doubleday, 1956), 137.

9. C. G. Jung, *Man and His Symbols* (New York: Dell Publishing, 1968), 84.

10. J. Campbell, *Myths to Live By*, 9.

11. Nietzsche, 137.

12. R. May, *The Cry for Myth* (New York: W. W. Norton & Co., 1991), 19.

13. J. Campbell, *A Joseph Campbell Companion*, 18.

14. J. Campbell, *The Power of Myth*, 182.

15. J. Campbell, *Primitive Mythology*, 263.

16. R. May, *My Quest for Beauty* (Dallas: Saybrook Publishing Company, 1985), 157.

17. P. Tillich, *The Essential Tillich*, ed. F. F. Church (New York: Macmillan Publishing, 1987), 45–46.

18. R. May, *My Quest for Beauty*, 153, 166.

19. Tillich, 42.

20. For example, see J. S. Bolen, *Goddesses in Everywoman* (New York: Harper & Row, 1984); and Bolen, *Gods in Everyman* (New York: Harper & Row, 1989).

21. C. P. Estes, *Women Who Run with the Wolves* (New York: Ballantine Books, 1992).

22. R. May, *The Cry for Myth*, 21.

23. R. May, *The Cry for Myth*, 21.

24. See J. Campbell, *Myths to Live By*. All quotations are from pages 9–13.

25. J. Campbell, *Myths to Live By*, 13. For those who wish a personal demonstration of the power of mythology to nourish the soul, I recommend the video tapes of Bill Moyers's interviews with Joseph Campbell. See *Joseph Campbell and the Power of Myth*, ed. Bill Moyers, prod. C. Tatge (New York: Mystic Fire Video, Inc., 1988), videocassettes.

Path Six – Nature

1. H. D. Thoreau, in *The Portable Thoreau*, ed. Carl Bode (New York: Penguin Books, 1977), 5.

2. Thoreau, 343.

3. Thoreau, 384.

4. Cited in M. Fox, *The Coming of the Cosmic Christ* (San Francisco: Harper & Row, 1988), 11.

5. R. Eisler, *The Chalice and the Blade* (San Francisco: Harper and Row, 1987).

6. See the following by M. Gimbutas: *The Goddesses and Gods of Old Europe: Myths and Cult Images* (Berkeley: University of California Press, 1982); *The Civilization of the Goddess* (Harper San Francisco, 1991); and *The Language of the Goddess* (San Francisco: Harper and Row, 1989). See also J. Campbell with Bill Moyers, *The Power of Myth* (New York: Doubleday, 1988), 165–183.

7. S. Keene, *The Passionate Life* (San Francisco: HarperSanFrancisco, 1983), 120.

8. L. Anderson, ed., *Sisters of the Earth: Women's Prose and Poetry about Nature* (New York: Vintage Books, 1991), 269.

9. See A. W. Watts, *Nature, Man, and Woman* (New York: Vintage Books,1970). All quotations here are from pages 3–5 and page 95.

10. See R. Carson, *Silent Spring* (Boston: Houghton Mifflin, 1962).

11. Thoreau, 384.

12. P. Devereux, *Earth Memory* (St. Paul, MN: Llewellyn Publications, 1992). Quotations from Devereux are from pages 12–14.

13. W. Whitman, "When I Heard the Learn'd Astronomer," in *Voyages: Poems by Walt Whitman*, ed. L. B. Hopkins (New York: Harcourt Brace Jovanovich, 1988), 30.

14. Watts, 80–81.

15. Watts, 82.

16. M. Buber, *I and Thou*, trans. W. A. Kaufmann (New York: Charles Scribner's Sons, 1970), 57–58.

17. Thoreau, 383.

18. Thoreau, 336.

19. D. N. Elkins, "Here the Animal is Sustained in Me: A Poem for Wyoming," in *Seaward Journeys of No Return*, by D. N. Elkins (Capistrano Beach, CA: Attica Publishing, 1996), 50.

20. D. N. Elkins, "To the Redwoods," in *Seaward Journeys of No Return*, 51.

Path Seven – Relationships

1. See R. N. Bellah, R. Madsen, W. M. Sullivan, A. Swidler, and S. M. Tipton, *Habits of the Heart: Individualism and Commitment in American Life* (Berkeley: University of California Press, 1985).

2. E. Fromm, *The Art of Loving* (New York: Bantam Books, 1956), 112.

3. See L. Behrendt, "Soul-to-Soul Friendships," (Psy.D. diss., Pepperdine University, 1994).

4. K. Gibran, *The Prophet* (New York: Alfred A. Knopf, 1983), 59.

5. See H. Kohut, *The Analysis of the Self* (New York: International Universities Press, 1971); and Kohut, *The Restoration of the Self* (New York: International Universities Press, 1977).

6. W. Shakespeare, *Hamlet, Prince of Denmark,* in *The Complete Works of William Shakespeare* (New York: Avenel Books, 1975), I, 3, 1076.

7. See R. Coles, *The Spiritual Life of Children* (Boston: Houghton Mifflin Company, 1990).

8. D. Chopra, *The Seven Spiritual Laws for Parents* (New York: Harmony Books, 1997), 21.

9. See S. Covey, *The 7 Habits of Highly Effective Families* (New York: Golden Books, 1997).

10. M. Eckhart, *Meister Eckhart,* trans. R. Blakney (New York: Harper & Row, 1946).

11. Chopra, 20.

12. P. Catalfo, *Raising Spiritual Children in a Material World* (New York: Berkley, 1997), 213.

13. Catalfo, 27.

14. Chopra, 27–28.

15. Gibran, 17–18.

16. S. Levine and O. Levine, *Embracing the Beloved* (New York: Anchor Books, 1995), 3.

17. H. Prather and G. Prather, *I Will Never Leave You* (New York: Bantam Books, 1995), 4.

18. Levine and Levine, 19.

19. See M. Friedman, *The Confirmation of Otherness* (New York: The Pilgrim Press,1983).

20. C. G. Jung, *The Practice of Psychotherapy,* vol. 16 of *The Collected Works,* Bollingen Series XX, trans. R. F. C. Hull (Princeton: Princeton University Press, 1954), 454.

Path Eight – Dark Nights of the Soul

1. S. Peck, *The Road Less Traveled* (New York: Simon and Schuster, 1978), 15.

2. R. M. Rilke, "The Fourth Elegy," in *The Selected Poetry of Rainer Maria Rilke,* ed. and trans. S. Mitchell (New York: Vintage Books, 1980), 173.

3. St. John of the Cross, "Dark Night of the Soul," in *The Poems of St. John of the Cross,* ed. W. Barnstone (New Directions Publishing, 1972), 38.

4. Cited in W. Barrett, *Death of the Soul* (New York: Anchor Press, 1986), 8.

5. See V. Frankl, *Man's Search for Meaning* (New York: Pocket Books, 1963).

6. See I. D. Yalom, *Existential Psychotherapy* (New York: Basic Books, 1980).

7. This version of Wiesel's Nobel Prize acceptance speech was reported in *The New York Times*, Dec. 11, 1986. Also see Wiesel's book *From the Kingdom of Memory: Reminiscences* (New York: Summit Books, 1990), 235–36, 233.

8. S. Rinpoche, *The Tibetan Book of Living and Dying* (San Francisco: HarperCollins, 1994), 25.

9. Rinpoche, 18–19.

10. W. Blake, "Eternity," in *William Blake: The Complete Poems*, ed. A. Ostriker (New York, Penguin Books, 1977), 153.

11. Rinpoche, 32.

12. H. S. Kushner, *When Bad Things Happen to Good People* (New York: Avon Books, 1981), 133–34.

13. Frankl, 191–93.

14. M. Oliver, "In Blackwater Woods," in *New and Selected Poems* (Boston: Beacon Press, 1992), 177–78.

15. J. Rumi, in *The Essential Rumi*, ed. and trans. C. Barks (San Francisco: HarperSanFrancisco, 1995), 281.

16. W. B. Yeats, "Sailing to Byzantium," in *Selected Poems and Three Plays of William Butler Yeats*, ed. M. L. Rosenthal (New York: Macmillan Publishing Co., 1986), 102.

17. Frankl, 141–42.

18. C. G. Jung, *Modern Man in Search of a Soul* (New York: Harcourt, Brace & World, 1933), 240–41.

Walking the Paths

1. J. Campbell with Bill Moyers, *The Power of Myth*, ed. Betty Sue Flowers (New York: Doubleday, 1988), 92.

Epilogue

1. K. Gibran, *The Prophet* (New York: Alfred A. Knopf, 1983), 78–79.

INDEX

A

aborigines, Australian, 61–62
acceptance. *See* unconditional acceptance
active imagination (therapeutic technique), 134
Adam and Eve, 212–13
adolescence, male, 106–7
Adventures of Huckleberry Finn, The (Twain), 130
affairs, sexual, 152–53
aging, 256–58
Alcoholics Anonymous, 17
aleitheia, 123
Allende, Isabel, 178–79
Allport, Gordon, 25
altruism, 35
Amphitryon 38 (Giraudoux), 127
ancient cultures, sexuality in, 141, 144–46
Anderson, Lorraine, 214
anima/animus, 45, 103–4
Apuleius, 37
archetypes, 20–21
   and depression, 185–89
   masculine and feminine, 46–47, 104
   and mythology, 46, 195, 203–4
   shadow, 50–51, 163
   and the soul, 46–47, 49–50
art therapy. *See* healing and art
artists, 123, 124–26
art(s):
   censorship and persecution of, 125
   defining, 122–28
   personal, 122
   and sacred power, 93
   and the soul, 38, 44–45
   as a spiritual path, 121–40
   See also creativity
Aruta tribe. *See* aborigines, Australian
astronomy as art, 128

B

baby boomers, spirituality of, 10, 18–19
Bacon, Francis, 214
Bali, art in, 122–23
Beethoven, Ludwig van, 138
being:
   and art, 124–26
   and peak experiences, 77–78
   and psychotherapy, 182–85
Bellah, Robert, 172, 228, 229
Berdyaev, Nicolas, 165
Berry, Thomas, 61
Bible:
   and nature, 212–13
   origins of, 12–13
   See also specific books/sections of the Bible
Big Horn Mountains (Wyo.), 222
bipolar disorder, 187
Black Madonna, 50, 163
Blake, William, 78
   poetry of, 126, 149–50, 255
Bly, Robert, 20

Bolen, Jean Shinoda, 119
Brahma in legend, 37
Brucke, R. M., 85–86
Buber, Martin, 243, 245
  types of relationships of, 70–74, 79,
    220
Buddha, 247

C

Cain and Abel, 213
Califia, 158
California Psychological Association,
    survey by, 32
Calliope, 128
Campbell, Joseph, 20, 126, 197, 212
  on loss of mythology, 196
  on mythology, 191, 194, 205–6
  on rituals, 199, 200
  on sacred places, 263–64
Care of the Soul (Moore), 17, 41
careers. See work
Carson, Rachel, 215
Carter, Jimmy, 148
Catalfo, Phil, 239–40
Catholicism, medieval, 11
children, raising spiritual, 237–42
Chopra, Deepak, 237, 238, 241
Christianity, 80, 228–29
  and child rearing, 239–40
  in history, 11–12
  patriarchal nature of, 46, 147
  rituals of, 49–50
  and sexuality, 142, 147–50, 163
Clemens, Samuel. See Twain, Mark
Clio, 129
codependency, 229
Coles, Robert, 237
collective unconscious, 20, 195
communities:
  breakdown of, 225–29
  spiritual, 244–45
compassion, 33
consciousness:
  secular, 88–90

states of, 86–90
cosmic meaning systems, 251
counseling. See psychotherapy
Covey, Stephen, 237
creativity:
  ex nihilo, 129–31
  and psychotherapy, 178–82
  and sexuality, 165
  See also art(s)

D

Dalai Lama, 23, 36
Dante, 21
dark nights of the soul as spiritual path,
    247–60
darkness and the soul, 50–52
David (biblical character), 247
death, 248, 253–56
  and art, 126–27
Death of a Salesman (Miller), 50
Death of Ivan Ilyich, The (Tolstoy), 50
Denfeld, Rene, 154–56
depression, 185–89
Descartes, René, 39
Devereux, Paul, 217
Don Quixote, Man of La Mancha, 95
duende, 92–94
Durkheim, Emile, 92, 98

E

Eckhart, Meister, 237
ego and crisis, 249
Eisler, Riane, 110, 118–19
  and Goddess religions, 145–46,
    211–12
Eliade, Mircea, 138, 141
  and the sacred, 65–67, 79
Elkins, David N., poetry of, 51–52,
    222–23, 224
Emerson, Ralph Waldo, 58
emotions. See mood and the soul
energy, sacred. See sacred energy

environment. *See* nature
Erato, 128
Eric Hermannson's Soul (Cather), 121–22
Eros, 40, 73–74
erotic energy. *See* sexual energy
erotic spirituality, 156–66
Estes, Clarissa Pinkola, 20
eternity and art, 126
Euterpe, 129
ex nihilo creativity, 129–31
existential crises. *See* dark nights of the soul as spiritual path
extrinsic religion, 25

F

faith, 29–30
See also over-beliefs
family relationships, 235–44
Faust (Goethe), 50
feminine, the:
    and the soul, 45–47
    as spiritual path, 103–20
feminism, 118–20, 153–56
Feuerstein, Georg, 142–43, 144–45, 158–59
Fletcher, Joseph, 55
focusing (therapeutic technique), 182
forgiveness of parents, 235–37
Fowler, James, 29–30
Fox, Matthew, 122, 142, 166
Frankl, Viktor, 175
    concentration camp experience of, 251, 252, 258–59
    on living fully, 257
    and reductionism, 96–97
    and self-actualization, 228
Freud, Sigmund, 20, 74, 158, 168, 176
Freudian psychology, 104–5, 133
Friday, Nancy, 151–52
Friedman, Maurice, 245
friendships, soul-to-soul, 231–35
Fromm, Erich, 1, 3, 122, 175, 230
Frost, Robert, 59, 125

Fulghum, Robert, 138
fundamentalism:
    damage to children by, 239–40
    and sexuality, 148–50
    and spirituality, 28

G

Gendlin, Eugene, 182
Genesis, 129, 212–13
Gibran, Kahlil:
    on children, 242
    on friendship, 231
    on God, 278
Gilligan, Carol, 55, 105, 119
Gimbutas, Marija, 145, 212
Giorgi, Amedeo, 169
God, patriarchal view of, 109–10, 212
Goddess religions, 145–47, 160–63, 211–13
Greece, ancient, 40, 128, 141

H

healing:
    and art, 131–35
    and sexuality, 165
    and shamanism, 136–38
Heidegger, Martin, 56, 123, 124, 184
Heraclitus, 42
Heyn, Dalma, 152–53
hierophanies, 66
hieros gamos, 162–63
Hillman, James, 53
    on destiny, 58
    on imagination, 48
    and psychology, 171–72, 175
    on the soul, 39, 41, 42, 47–48, 138–39
    and soul and spirit, 18, 43
Hindu legend, 37–38
history as art, 128
Hitler, Adolf, and art, 125
homosexuality and women, 151–52

Horney, Karen, 58
human potential movement, 16, 19

I

I-It and I-Thou relationships, 70–74,
    220
Idea of the Holy, The (Otto), 64
idealism, 35
idols vs. symbols, 201
imagination and the soul, 47–49
impermanence, 253–55
individualism and community, 228–29
Inhibited Sexual Desire, 157
institutional religion, 25
intrinsic religion, 25
isolation. *See* loneliness

J

James, William, 25, 53
    on consciousness, 88
    and primal truths, 30–31
    and religious experience, 76
    unseen order of, 68–69
Jamison, Kay Redfield, 187
Janus Report on Sexual Behavior, 151
Jerome (early church father), 142
Jesus, 27–28, 55, 247
jobs. *See* work
John, Gospel of, 126
Johnson, Robert, 23–24
journaling, 139
    See also Soul Journals
Joyce, James, 38, 40, 60, 124
Judaism,   patriarchal nature of, 46, 147
Jung, Carl, 3, 19–20, 23, 52, 162, 170,
    205–6
    and the anima/animus, 45, 104, 111
    and archetypes, 20, 49, 50, 104, 163,
        185, 195
    and art therapy, 134
    developmental theory of, 21
    on imagination, 48
    on loss of mythology, 195
    on relationships, 245
    on sexuality, 142, 158
    on the soul, 50
    on suffering, 247, 259
Jungian psychology, 46
    and art therapy, 134–35
    and spirituality, 19–21

K

Kasl, C. S., 225
Kaufmann, Walter, 72
Keene, Sam, 213
Ketcham, Katherine, 25
Kierkegaard, Sören, 57, 169, 261
Kleinplatz, Peggy, 157–58, 165
Kohut, Heinz, 233
Kurtz, Ernest, 25
Kushner, Harold, 255–56

L

Lao-tzu, 103
Laski, Marghanita, 143
L'Engle, Madeleine, 118
Levi Strauss company, 245
Levine, Ondrea, 243
Levine, Stephen, 243
life, meaning in, 34
Like Water for Chocolate, 94
literature:
    archetypal themes in, 50
    and the soul, 38
loneliness, 229–30
Lorca, Federico, Garcia, and duende,
    92–93, 163
"Lottery, The" (Jackson), 51
love and loneliness, 230

M

manic depression. *See* bipolar disorder
marriage, 242–44

Mary. *See* Virgin Mary
masculine, the, 104
masculinity and men, 108
Maslow, Abraham, 95, 169, 171, 173
    and Being-values, 175
    on desacralization, 89
    and peak experiences, 74–78, 83
    on religion and spirituality, 16, 25
    and self-actualization, 19, 58, 74
Masters and Johnson, 165
material realm, 24
materialism, 227
May, Rollo, 125, 180, 181, 182
    on imagination, 48
    on loss of mythology, 197
    on mythology, 192–93
    and symbols, 201, 202
McNiff, Shaun:
    and art therapy, 131–34
    on psychic illness, 137
    on the soul, 57
meaninglessness, 250–52
medicine and psychology, 168, 170,
        173, 174
megatrends, 9–10, 172
Melpomene, 128
men and the feminine, 104–15
mental illness and art, 131–35
metaphysics, 80
Micah (biblical character), 27
midlife:
    men in, 113–15
    spirituality in, 18–19, 20, 21
Miller, Alice, 58
mood and the soul, 56–57
Moore, Thomas, 39, 41, 57
morality, 54–55
"more, the," 53–56
mortality. *See* death
Moses, 85
movies, passion and power in, 94
Murdock, Maureen, 116–17, 120
muses, Greek, 44, 128–29
music and sacred power, 93
mystical experiences, 53, 76–77, 84–86

See also peak experiences
mystery and the soul, 52–53
mythology:
    breakdown of, 195–97
    defining, 191–95
    literal interpretations of, 205–7
    personal, 204
    as spiritual path, 191–7

N

Naisbitt, John, 9–10, 172
Nanpoku, 209
Native Americans, destruction of, 197
nature:
    abuse of, 213–15
    communion with, 72–73, 217–24
    early man and, 210–11
    estrangement from, 211–13
    objectification of, 214–16, 220
    as spiritual path, 209–24
New Age Journal, 16–17
New Age movement, 16–17, 19, 217
New Testament, 27–28
Nietzsche, Friedrich:
    on loss of mythology, 195, 196
    on meaning, 251
    on the self, 57–58
Nin, Anaïs, 119
nonmaterial realm, 24–25, 68–69,
        80–81

O

objectivity vs. subjectivity, 219
Oedipal phases, 104–5
O'Hara, Maureen, 173
Old Testament, 27
Oliver, Mary, poetry of, 257
ontological thirst, 79–80
organized religion. *See* religion(s)
Otto, Rudolph, and the sacred, 64–65
over-beliefs, 69

P

parents, forgiveness of, 235–37
Pascal, Blaise, 250
Paul (apostle), 80, 85
peak experiences, 74–78, 84, 86
Peck, Scott, 247
perception, transcendent. See transcendent perception
Perls, Fritz, 186
personal mythology. See under mythology
personal religion, 25, 68
personification in mythology, 199
Phantom of the Opera, The, 163, 177–78
Picasso, Pablo, 58, 121, 125
Place of Refuge (Hawaii), 91–92
Plato, 80
poignant moments, sacred in, 83–84, 86
Pollyhymnia, 128
Postman, The, 94
postmodernism, 13
Prather, Gayle, 243
Prather, Hugh, 243
prehistoric man and mythology, 191
primal truths, 30–31
Prinzhorn, Hans, 132
program for spiritual growth. See spiritual growth, program for
Protestant Reformation, 11, 148
Protestantism, 12
Psalms, 247
psyche, 40, 45, 68, 74
psychologists, spirituality of, 32, 172
psychology:
    misdirection of, 137, 167–70
    and mythology, 205–6
    as spiritual path, 167–89
    and spirituality, 69–70
psychopathology, 168, 175–76
psychotherapy:
    as creative process, 178–82
    defining, 175
    misdirection of, 180–81
    and spirituality, 172–75, 176–89

Q

Qualls-Corbett, Nancy, 146, 160–62

R

Rank, Otto, 139
reality:
    and culture, 13–14
    dimensions of, 24–25, 68–69, 80–81
recovery movement, 17
reductionism, 96–97
relationships:
    and erotic spirituality, 166
    I-It and I-Thou, 70–74, 220
    men in, 111–13
    as spiritual path, 225–45
    therapist-client, 176–77
religion(s):
    acceptance of multiple, 14
    archetypes in, 49–50
    as cosmic meaning systems, 251
    damage to children by, 238–40
    movement away from, 9–10, 15–17, 24, 26
    and mythology, 191–93
    origins of, 77
    patriarchal nature of, 46, 109–10, 146–47, 211–13
    and sexuality, 141–42
    vs. spirituality, 4–5, 25–26, 27
    types of, 25
    See also Christianity
Renaissance, 11, 12
rhapsodic communication (research technique), 75
Riga, Adi al-, poetry of, 39–40
Rilke, Rainer, Maria, 40, 45
    on death, 248
    poetry of, 60, 98
Rinpoche, Sogyal, 253–55
rites of passage, male, 107–8
ritual and mythology, 199–200
Rogers, Carl, 124
    and psychotherapy, 42, 94, 183–84

Romantic Movement, 96
Roof, Wade Clark, 10
Rosen, David, 138, 185, 186
Rumi, 53, 55, 86–87
    poetry of, 59, 87, 257–58
Russia, art in, 125

S

sacred, the, 31, 61–99
    and consciousness, 86–90
    definition of, 66
    loss of, 62–63
    nature of, 82–83
    and the soul, 98–99
Sacred and the Profane, The (Eliade), 65
sacred energy, 33, 64–65, 92–94
sacred experience, continuum of, 83–86
sacred objects, 61–62, 67
sacred places, 90–92, 263–64
sacred power. *See* sacred energy
sacred prostitutes, 146, 160–62
St. Francis of Assisi, 216
St. John of the Cross, 50, 248
sand trays, 134–36
science:
    and mythology, 193, 196, 205, 206
    and nature, 213–14, 217
    and psychology, 168–70, 205–206
    and religion, 12–13
self-actualization, 74, 228–29
    See also human potential movement
self psychology (therapeutic technique),
    233
self, true, 57–60
sensate focus (therapeutic technique),
    165
sexual energy, 156–59
sexual revolution, 150–53
sexuality as spiritual path, 141–66
Shakespeare, William, poetry of, 131
shamanic images, 136–38
soul, 37–60
    and archetypes, 49–50
    and art, 44–45, 127–28

and darkness, 50–52
defining, 40–41, 47
and depth, 42–44
and the feminine, 45–47
and imagination, 47–49
loss of, 38–40
and mood, 56–57
and "the more," 53–56
movement toward, 17
and mystery, 52–53
and the sacred, 98–99
and spirit, 18–19, 43–44
and the true self, 57–60
Soul Journals, 264–65, 273–74
soul retrieval, 136–37
spirit and soul, 18–19, 43–44
spiritual growth, program for, 261–75
    exercises, 265–72
Spiritual Orientation Inventory, 35–36
spiritual realm. *See* nonmaterial realm
spirituality:
    characteristics of, 32–33
    components of, 33–35
    content of, 26–28
    defining, 24–25, 26
    measuring, 35–36
Stone, Merlin, 145, 160
Stonehenge, 90
stories and mythology, 197–99
Styron, William, 138
subjectivity. *See* objectivity vs. subjec-
    tivity
suffering, 247–48, 252–53
Susya, Rabbi, 59
Sutich, Anthony, 171
symbols, 201–3

T

Tart, Charles, 88, 167
Terpsichore, 128
terrestrial meaning systems, 251
Thalia, 129
theology and spirituality, 28–31

therapist-client relationships. *See under* relationships
Thoreau, Henry David, 56, 227
    and nature, 209–10, 216, 220–21
    on perception, 97
Tillich, Paul, 56
    on acceptance, 184–85
    on depth, 42–43, 177
    and faith, 29, 31
    and Ground of Being, 42–43, 53, 183
    on self, 58
    on symbols, 67, 201, 202
tragic, the, 35
transcendent dimension, belief in, 34
transcendent perception, 94–97
transpersonal psychology, 171
troubadours, medieval, 96
truth:
    art as, 123
    in mythology, 192–93
    See also primal truths
Twain, Mark, 130
Twelve Step programs, 17

U

unconditional acceptance, 184–85
Urania, 128
urbanization, 226–27

V

values. *See* morality
Van Gogh, Vincent, 125, 127
Variety of Religious Experience, The (James), 68, 76, 85–86
violence, 51
Virgin Mary, 46, 160

W

Walden (Thoreau), 209, 220
Watts, Alan, 214–15, 219
wedding ceremonies, ritual of, 199–200
Wheelwright, Jane, 186–87
Whitman, Walt, poetry of, 143, 218
Wiesel, Elie, 252–53
wild woman/man archetypes, 20, 203–4
Williamson, Marianne, 120
women:
    affairs by, 152–53
    and the feminine, 115–20
    and homosexuality, 151–52
    working, 116–19
Women Who Run With Wolves (Estes), 20, 203
women's movement. *See* feminism
work:
    and relationships, 226–27
    and women, 116–19
written language and storytelling, 198

Y

Yahweh, 211–12
Yalom, Irvin, 175, 176, 251
Yeats, William Butler, poetry of, 197, 198, 258
Yirrkala, Narritjin Maynuru, 210
youth, spirituality in, 18–19

Z

Zorba the Greek, 94

QUEST BOOKS
are published by
The Theosophical Society in America,
Wheaton, Illinois 60189-0270,
a branch of a world organization
dedicated to the promotion of the unity of
humanity and the encouragement of the study of
religion, philosophy, and science, to the end that
we may better understand ourselves and our place in
the universe. The Society stands for complete
freedom of individual search and belief.
For further information about its activities,
write, call 1-800-669-1571, or consult its Web page:
http://www.theosophical.org

The Theosophical Publishing House
is aided by the generous support of
THE KERN FOUNDATION
a trust established by Herbert A. Kern
and dedicated to Theosophical education.